American Betrayal

**Franklin Roosevelt
Casts Poland
into Communist
Captivity**

Franklin Roosevelt
Casts Poland
into Communist
Captivity

FRANCIS CASIMIR KAJENCKI

SOUTHWEST POLONIA PRESS
EL PASO, TEXAS

American Betrayal: Franklin Roosevelt Casts Poland into Communist Captivity
Copyright © 2007 by Francis Casimir Kajencki

FIRST EDITION

Published by Southwest Polonia Press, 3308 Nairn Street, El Paso, Texas 79925-4126.

Printed in the United States of America

Cataloging-in-Publication Data

Kajencki, Francis Casimir
American Betrayal: Franklin Roosevelt Casts Poland into Communist Captivity

Bibliography
Includes index

1. United States—History—World War II (1939-1952)
2. Poland—History—(1386-1990)
3. Great Britain—History—(1918-1950)
4. Russia—History—(1918-1990)
5. Germany—History—(1918-1950)
6. France—History—(1918-1950)
7. Biography—Franklin Delano Roosevelt, Harry S. Truman, T. S. Eliot, Arthur Bliss Lane, Clayton Bissell, John H. Van Vliet, Jr., George Howard Earle II, Henry Ignatius Szymanski, Edward Joseph York, Alfred B. Wisniewski, Winston Churchill, Josef Stalin, Jozef Pilsudski, Wladyslaw Sikorski, Helena Sikorska, Stanislaw Mikolajczyk, Wladyslaw Anders, Janusz K. Zawodny, Stefan Korbonski.

Library of Congress Control Number: 2007900074
ISBN 978-0-9627190-8-0

STANISLAW MIKOLAJCZYK,
Prime Minister
of the Polish Government-in-Exile
(London) (July 1943–November 1944)
and Vice Premier of the Polish Provisional
Government of National Unity
(1945–1947).

ARTHUR BLISS LANE,
first American Ambassador
to the Polish Provisional Government
(1945–1947).

*For their valiant try
to insure "free and unfettered"
national elections in Poland.*

BOOKS BY
FRANCIS CASIMIR KAJENCKI

Star on Many a Battlefield:
Brevet Brigadier General Joseph Karge in the American Civil War
1980

"Uncle Billy's War":
General William T. Sherman's Changing Concept of
Military-Civilian Relations during the Civil War—
from Staunch Civilian Protector to "Cruel Plunderer"
1989

Poles in the 19th Century Southwest
1990

Across the generations:
Kajencki Family History
1994

Thaddeus Kosciuszko:
Military Engineer of the American Revolution
1998
(Recognized for merit by the International
Commission on Military History, 2001)

Casimir Pulaski:
Cavalry Commander of the American Revolution
2001

Discordant Trumpet:
Discrimnation of American Historians
2003

The Pulaski Legion in the American Revolution
2004

American Betrayal:
Franklin Roosevelt Casts Poland into Communist Captivity
2007

PREFACE

*T*HE MOMENTOUS EVENTS of World War II (1939-1945) may have been largely forgotten by the American public after a passage of some seventy years. The cruel conquests, savage oppression, and murders of millions of innocent civilians by both Germany and Russia have probably receded from memory. During the war, Adolf Hitler and Josef Stalin repeated the reckless violence in earlier centuries of Attila the Hun and Genghis Khan. Perhaps it was natural to associate the term "Hun" with the German in World War I (1914-1918).

Of all the countries of Europe swept up in this maelstrom of destruction during World War II, Poland undoubtedly suffered the most. Three million Christian Poles and three million Polish Jews were starved, worked to death, and murdered outright by Nazi Germany and Soviet Russia. With a population of some twenty-eight million in 1939, Poland lost more than one-fifth of its population, not counting its loss of precious freedom and substantial damage to its intelligentsia and cultural treasures, as well as the loss of the opportunity to make normal progress over a period of fifty years of captivity.

Russia, the Evil Empire, which paradoxically became an ally of the United States and Great Britain in 1941, played a major role in the destruction of Poland. Even though Germany and Russia were natural enemies, Russia could not resist the temptation to join Germany in an attack and partition of Poland in 1939. The planned German-Russian strategy was diabolically clever, designed to overwhelm Poland in one massive attack from all directions of the compass—south from East Prussia, east from Germany, north from Slovakia, and west from Russia. Regrettably, Poland's Slavonic neighbor, Slovakia, joined Germany to stab Poland in the back. On 1 September 1939, massive German armies invaded Poland. Sixteen days later, on 17 September, Russian armies crossed the border into Poland. Thousands of Polish soldiers were taken prisoner by the German and Russian armies. The two enemies imposed harsh conditions on the subjugated country. They tried to stamp out all resistance and crush the spirit of freedom.

This author was fortunate to have excellent primary source data for his research in the personal accounts of individuals who participated in and experienced the events of World War II. Zoe Zajdler's book *The Dark Side of the Moon* (1947) reveals the suffering of thousands of Polish civilians, innocent victims of the bestial treatment by the Russian captors. Large numbers were starved and worked to death in the Russian gulags. The Nobel Prize-Winning Anglo-American critic T. S. Eliot vouches for Zajdler's objectivity.

Janusz K. Zawodny's *Death in the Forest* (1962) describes the monstrous Russian crime of the murder of some 15,000 Polish prisoners of war, including 5,000 in the Katyn Forest near Smolensk, Russia, in the spring of 1940. Katyn resembles Auschwitz in its evil result. Politically, Katyn caused an upheaval in the relations among the United States, Great Britain, Russia, and Poland. In 1978, Stefan Korbonski wrote *The Polish Underground State, 1939-1945*, which he helped to organize. The Underground State was more than an Underground Movement. It was a complete functioning government. In *Hitler's Last Weapons* (1978), Jozef Garlinski describes how the Polish Home Army, among its many activities, tracked and reported to London the launchings of the V-2 supersonic rocket from a German rocket testing center in occupied-Poland.

The excellent account of Stanislaw Mikolajczyk's memoir, *The Rape of Poland* (1948), reveals the cavalier treatment by the Western Allies of the Polish Government-in-Exile (London). Mikolajczyk served as the prime minister of the Polish Government. Following the lead of the United States, Great Britain handed over one-half of Poland's territory to Russia at the Yalta Conference. Winston Churchill's six-volumes of the Second World War are a treasure trove of historical data. Churchill frequently discusses the relationship of Great Britain and the Polish Government-in-Exile (London). Likewise, the author found the two-volume *Memoirs of Harry S. Truman* (1955) a valuable source of information, especially the first volume *Year of Decision* that includes the agreements of the Potsdam Conference as they affected Poland.

The author studied the fact-filled account of Arthur Bliss Lane, *I Saw Poland Betrayed* (1948). Lane presents an American point of view, having served as the first American Ambassador to the Polish Provisional Government of National Unity (1945-1947). He records the machinations of the Communist-controlled Polish government that led to the fraudulent national elections of 19 January 1947. Added to the specific sources above, the events of World War II caused a mass of published books by military and diplomatic individuals. Many relate to the author's research.

Poland's terrible ordeal lasted through five years of warfare and forty-five years of Russian captivity. In *American Betrayal*, the author attempts to remind present generations of the agony of the Polish nation—betrayed by its Allies and oppressed by its enemies. Nevertheless, Poland survived and emerged proud and independent again.

FRANCIS CASIMIR KAJENCKI
El Paso, Texas

ACKNOWLEDGEMENTS

THE AUTHOR expresses his deep appreciation to individuals and staffs of libraries and historical societies for providing data and other documents during the author's intensive research. In particular, the author thanks his daughter Dr. AnnMarie F. Kajencki, Professor of English at Bismarck State College, North Dakota, who critically reviewed my manuscript. My cousin Marzena Piasecka of Sopot served ably as a contact with scholarly institutions in Poland.

I would also like to thank Richard P. Poremski of Baltimore, Maryland. Serving as a member of the National Katyn Memorial Committee, he provided the author with many documents and newspaper articles relating to the project of erecting the Katyn National Memorial in Baltimore. He now heads The National Katyn Memorial Foundation.

The list of additional individuals and agencies that assisted the author is shown in Appendix D.

—FRANCIS CASIMIR KAJENCKI

CONTENTS

ILLUSTRATIONS

American

Betrayal

Franklin Roosevelt
Casts Poland
into Communist
Captivity

CHAPTER ONE

GERMANY AND RUSSIA PLUNGE THE WORLD INTO WAR

*V*AINLY ATTEMPTING to insure "Peace in Our Time," Great Britain and France cavalierly ceded the Sudetenland of Czechoslovakia to Germany at the Munich Conference, 28-29 September 1938. The Czechs had no say in the loss of their own land. Shortly afterward, Germany invaded Czechoslovakia and seized the rest of the country, 15 March 1939. Emboldened by its easy successes, Germany next demanded that Poland hand over the Polish Corridor and the Free City of Danzig (Gdansk). Prime Minister Neville Chamberlain, becoming alarmed by the blackmail tactics of Adolf Hitler, was forced to demonstrate some sign of strength and opposition to Hitler's continuing demands. Consequently, Great Britain and France, too, declared on 31 March 1939 their total and unqualified support to Poland should its independence be threatened. Notwithstanding, Hitler ordered his military commanders to plan a massive attack on Poland set for 1 September 1939.

(NOTE: The Polish Corridor was not German land ceded by the Treaty of Versailles to Poland. The Corridor was part of the Kingdom of Poland before the infamous Partitions of Poland in the late eighteenth century. The natural outlet on the Baltic Sea which the Poles rightfully should have received was the port of Gdansk. However, British Prime Minister Lloyd George, hostile to Poland, denied Poland the port of Gdansk by creating a Free City of Danzig. During the 125-year German occupation of Gdansk (since 1793), Gdansk became colonized with Germans. Lloyd George's action reduced Poland's sea access to nothing but a sandy beach. The enterprising Poles, however, expanded a small fishing village into the thriving port city of Gdynia whose population grew to 100,000 in a period of fewer than twenty years. Following the development of the port of Gdynia, the Germans of Danzig complained that Poland discriminated against them by favoring Gdynia for its export trade. The Germans were dissatisfied that Poland exported "clean" products through Gdynia and its "dirty" products, like coal, through Danzig.

In August 1939, the massing of German armies along the Polish frontier became more than saber rattling. The Polish High Command recognized the urgency of calling up the reserves. France, however, pleaded with the Poles not to mobilize for fear of "offending" the Germans. The Poles delayed the mobilization a few days in order to cooperate with its military ally. Unwilling to delay any longer, the Polish High Command ordered a quiet mobilization of the reserves. The call-up was not completed and still in motion when the Germans attacked on 1 September 1939. In the air, German pilots bombed not only military targets but civilian installations as well. People fled the cities and towns, clogging roads and impeding the travel of reservists trying desperately to reach their assigned units. In a display of raw German barbarism, Stuka dive bombers strafed the fleeing civilians on the roads.

Although most Europeans believed that Germany was about to start World War II, Hitler's Propaganda Minister Josef Goebbels fabricated a plot that was executed ostensibly by Polish soldiers on the German radio station in Gleiwitz (Gliwice) close to the

Polish border. Alfred Helmut Naujocks of the German Security Service, leading about a dozen or so convicted criminals dressed in Polish Army uniforms, attacked and seized the station at 8 P.M. on 31 August 1939. They fired a few shots and broadcast an announcement in Polish. Although the criminals were promised their freedom for participating, they were machine gunned upon exiting the radio station. Their blood-soaked bodies were left lying on the street where the local police shortly found them. The next morning, 1 September, the world was surprised to learn that Poland had made an unprovoked attack on Germany. This thinly-veiled plot was quickly exposed. Just eight hours later, at 4:40 A.M., 1 September, the German battleship *Schleswig-Holstein*, in Danzig harbor on a "friendly" visit, opened fire on the Polish-held Westerplatte peninsula (in Polish hands by treaty). At the same time, powerful German armies massed on three flanks of Poland attacked ferociously.[1]

The Polish defensive strategy called for the army to meet the Germans at the frontier. Then, executing a fighting retreat, the Polish divisions would withdraw to the Pripet marshes in eastern Poland where German tank warfare would be impeded. In the rearward positions the Poles would continue the fight while awaiting the French offensive in the West. British military historian John Keegan takes issue with Poland's forward strategy. He would have advocated a deployment further to the east. However, if Poland had conducted a defense favored by Keegan, the Poles would have given up practically without a fight the industrial heart of the country containing some twenty-two million citizens. Rear deployment, indeed, would have been a hard choice. However, a key diplomatic reason made forward deployment necessary. Since Great Britain and France had openly declared their commitment to the independence of Poland, the Poles felt it necessary to explode Germany's attack into full-scale warfare immediately so as to force the two Western allies to live up to their commitments. Poland did not want a repetition of the case of Czechoslovakia, a piecemeal acquisition of land. Seizing western Poland quickly, Germany could then have halted the offensive before Poland's two allies declared war. Endless negotiations would follow and, finally, Germany's seizure of the remainder of the country. The rear deployment of Polish forces probably would not have succeeded because Russia attacked the country from the east on 17 September 1939. The Polish government was unaware of the secret treaty between Germany and Russia to attack and divide the country between them. About ten days before the movement of the German armies, Foreign Minister Joachim von Ribbentrop flew to Moscow where he and Josef Stalin plotted the destruction of Poland (reminiscent of the meetings of the Prussian, Austrian, and Russian ministers in Warsaw in the late eighteenth century, when they secretly agreed to carve up the Commonwealth of Poland). Although Germany and Russia were natural enemies, they found it expedient to cooperate, at least temporarily, on eliminating Poland from the map. The resulting Von Ribbentrop-Molotov Agreement of 23 August 1939 called for the Russians to join the German attack on Poland and rewarded Russia with the eastern half of Poland.

Coming from all directions at once, the attack on Poland was overwhelming. Hitler marshaled his entire armed forces against Poland. He stripped divisions from the Western front facing France, having concluded correctly that the French would not fight. Poland faced an impossible situation. Even withdrawing to the Pripet marshes was not feasible; the Russian invasion eliminated any possibility of fighting in eastern Poland. On 1 September 1939, massive armies of German tanks, artillery, and soldiers rolled over the dry plains of Poland, all aimed toward the capital Warsaw.

The directions of attack of German and Russian armies are shown on the map (page 5). Opposing the Germans, Poland's top commander, Marshal Smigly-Rydz, deployed seven small Polish Army Groups and several reserve forces. The Polish armies were no match for the overwhelming numbers of German planes, tanks, and soldiers. Hitler was eager to spring a new type of warfare on the world called *Blitzkrieg* (lightning war), and he ordered his generals to race toward Warsaw. Despite German propaganda,

UNPROVOKED ATTACK ON POLAND
From All Directions of the Compass
September 1939

BALTIC SEA

LITHUANIA

Free City of Gdansk

Wilno

EAST PRUSSIA

GERMANY

RUSSIA

• Poznan

• Warsaw

POLAND

CZECHOSLOVAKIA (Occupied by Germany)

• Lwow

Russian Armies Attack 17 September 1939

German Armies Attack 1 September 1939

HUNGARY

ROMANIA

Map by Vicki Trego Hill

Note: France fails to open western front and abandons its military treaty with Poland.

the German advances were hotly contested. On the River Brzura, General Tadeusz Kutrzeba's Army fiercely battled General Blaskowitz's VIII Army for three days. Kutrzeba inflicted severe losses on the Germans. Outflanked on the north and south, however, Kutrzeba was forced to retreat.

By the end of the second week, German soldiers surrounded

Warsaw. On 17 September Russia struck from the east. The situation now became hopeless. Warsaw surrendered on 27 September. At Kock in eastern Poland, General Franciszek Kleeberg with 12,000 soldiers battled the German 13th Motorized Infantry Division for three days until forced to surrender on 5 October 1939. Thousands of Polish soldiers were captured by the Germans and Russians. Many additional thousands escaped into Romania. The Polish government fled the country but was reconstituted in France and later in Great Britain. For the next five years, the Germans and Russians inflicted hellish oppression on the Poles. Notwithstanding, the Poles never doubted that one day they would be free again. They fought on—in France before the French wilted, in the Battle of Britain, in Africa with the British, in Italy at the Battle of Monte Casino, and in the Normandy campaign, fighting to the end.[2]

During the Polish campaign, German propaganda spread myths about German invincibility and the ineptitude of Polish arms. One of the most enduring tales centered around the Polish horse cavalry charging German tanks, a myth that American editors eagerly accepted and propagated. Time-Life Books, among others, perpetuates the myth in *Blitzkrieg* (1977). Robert Wernick and the editors of Time-Life Books narrate the attack by the crack Pomorska Cavalry Brigade which attempted to break out of the encircling arms of General Heinz Guderian's Panzer Division. Indulging in poetic license, Wernick describes the scene with precision, as if he were an eyewitness: "Like an animated page out of an old history book, the brigade came forward across open fields, at a steady earth-shaking gallop, lances at the ready, straight into the fire of Guderian's tanks."[3]

Time-Life Books' portrayal of the employment of Polish cavalry is inaccurate. Fortunately, there are other accounts for comparison. Authors Steven Zaloga and Victor Madej relate the same attack in their book *The Polish Campaign 1939*, published in 1985. Colonel Kazimierz Mastelarz, they write, commander of the 18th Lancer Regiment, sought to withdraw his unit to defensible positions on the east bank of the Brda River. His regiment had suffered severe losses in daylong fighting with the 20th German Motorized Infantry Division. However, the colonel's superiors ordered him to stay and fight.

Colonel Mastelarz decided to swing around the German infantry positions and strike them from the rear with two under strength squadrons (one-half of his available force). Counting on the element of surprise, the Poles galloped out of the forest and rode down an infantry battalion. The saber charge wiped out the Germans. Meanwhile, several armored cars arrived unexpectedly at the position and opened fire with automatic cannon on the mounted Poles. Mastelarz and about twenty lancers were killed before the two squadrons could withdraw. The fighting was a normal combat action. The next day Italian war correspondents visited the battle site. Their German escorts told them the Polish cavalrymen had been killed while charging tanks. The story, embellished with each telling, became a source of continuing German propaganda.[4]

British historian Norman Davies has attempted to stem the tide of erroneous belief. He writes in *God's Playground: A History of Poland* that every popular history of the September campaign portrays the "brave but foolish" Polish cavalry charging German tanks on horseback. Davies says the image rests on a grain of truth. "In one or two places," he explains, "isolated squadrons of Polish cavalry found themselves surprised by tanks and, despite their orders to the contrary, did try to fight their way out in the traditional fashion. Short of surrender, it was the only action available."

While no one ever believed that horse cavalry was a match for armored vehicles, cavalry in the Polish army during the 1930 decade was a necessary arm, given the nature of Polish terrain. The Germans were fortunate that the month of September 1939 turned out to be very dry. The ground was firm, and most rivers were fordable for truck and other wheeled vehicles. In the Russian campaign two years later (Operation Barbarossa), cavalry and horse transport proved their worth, even to the Germans.[5]

In 1942, the United States Military Academy published a

booklet for the instruction of cadets entitled *The Campaign in Poland 1939*. The data are based on a careful and objective study by American officers. The West Point analysts concluded that it would be unfair, with only incomplete evidence at hand, to condemn too severely the strategy of the Polish High Command. "We do not know for certain," the analysts state, "whether it was the intention to accept battle at the frontier or merely to fight a series of delaying actions and then withdraw to the strong Narew-Vistula-San River line." Historians Zaloga and Madej clarify this point. The deployment was the series of delaying actions. To begin with, Poland does not have natural boundaries on the east with Russia nor on the west with Germany. Protection against its stronger enemies was very difficult and became nearly impossible when Germany seized the remainder of Czechoslovakia in March 1939. The conquest exposed Poland's southern flank. (One of Germany's army division, the 14th, attacked from Slovakia with the help of Slovak troops.)

For the Poles to man the Vistula River line immediately would automatically give up one-half of the nation to the enemy. This strategy would prevent the mobilization of reserves from the western half, which was the more developed and progressive area of Poland, an area essentially all-Polish ethnically. The strategy of initial rear deployment was politically unacceptable.

German propaganda portrayed the attack on Poland as a lightning thrust that overcame the Polish army quickly and easily. Their superiority in numbers of soldiers and armament lends support to their claim. However, both the West Point study and Zaloga and Madej counter the erroneous impression of the campaign being anything more than a maneuver which did not provide a real test of German battle efficiency. According to West Point, the erroneous view overlooks the large number of German casualties. As reported by the Germans themselves, they suffered 10,000 soldiers killed, 30,000 wounded, and 3000 missing. Since most of the casualties occurred in the first eight days of fighting, "the campaign in Poland," West Point concluded, "can be recognized as a major military operation, in which the Polish army offered a stubborn resistance, and which required a major effort on the part of Germany."

Zaloga and Madej place the German dead at 16,000 plus about 32,000 wounded (forty-three years after West Point's available data in 1942). German losses in equipment were heavy, too. In the matter of their favorite weapon, for example, the Germans lost a total of 674 tanks, either completely destroyed or severely damaged.[6]

The Poles never expected to bear the brunt of German aggression alone. They had a military alliance with France since World War I, and that country was committed to opening a major offensive in the West within two weeks of the outbreak of hostilities. France, however, proved to be a worthless ally. Infected with despicable appeasement, the French had allowed Germany to re-militarize the Rhineland in 1936 in violation of the Treaty of Versailles, annex Austria in 1938, grab the Sudetenland of Czechoslovakia in 1938, and next destroy that country entirely. As late as 30 August 1939 (two days before Germany attacked Poland), France was pressuring Poland not to mobilize its reserves for fear of provoking Hitler. Clearly the French had lost the will to fight. After reluctantly declaring war on Germany, 3 September 1939, the French sat cowed behind their Maginot Line while superior German forces destroyed Poland. Two years later, 1940, German armies stormed into France and swept the battlefields clear of French troops, like autumn winds sweeping the leaves away. The French quickly surrendered under the authority of Marshal Philippe Petain, 10 June 1940. The rush to surrender caused France to abandon a British Expeditionary Force (B.E.F.) of 325,000 soldiers that had been sent to support France. Almost miraculously, the British nation rescued the B.E.F from the beaches of Dunkirk. A corps of 40,000 Polish troops who had eagerly joined the French Army to fight the enemy was surrendered to the Germans.

British military historian B. H. Liddell Hart states bluntly that France and Great Britain failed in their commitment to Poland:

Not only did they fail to prevent Poland from being overcome in the first place, and partitioned between Germany and Russia, but after six years of war which ended in apparent victory, they were forced to acquiesce in Russia's domination of Poland—abandoning their pledges to the Poles who had fought on their side.[7]

For the Polish nation, the month of September 1939 was a period of brutal aggression by the Germans and the Russians, as well as a calloused betrayal by Poland's allies, Great Britain and France. The Poles alone stood up to Adolf Hitler in sharp contrast to the weak-kneed behavior of the British and French. Czechoslovakia was also betrayed by the two European nations, but Czechoslovakia did not fire a single round in her own defense. It was for the Poles to call a halt to Nazi Germany's rapacious actions. Poland's fighting response to aggression made the Western countries realize at last that Adolf Hitler must be destroyed for the good of mankind.

It is amusing, if not frustrating, to note the reaction of some top British leaders to the fall of Poland. General Adrian Carton de Wiart of the British Military Mission in Poland arrived in London by way of Romania and reported to Field-Marshal Lord Ironsides, Chief of the Imperial General Staff. Ironsides made a condescending remark about the Poles not putting up much of a fight. As for Prime Minister Neville Chamberlain, he merely inquired about the effectiveness of British leaflets dropped on Germany that warned it of dire consequences.[8]

CHAPTER TWO

RUSSIA TRIES TO DESTROY THE SOUL OF POLAND

*A*UTHOR'S COMMENT: Perhaps the most shocking exposé of the cruelty and barbaric behavior of Russians in World War II may be found in the book *The Dark Side of the Moon*, published by Charles Scribner's Sons in 1947. The author, Zoe Zajdler, had access to official documents and hundreds of letters of Poles who survived Russian torture and subsequently recorded their harrowing experiences. Helena Sikorska, wife of General Wladyslaw Sikorski, writes in a short introduction that the author completed her manuscript in the winter of 1944 after an enormous amount of collecting, sifting, and checking of material and evidence. As Prime Minister of the Polish Government-in-Exile (London), General Sikorski gave the author permission to examine government documents. Unfortunately, General Sikorski did not see the completed text, having been killed in an airplane crash at Gibraltar on 4 July 1943.[1]

For unknown reasons, author Zoe Zajdler's name does not appear on the title page of *The Dark Side of the Moon*. However, when Harvester and Wheatsheaf published a new edition of the book, the author's name is imprinted on the title page as Zoe Zajdlerowa, the Polish feminine name of Zajdler.

T. S. Eliot, eminent Anglo-American poet, critic, and Nobel Prize Winner, reviewed *The Dark Side of the Moon* and wrote the Preface. Eliot says: "I think that the author displays admirable moderation." Continuing, Eliot adds: "The aim of the book is to provide a record and to state a case as dispassionately and as fairly as is possible for a book, written by one of the people who have suffered so deeply as the Poles have suffered." Eliot writes further that *The Dark Side of the Moon* is not a political book, but a study of the methods for destroying a culture. Eliot's conclusion about the clash of cultures remains relevant today. He explains that "the culture conflict is the religious conflict on its deepest level: it is one whole pattern of life against another." (Eliot received the Nobel Prize for Literature in 1948.)[2]

During World War II, the overwhelming masses of Russians, almost eighty percent, were so backward that they seemed to be living in the Dark Ages. In 1917, the Communists murdered Tsar Nicholas II and his family and abolished the Russian Empire. Very little changed, however, between the two World Wars. The Frenchman Paleologue, ambassador to the last tsar, describes the Russia of the years of 1900 to 1914 to be unlike any other Western European country that existed several hundred years ago. "Scratch underneath the surface of the cultural St. Petersburg circle," he says, "and you are back in a country which is what a *Western European country may have been four or five centuries ago.*" (The period occurred before the French Revolution, the Reformation, the Renaissance, back to a country that is still in the darkness of the Middle Ages.) This utter backwardness may help explain the barbaric behavior of Russians, although it cannot excuse their cruelty.[3]

When Russian armies seized the eastern half of Poland in September 1939, the security police followed on their heels. These security personnel were the dreaded NKVD agents, the forerunners of the KGB. They came with prepared lists of thousand of Poles that they arrested as posing a danger to Russia.

Every Pole who held a position of some responsibility (showing leadership) was seized and hauled away. The NKVD added thousands more as they scoured the cities and countryside. Professionals —doctors, lawyers, religious members, teachers, officers of political parties, officials of cities, towns, and villages, merchants, artists, and others—were rounded up. Even ordinary lay people were seized by the security agents, all destined for Russian slave labor camps.

The author writes that the Russians carried out four mass deportations of Poles. The first on 10 February 1940 included whole villages of small farms and farm laborers, forestry workers, ex-soldiers from World War I who had received grants of land, civil servants, local government officials, and members of the police forces. The other mass deportations occurred in April and June of 1940, and June 1941. The first deportation on 10 February 1940 caught the Poles by surprise, and it occurred in the worst weather in memory. When other Poles learned what the hated Russians were doing to them, they prepared for the round-up with more attention to the personal items they would take with them.

Russian soldiers and NKVD agents pounced on the unsuspecting Poles in the middle of the night, firing their weapons in the air, shouting and pushing the bewildered Poles around in a climate of fear and confusion. A family was allowed only thirty minutes to dress, pack one suitcase, and be marched off to a railroad siding, where, with hundreds of others, they were packed into cattle cars and transported to the far reaches of European Russia and Siberia. Thousands of other Poles were transported to the Pacific coast of Siberia to work in the slave labor camps (gulags) along the Kolyma River.

The Russians callously ignored humane treatment even for the sick, pregnant women, and children. One narrow opening at the top of the railroad car allowed the entry of fresh air. The prisoners did not receive any food for days, only at planned stops along the way. The "bathroom" consisted of a hole in the floor of the car for both men and women. There was no privacy. A former member of the Polish Resistance Movement describes an incident where a lone woman, a countess, found herself in a packed car with men. To give her a measure of privacy, a group of men formed a wall around the "bathroom," facing outward, so that the countess was spared embarrassment. This simple act of kindness demonstrated the vast difference between Polish Western culture and the barbaric behavior of Russians.[4]

The author of *American Betrayal* is able to describe the tragedy of his mother's sister Stanislawa, husband Aleksander, and four children. They lived in the village of Podgorze, about five miles south of the city of Lomza, Poland. The first mass deportation of 10 February 1940 caught them by surprise. Breaking into their home at night, Russians soldiers ordered the bewildered family to pack one suitcase quickly. Forced to abandon their home and family possessions, they were marched, with hundreds of other Polish civilians, to a railroad siding and packed into dirty freight cars. They completed their final journey to a camp on trucks, sleighs, or on foot, sometimes as much as 100 miles. After two weeks of travel, Aunt Stanislawa and her family reached a logging camp somewhere in the vicinity of Archangel, located on the White Sea and near the Arctic Circle. The camp commandant assigned them to crude barracks where they slept on wooden beds without mattresses. The Poles were starved on meager rations as they labored to cut down the dense forest and provide lumber for the Russians. During the long ordeal, father Aleksander died of overwork, malnutrition, and exposure to the cold climate.

A dramatic change in the wartime situation in Europe favorably influenced Aunt Stanislawa's family. On 22 June 1941, Germany attacked its erstwhile ally, Russia. The United States and Great Britain came to the support of Russia, and the Polish Government-in-Exile resumed diplomatic relations with Russia. Prime Minister General Sikorski persuaded Stalin to alleviate the lot of the oppressed Poles. Consequently, Aunt Stanislawa's family and others left the logging camp for southern Siberia where they picked cotton. The work was easier. Sikorski now negotiated the release of all Poles in Russia and gained permission to organize on Russian soil a Polish Army which became the Second Army Corps under the command of General Wladyslaw Anders. When the Second Corps and thousands of Polish civilians reached Persia (Iran) and British-controlled territory, Stanislawa's sons Jozef and Franciszek joined the British Navy, and son Aleksander, Jr. enlisted in General Anders' Corps that later fought in the Italian campaign. The civilians were evacuated to a resettlement camp in Rhodesia, Africa. Daughter Genowefa worked in an aircraft plant producing equipment for the Royal Air Force. From the Polish Refugee Settlement in Rusape, Rhodesia, Stanislawa contacted her sister Antonina in Erie, Pennsylvania. At the end of World War II, my parents began the long administrative process with the U.S. State Department to bring Stanislawa and Genowefa to the United States. The two wayfarers departed Africa for Italy from where they sailed to New York. While in Italy, Stanislawa learned the sad news that son Aleksander, Jr. was killed at the Battle of Monte Cassino. On 26 April 1950, mother and daughter sailed past the Statue of Liberty. The next day at Union Depot in Erie, my parents greeted them joyously. Sisters Stanislawa and Antonina had not seen each other since 1913.[5]

The release of Polish prisoners was carried out by local Russian officials with varying degrees of compliance—some promptly but others with disbelief and long delays. Many officials could not accept the fact that prisoners in the jails and gulags would ever be allowed to enter the community as free individuals. Polish relief agencies had difficulty finding the Poles, scattered over the vast area of Russia and Siberia. In poor health and devastated by malnutrition and overwork, the Poles desperately needed medical help and sustenance. Large numbers of the displaced Poles were children who were mostly orphans. Other children had become separated from their parents in the confusion or by Russian officials at an earlier stage of captivity.

When General Anders was released from Lubianka prison in Moscow, he was weak and physically devastated from wounds that had never healed properly during his long imprisonment.

Anders needed weeks of care, adequate food, and medical attention to recover to the point where he could appear in public.
Despite the dehumanizing conditions of the Russian prisons, they
could not dampen the surging emotion of the Poles who witnessed
the organization of a Polish Army in the land of the enemy—the
sight of Polish uniforms of the Polish soldiers, the Polish flag,
and the presence of General Sikorski who came to see them in
Russia. Author Zajdler quotes the Russian writer Ilya Ehrenburg
who describes his visit:

> I have been for a week among the Poles. I have seen them parade
> in deep snow before General Sikorski. These men who march
> past have come out of profound suffering. A human tragedy looks
> out of every pair of eyes; these men had lost everything. But
> they hold their rifles with pride and joy. I have seen grey-haired
> soldiers and young boys kissing the arms they had just received,
> holding their weapons tight in their hands, radiant with happi-
> ness, as a man holds a beloved woman.

NOTE: In *The Dark Side of the Moon*, Zoe Zajdler narrates many
accounts for three types of Russian oppression—the dehumanizing conditions of Russian prisons, the back-breaking work in
the gold mines along the Kolyma River in Eastern Siberia, and
the imprisonment in a so-called "free exile" where Poles were
left in primitive Asiatic villages to survive as best they could. In
American Betrayal, this author describes a typical experience
of Poles in each of the three types of enslavement.

A young Polish woman was jailed in the Polish city of Lwow
(in Russian hands since the invasion). Russian soldiers broke
into her apartment, escorted her to a jail, and placed her in a
cell that already held nine individuals. The cell was meant for
one prisoner. She endured horrors of insomnia for six weeks.
Her cellmates assured her that the insomnia would pass, and
sleep would become the only consolation. Prison regulations
would allow an inmate to be escorted to the latrine twice in twelve
hours. At other times, no explanation and no pleas had any effect on the guards. Under this condition, the young woman had

no other outlet than to relieve herself on the floor of the cell while Russian guards looked on, laughed derisively, and cracked crude jokes. Great self-control and moral courage were needed to endure the degradation and retain her self-control.[6]

Prison regulations allowed a walking exercise of twenty minutes each day, but almost no one was granted the exercise. The young woman got her first chance after six weeks confined in the crowded cell. A widow with a six-month-old child waited in her cell six months before getting her first chance of walking for just twenty minutes. A pregnant woman was held in her cell until the last moment before the birth of her child. Pregnant women were mistreated like all the other cellmates. Young, inexperienced mothers were able to care for their infants in a hospital for only a few days, or, at most, for a few weeks before the infants died. The dead infants were taken away immediately from their mothers who were then returned to the overcrowded cells. The loss and maltreatment devastated the women. The Russians tortured political prisoners. The term "political" applied to any Pole whom the Russians chose to label political. The young woman who provided the account wrote: "For hours at a time I listened to their fearful cries. After a time I ceased to feel either horror or pity." She relates an incident that occurred in her prison in January 1941:

> Women and young girls were beaten to a pulp and thrown into the cells. Their hair was torn out from their scalps; their fingers broken; their toes crushed; skin broken open. They were beaten on their heels and kicked in the stomach; their kidneys were laid open by the beatings.

In June 1941, the young woman was taken from her cell for political prisoners and locked up in another cell with thieves, prostitutes, and murderers. She wrote that they were searched repeatedly in the most intimate ways. The death rate of the prisoners was high. Of the 130 women in the cell, at least seven were officially known to be syphilitic, stinking horribly from open sores that were continually putrefying. Girls of fourteen and fifteen years of age were witness to the appalling scene in the cell, and they were affected by the venereal disease, vile language, and corruption of all kinds.

In Russian prisons the Poles were constantly being examined by Russian judges and the NKVD agents who lacked skill and subtlety. These officials "as often as not displayed the most grotesque ignorance of what life and its social structure was really like in Poland." These Russians were submerged in the ignorance of the Dark Ages.

A prisoner in a Russian penal colony described conditions that could well apply to the logging camp where the family of my Aunt Stanislawa was confined. The prisoner said that Poles lived in tents without floors and that stood on frozen mud. The camp inmates daily walked about six kilometers to the area in the forest where they worked and returned at night, chilled and soaked to the bone. They sank up to their knees in mud inside the tent because the stoves, such as they were, thawed out the ground under the canvas. At night, they lay in their clothing along the shelves and managed to dry out partially. At dawn, guards with dogs came to drive them out to another day's work. When one inmate died, the others concealed his body beneath a bunk for as long as they could stand the stench, so as to receive the dead man's ration of bread.[7]

When Stalin ordered the release of Polish prisoners in 1941, one Pole told a friend whom he met again: "As for me, I am no longer a human being. After what I have experienced and what I have seen, every imaginable human feeling...has been purged out of me forever...." The ordeal under the Russians, author Zajdler explains, "is very different from hardship or exposure over a limited period of time that one may experience." The torture is Russian barbaric behavior at its criminal worst. Every single influence to which the individual is subjected to is deliberately aimed at destroying the person as an individual.

The Russian prison camps had some doctors and hospital facilities. However, they were practically devoid of medical supplies and other normal items. The commandant allowed the doctor to excuse only a limited number of sick workers on any given day. Patients admitted to the hospital had to bathe first, whether suffering from pneumonia or a putrefying limb. There was no appeal from this strict rule. And in many cases the result was death. A patient with a high fever, for example, waited his turn for the bath. Next, the patient must wait, perhaps the entire day, for a bed or a space to lie down on the floor. Then he waited for a blanket. The only thing he did not have to wait for was death. Despite all the disadvantages, hospitals were considered a paradise compared to the daily ordeal. The prisoners were willing to inflict on themselves almost any injury in order to get admitted to a hospital and remain there as long as possible.[8]

The prolonged imprisonment and undernourishment caused sickness and failing vision that led to blindness. The prisoners were also exposed to snow blindness. The bite of gnats caused blindness, too. The author writes that human beings and animals attacked by thousands of gnats could lose so much blood that they died within a few minutes. In the forests especially, gnats attacked faces, legs, and arms or other exposed parts of the body, and devoured the flesh to the bone. Camp commanders were required to provide the workers with netting, but they seldom did. Russian overseers often denied netting as punishment for some infraction.

Medical commissions visited the camps occasionally. In September and October of 1941, a medical commission from Magadan, Siberia, visited some of the mining camps along the Kolyma River. In Magadan, a long procession of human derelicts boarded ship. People who saw them could not believe they were human beings. The majority had neither noses, lips, nor ears. Many were armless and legless. There were a few Poles in the group; the rest were Russians. The medical commission declared these physical wrecks unfit to work. People in Magadan whispered that once aboard ship they were taken out to sea and drowned, although there was no proof of this suspicion.[9]

.   .   .

The author discusses a number of firsthand accounts of Poles who survived the cruelty of the coarse Russians. The evidence of great suffering was uniformly similar in each account. She says, "All might have been set down by the same hand and signed with the same name." The author of *American Betrayal* selects a few examples. The first concerns a member of the Executive Council of the Polish Socialist Party. On 27 September 1939, just ten days after Russia invaded Poland, the Russians ordered him to attend a meeting of all workers organizations for the purpose of dissolving existing Polish organizations. At this meeting the NKVD handed the assembled representatives of workers a resolution expressing satisfaction at the incorporations of the invaded Polish territory into Russia. The Polish Socialist refused to sign the resolution. He was promptly arrested and thrown into jail in the town of Drohobycz, Poland. A Russian military tribunal condemned him to ten years of hard labor. The Russians moved him from Drohobycz to Lwow to Odessa, Russia, and confined him to a prison that overflowed with Poles. He was thrown into a cell with twelve others, although the cell was meant to hold two prisoners. In April 1940 he was aboard a convoy for Vladivostok, Siberia, on the Sea of Japan.[10]

There were 25,000 prisoners camping in the open at Vladivostok, which served as a temporary stop. On 20 May 1940, a large number of fellow prisoners and he were transported through the Sea of Japan and into the Sea of Okhotsh to the port of Magadan. Continuing, the prisoners were further trucked north some 1700 kilometers (about 1000 miles) to a site called Maldiak on the Kolyma River. Four camps of 2500 prisoners each were located here. The prisoners were housed in huts covered with tenting, 100 in each hut. They slept with their clothes on bare bunks made of logs. The 10,000 prisoners worked in the mines, digging gold for the Russians.

The area surrounding the camp was totally deserted. The narrator speaks of flies, like mosquitoes, that caused the prisoners misery. The tiny, blood-sucking insects kept impacting on their

Russian Gulags along the Kolyma River where Polish civilians suffered and died.

Map by Vicki Trego Hill

eyes and biting them elsewhere. By the middle of September snow covered the ground. Fortunately, the prisoners had been handed winter jackets while in Magadan. The prisoners were roused each morning at 5 A.M. and fed a meager breakfast—a piece of bread and a portion of gruel. They were then marched under guard to the mines that were from 120 to 150 feet below the surface. They dug the earth with crowbars, picks, and shovels. In the winter, when the ground was frozen, they used chisels. The ceilings of the narrow tunnels were not supported, and accidents were frequent, as many as five or six a day. The unfortunate victims of accidents were brought to the surface where the guards coarsely cut off their hands as proof to the camp authorities of their death. The dead bodies were thrown into the brush.

At 12:30 each day the prisoners were given a thirty-minute break for dinner, consisting of a small piece of bread (about five ounces) and a thin skilly. The digging continued until 8 P.M. Those individuals who had not reached their workload for the day continued for another two hours. Returning to the camp in late evening, the prisoners had chores to do, bringing food and fire wood to the camp. They received a piece of bread and soup for the evening meal.

The Russians mocked their prisoners with music played by an orchestra. As the musicians performed, guards called out the names of those whose output of work was feeble. Without delay the guards shot them and buried the bodies under the brushwood. The Polish survivor wrote about a Jew from Lwow who worked alongside of him. Becoming exhausted from overwork, the Jew fainted repeatedly. A guard ordered him to fall out and led him to a shed where the guard killed him without any scruples. The Pole said he heard the shot and saw the dead body a few minutes later. Prisoners were shot for the slightest breach of regulations, such as moving a few steps from an assigned place of work or not keeping in line while marching. As a prisoner began to falter at work, a guard beat him with his rifle butt, placed him in solitary confinement, and, finally, murdered him. In a camp of 10,000 men, some 2500 died every year. The Polish survivor said that he was in a group of twenty Poles. In the first two and half months, only four survived, including himself. All prisoners reached the same conclusion, "Kolyma means death."

There was no pause in the work due to severe weather of winter. The prisoners were forced to work even when the temperature stood at minus 65 degrees Celsius. Clothing wore out quickly so that the prisoners had to wrap themselves in rags. They seldom removed their clothes, only rarely in the bath house. To escape the deadly working conditions, prisoners sought desperately to be admitted to the hospital, even though the hospital provided very little medical help. The environment there offered some relief in contrast to digging for gold. Self-inflicted wounds were abundant. A prisoner willingly cropped off his fingers. The survivor writes: "I myself with another Pole shortly before our release decided to cut off our fingers and toes. We had come to the end of our endurance."

After several months the Polish survivor was transferred from Maldiak to Berliach, where he worked as a blacksmith in a motor pool. He never saw bread for three and a half months. He lived entirely on herring. By chance he learned of the Polish-Russian Pact of 30 July 1941 and the amnesty for all Polish prisoners. He asked the commandant about the amnesty, and the commandant punished him for impertinence. The Pole was forced to stand in the open without food for twenty-four hours. On 20 September 1941, he was among a group of Poles that was returned to Magadan where he met some 1200 other Poles. He learned from them that about sixty percent deported to camps along the Kolyma River had died. Despite the amnesty, conditions for the Poles in Magadan did not change much.

NOTE: The following account deals with the status of "free exile" as the Russians called it.

Hundreds of thousands of Poles were transported to the far reaches of Kazakstan in Asia near the border with China. The natives of this region, described by vast treeless plains, were nomadic tribes which the Russians forced into collective farms, a condition that was unnatural to their culture. The NKVD hauled the Poles to these Asiatic peoples—Kazaks, Khirgizi, and Uzbeks —to work for them as cheap labor. On their way to unknown settlements, after twenty, thirty, and sometimes forty days spent on the dirty trains, hundreds of Polish exiles from the grain fields, friendly towns, and ancient parishes of Poland waited for days on the naked steppes for the convoys to take them on the last stage of their journey. The despicable Russians had evicted them from Poland, and as the author writes, "never again, at sunrise or sunset, to watch with joy the scented wood smoke rise above the Polish villages, the windows of Polish homes beckon with hospitable lights, or the great, white, fraternal Polish storks sink down upon their roof-top nests with serene and fondly familiar deployments of their immaculate wings."[11]

The narrative of a Polish survivor of "free exile" begins on 29 April 1940 at a site called "Ayagouz," a day's journey from the ancient city of Alma Ata near the Chinese border. The Poles were ordered to climb into high-riding trucks with their baggage. Many found it difficult because they could barely crawl from the exhaustion of long travel, camps, dysentery, and the like. One Pole was eighty-four years old and his wife, eighty. There were other old individuals. In the confusion, families and groups of friends became separated. Some of the valuable baggage was mislaid and lost. The journey to their destination lay across land that was gray and flat and without a single tree. At first, there was a road of sorts, but it soon entered open country. The Poles saw only one settlement along the way. It was a huddle of dirty mud huts with a few ragged and dirty Kazaks standing at the doors. At the next settlement the Poles were literally dumped off.

The settlement consisted of ten small, very dirty huts, with no garden of any kind and not a single tree. The Kazaks were repulsively ugly, syphilitic, and very unfriendly. They spoke very little Russian. They resented the Poles, and the Russians, too, for bringing the strangers to their village. At first, they did not want to help their unwanted guests. The enterprising Poles managed to get a measure of cooperation. The Europeans possessed some personal items, very normal but immensely better than what the Kazaks had or had seen previously. Negotiating with them, the Poles traded for a small jug of thin whey, the only available food. The Kazaks were expected to house the Poles in the corners of their huts. Neither side was satisfied with such an arrangement. By bribery and determined persuasion, the Poles were able to obtain an empty hut from the Kazaks. There were four small rooms in the hut, like cells, with earthen floors. The Polish group consisted of 160 individuals, too many for all to fit into the hut. But, six older persons, the sick, and women with children gained a shelter. The hut held forty persons maximum, ten per room, and crowded into each room measuring three meters by four. The new residents placed their suitcases on stones to make something of a bed. The nearest water supply was a brook, a half mile away. At first, there was no vessel to carry the water to the hut.

The Poles followed the practice of the Kazaks for their source of fuel. They collected dung from the pastures and shaped it into small cakes or bricks. The bricks were next baked in the sun until they became solid. These bricks gave off little flame but much heat. (This author understands how the Poles converted dung into solid bricks for fuel. In 1968, he made a NATO training inspection of Turkish Army units in far eastern Turkey, near the border with Iran. The region was inhabited by Kurds who lived in small villages of mud huts. While traveling in a jeep with a Turkish Army officer, we passed a Kurdish village. I saw small pyramids of black bricks placed near the entrance to the huts. I asked my Turkish officer, "What are those pyramids?" He answered: "They're fire wood made of dry dung," and I commented, "When burning, those bricks must give off an awful stench.")

The Kazaks baked bread in a central bakery. Only those Poles who worked were able to buy bread. However, the supply of bread occurred irregularly. The Kazaks sought to barter with the Poles for European items. For a few pieces of cotton ribbon, the Poles obtained s few eggs and a glassful of flour. The Kazaks ran a small cooperative store where the Poles bought a lantern, a packet of apple tea, and eagerly bought a few copies of a geography book. Because the Poles were brought to the village as cheap labor, the Kazaks put them to work digging latrines and plowing the earth. Some of the Poles, such as a judge or university professor, had never done manual labor, and they performed their work most unskillfully, much to the malicious pleasure of the Kazaks who jeered and mimicked them. The women were put to work digging over and shifting an enormous amount of dung. The Poles brushed off the jeers of the Kazaks. The cruelty of the Russians, however, was unbearable. (It appears that the Russians, so-called Europeans, exhibited a culture much lower than that of the nomadic and primitive Asians.)

The Russian secret police came periodically to the Kazak settlements to check on the Poles. The Russians always asked the same questions, but left the Poles to the whims of the Kazaks. In time, a few Kazaks became a bit friendly. Nevertheless, they did not want the Poles with them because they were the cause of the visits of the Russians whom they resented, as well. Left alone without the cruel and oppressive treatment of the Russians, the Poles were able to live with the Kazaks and survive their ordeal.

The lot of Poles in other Asiatic regions of Russia was affected by local conditions. As a result of the Russian amnesty, massive numbers of Poles were released from jails and gulags. They trekked over vast distances in various ways to reach the recruiting station of the Polish Army at Buzul'uk or the newly-established Embassy of Poland in Kuibyshev, which became the capital of Russia when the Germans threatened to capture Moscow. The Polish Ambassador began an immense relief effort on behalf of his starved brethren. In southern Kazakstan, thousands of Poles found themselves stranded and without means of livelihood. In the immediate period following the amnesty, the local authorities of Kazakstan cooperated with the Poles, allowing them to establish medical stations for the treatment of the emaciated Poles (although there was an acute shortage of doctors and medical supplies). The Poles were permitted to open orphanages for the massive number of children without parents—those who died and others who became separated from their children. Polish communities in Kazakstan opened up Polish grade schools for children. The Poles also organized themselves to carry out work programs to obtain supplies for themselves and also to sell them for needed cash. When the Polish Army of General Anders entered Kazakstan, thousands of Polish civilians came with them. The soldiers remained temporarily, as they continued to their destination of Persia.

The Russian government changed its mind about organizing a Polish Army to fight alongside the Russians. Russia now ordered Anders to leave Russia. The change affected the officials in Kazakstan, too. They proceeded to close down all the activities of the Poles and to carry out repressive measures. Some Poles were returned to prison. Others were forced into the Russian Army or labor battalions. The Russian amnesty turned out to be a hollow gesture. The suffering of the Poles in Russia continued.

NOTE: The remainder of Zajdler's book discusses the German attack on Russia, 22 June 1941, and the reconciliation of Russia and the Polish Government-in-Exile that brought some relief to the cruel life of most Poles in Russia. The author continues with the dramatic events of World War II and the final Russian enslavement of Poland. The publisher added an epilogue, a summary of events written by an unnamed Englishman [Spencer Curtis Brown] who is very knowledgeable with the events of World War II.

EPILOGUE

The English writer establishes at the outset that Communism never took hold in Poland. The Poles rejected Communism for its attack on Western values. A large number of Polish workers were organized into the Socialist Party. It played a leading role in the life of the nation, as it had demonstrated when it fought

for Poland's independence in World War I. As did the other political parties, the Polish Socialist Party wholeheartedly opposed
the Communist invasion of Europe in 1920 when the Polish Army
under Marshal Jozef Pilsudski decisively defeated the Russian
Army of Marshal Mikhail Tuhkachevsky at the gates of Warsaw,
15 August 1920. The Poles saved Europe from the evil of Communist rule. The Englishman Lord D'Aubernon called the Battle
of Warsaw the "18th Decisive Battle of the World." For Poles, the
Communist practice of the collectivization of land was extremely
unpopular since the nation was a land of small farmers. They
also strongly opposed the anti-religious and godless policy of the
Communists. Catholicism was intertwined with the history and
daily lives of workers and peasants. As the English writer observed: "The Party had, in fact, become so useless that it was
formally abolished by the Comintern in 1937." Finally, the misery and destruction caused by the Russian invasion in 1939 made
the Communists most loathsome to the Poles.[12]

Following the Russian conquest of eastern Poland, the few
Polish Communists in Moscow had to move carefully and deliberately to reconstruct the Communist Party in Poland. They
sought to recruit two classes of individuals: writers and officers—
the first to write Communist propaganda and the second to form
the nucleus of a Polish military unit. A school of Communist
writers was opened in Lwow under the direction of Wanda
Wasilewska, a Communist who became a Russian citizen and
married Korniechuk, Russian Commissar for Foreign Affairs. The
recruiting of Polish officers took place in Russia at Malakhovka
where the secret police questioned some 9400 captured Polish
officers. The secret police culled some seventy-four, or less than
one percent, as potential Communist converts. The most senior
was Colonel Zygmunt Berling who signed a document of loyalty
to Russia.

When the German attack on Russia on 22 June 1941 expelled
the Russians from eastern Poland, the Communists set up two
plans for the control of Poland in the future. The first dealt with
organizing a coterie of Polish Communists that would accom-

pany the Russian armies into Poland during the expected counter-offensive against the Germans. This small group of dedicated Communists would serve as a ready-made government. The second plan called for agents to be placed in Poland and, at the proper time, invite the ready-made government into Poland. Boleslaw Bierut and a few accomplices were dropped into Poland by parachute and lay low until the Russian Army returned to Poland. The Russians considered the presence of Communist agents in Poland to be necessary because a well-organized and functioning Polish Underground Government was a reality and had to be circumvented. The Underground Government was an extension of the Polish Government-in-Exile in London, and a Deputy Prime Minister served in Poland. (The Underground Government is treated more fully in Chapter 4.)

In Russia, Stalin set up the so-called Union of Polish Patriots, 1 March 1943, well before the Tehran and Yalta Conferences when Stalin sprang his demand for the eastern half of Poland. Stalin designated Zygmunt Berling and Wanda Wasilewska as leaders of the Union of Polish Patriots. Of the ten members, four were Russian citizens and six were Communists. Having set up a ready-made government for Poland, Russia dropped all adherence to the Polish-Russian Pact of 30 July 1941 when the United States, Great Britain, and the Polish Government-in-Exile joined to support Russia against Germany.

At the time the German press announced the discovery of the corpses of 11,000 Polish officers murdered in the Katyn Forest in Russia, Prime Minister General Wladyslaw Sikorski asked the International Red Cross to visit the site. The Russians seized on Sikorski's request as a pretext to break off diplomatic relations with the Polish Government-in-Exile. The Russians reasserted their false claim to eastern Poland. They also accused Sikorski and his supporters inside and outside Poland of being German collaborators.

The Polish Government-in-Exile categorically rejected the Russian lies. In its statement, the Polish Government declared: "No traitor, Quisling, has sprung from the Polish ranks." [As did

Quisling in Norway and Petain in France] "All collaboration with the Germans has been scorned," the Polish reply reads. "In the light of facts which are known throughout the world, the Polish government and the Polish nation have no need to defend themselves from any suggestion of contact or understanding with Hitler." [This statement can also serve as a rejection of the false claims of some American Jews that the Poles collaborated with the Germans to exterminate Polish Jews.]

In December 1943, Franklin Roosevelt, Winston Churchill, and Josef Stalin met at the Tehran Conference. The three restated their support of the Atlantic Charter (formulated by Roosevelt and Churchill at a meeting at sea) that "no territorial changes shall be made which are not in accordance with the freely expressed wishes of the population involved in such changes." Notwithstanding, Roosevelt and Churchill restated the Atlantic Charter even though they had just agreed to give Stalin half of Poland without the "freely expressed wishes of the population."

Meanwhile in Poland, Communist Boleslaw Bierut divided his skeleton Polish Workers Party into a number of sub-parties in order to give the appearance of support from several areas of the country. On 1 January 1944 the Workers Party transformed itself into the National Council of the Homeland, and in May 1944 Stalin invited the National Council to Moscow, headed by Edward Osubka-Morawski. On 22 June 1944, Russian armies, forcing the Germans back, crossed the so-called Curzon Line. Stalin was now ready to execute his carefully laid plan to subjugate Poland. The few Polish Communists of the so-called "Union of Polish Patriots," following on the heels of the Russian armies, were welcomed into Poland by Bierut. They established the Committee of National Liberation, with Osubka-Morawski as chairman and Wanda Wasilewska, vice-chair. Shortly thereafter, the Committee proclaimed itself the Provisional Government of Poland. Bierut was elected president by acclamation, and Osubka-Morawski became premier.

Moving quickly, Stalin urged Roosevelt and Churchill to deal with the Communist Provisional Government, but the two Western leaders would not recognize it as representing the will of the people. They held the view that the Communist group was only one faction to be considered along with other Poles inside and outside the country. Nevertheless, Stalin marginalized the other non-Communist parties so that the Communist coterie now ensconced in Poland remained dominant.

As the Russian armies approached the Vistula River, and German units were retreating from Warsaw, Moscow Radio on 30 July 1944 beamed a message to the people of Warsaw to rise up and expel the Germans. The message read:

> People of Warsaw, to arms! The whole population must gather around the National Assembly and the Underground Army. Attack the Germans. Stop the Germans from destroying public buildings. Assist the Russians in crossing the Vistula. Give it information and lead it to the best fords. The more than a million inhabitants of Warsaw must become an army of a million men fighting for liberation and destroying the German invaders.

Two days later, 1 September 1944, General Bor (Komorowski) ordered the Polish Underground Army to rise up and attack the Germans. General Bor's soldiers were equipped with only small arms and a supply of ammunition for about seven days of fighting. The Polish effort, however, would be sufficient to allow the Russian soldiers to cross the Vistula and join the fighting. The Russian call to arms, however, was a monstrous hoax that led to the death of more than 200,000 men, women, and children of Warsaw. Russian troops reached the east bank of the Vistula River and sat idly by as the Polish fighters and civilians were being massacred by superior German forces. The United States and Great Britain tried to help by airlifting ammunition, food, and medicine to the hard-pressed Poles. Some supplies got through, but the Western Allies suffered exceptionally heavy losses of aircraft and crews. Roosevelt and Churchill appealed to Stalin to allow transport planes to land in Russian-controlled territory and refuel for the return flight to bases. Stalin refused. He wanted the Polish Home Army exterminated, and he employed his

German enemy to carry out the diabolical scheme. Although the Poles had planned to fight the Germans for a maximum of seven days alone before Russian units entered the fight, they battled the enemy alone for a total of sixty-three days. The Warsaw Uprising of 1944 became an enormous tragedy, deliberately perpetrated by a barbaric and scheming Russia that used the German enemy in an attempt to achieve its eventual goal of world domination.

Several days after the fighting in Warsaw erupted, the Polish Communists in Moscow broadcast the lie that no fighting was taking place in Warsaw and claimed it was a fabrication of the Polish Government in London. The Uprising revealed the few Polish Communists to be slavish puppets of Russia. Still, Russia formally recognized the Communist Provisional Government to be the real government. At the Yalta Conference in February 1945, Roosevelt and Churchill agreed to Stalin's demands. The Big Three also reaffirmed their commitment to a "free and independent Poland." (Stalin always agreed to statements about freedom and democracy which he had no intention of carrying out.)

The United States and Great Britain now abandoned the legitimate and recognized government of Poland in London. And they proposed to form a body of Polish officials from London and the Underground State and merge them with Stalin's hand-picked Communists as the basis for a Provisional Government of National Unity. Despite the good intentions of the Western leaders, no member of the Underground Resistance—the strongest in Europe—was included. The English writer of the Epilogue concludes that the Russian policy toward Poland had not changed since September 1939, and, indeed, had not deviated since the time of the Tsars and the Partitions of 150 years ago. He continues with a description of the reign of oppression by the Communists in Poland that led to the fraudulent national elections of 19 January 1947 when the Communists seized total control of Poland.

CHAPTER THREE

RUSSIA MURDERS
15,000 POLISH
PRISONERS OF WAR

*A*UTHOR'S COMMENT: Dr. Janusz K. Zawodny's book *Death in the Forest: The Story of the Katyn Forest Massacre* is perhaps the best researched and accurate account of the mass murder of 15,000 Polish prisoners of war by Russia in the Spring of 1940. *Death in the Forest* was published by the University of Notre Dame Press in 1962. Zawodny calls the Russian mass murder "the largest assassination of prisoner-soldiers since Genghis Khan." Germany and Russia each accused the other of the horrendous crime. Zawodny asks the question: Why did the United States, Great Britain, and France fail to pursue the Katyn Forest Massacre at the Nuremberg Trial of German war criminals in 1945-1946?

In 1951-1952, the Select Committee of the United States Congress assembled heretofore suppressed documents from the State and War Departments that provide a clear-cut picture of the tremendously important part the Katyn Forest massacre played in shaping the future of postwar Europe.

. . .

Russia had no qualms about collaborating with its enemy, Germany, when it led to the destruction of Poland. Germany and Russia concluded the secret Molotov-Ribbentrop Agreement of 23 August 1939 for simultaneous attacks on Poland and carving up the country between them. In an unprovoked attack on 1 September 1939, Germany invaded Poland with its total and overwhelming military forces. In accordance with the secret agreement, Russia also invaded Poland from the east on 17 September 1939.

As the Russian armies advanced into eastern Poland, they captured some 230,000 Polish soldiers of all ranks. About 20,000 reserves who had not the time to join their units were seized in their homes, placing the total number of prisoners of war at 250,000. Ten thousand of these were officers. The Russians were not content to take prisoners, a valid objective of warfare. This brutal enemy also invaded Polish homes and seized some 1,200,000 civilians who were then packed into cattle cars and transported deep into European Russia and Siberia to labor and die in Russian gulags.[1]

Once its sinister purpose of destroying Poland had been achieved, Germany attacked Russia on 22 June 1941 and advanced deep into the country. Russia became Germany's enemy, a condition that abruptly changed the international situation. Great Britain and the United States declared their support of Russia, and the Prime Minister of the Polish Government in London, General Wladyslaw Sikorski, negotiated a resumption of diplomatic relations with Russia, 30 July 1941. The Maisky-Sikorski Agreement freed the prisoners of war and the enslaved Polish civilians. Sikorski also obtained Stalin's concurrence to organize a Polish Army on Russian soil. General Sikorski appointed General Wladyslaw Anders, who also had been held as a prisoner of war, commander of the Polish forces in Russia. The British and American governments were pleased that General Sikorski sought reconciliation with Russia, despite Russia's

RUSSIAN KILLING FIELD OF
POLISH POWS – Katyn, Spring 1940
Prisoner of War Camps: Ostashkov, Kozelsk, Starobelsk

Map by Vicki Trego Hill

treacherous attack on its Slavic neighbor. Following the signing of the Sikorski-Maisky Agreement of 30 July 1941, British Foreign Minister Anthony Eden handed Sikorski a note that read:

> In connection with today's signing of the Polish-Soviet Agreement, I desire to take the opportunity of informing you that, in accordance with the provisions of the Treaty of Military Aid between Poland and Great Britain, dated the 25th of July 1939, His Majesty's Government in the United Kingdom has not undertaken any obligations to the U.S.S.R., which would affect the relations between that State and Poland. I desire also to assure you that His Majesty's Government does not recognize any territorial changes made in Poland since 1939.

Like Great Britain, the United States made a similar statement of support and lauded Poland for its demonstration of "immense national discipline." The American statement read:

> In the whole history of nations there was no parallel to what had now happened. The population of almost one-half of Poland, since 1939, had had their homes burst open and destroyed, their families and friends deported, everything that was most dear and most sacred to them cut down and rooted out, by order of the Soviet Union. The Polish Forces everywhere, fighting on the Continent, in the Battle of Britain, in Africa and on the high seas, were fighting to liberate not only the people of Warsaw and Cracow but also of Wilno and Lwow. It was not a simple thing now to turn and once again hold out hands in friendship to the men who had done these things. But this act of immense national discipline was undertaken. For the second time in just over twenty years the offer of friendship was made. The war aims, the articles of faith, the great Christian principles, so often invoked, from platforms of every description, by the Western allies, blazed forth for a few magnificent seconds into passionate life and reality; and that within the almost fabulous territory of the Soviet Union.
>
> Out of so unparalleled a situation what might not be expected to develop? The opportunity was supreme. The future was looked into ardently, and with immense hope.

The United States Government issued a noble statement. Regrettably, this sentiment eroded rapidly.

Establishing his recruiting station in Buzul'uk, Russia, General Anders received a flood of Polish prisoners and civilians from all over Russia. As the ranks of his corps grew, General Anders noted that none of the 15,000 prisoners of war held at the Russian internment camps of Kozelsk, Ostashkov, and Starobelsk showed up at Buzul'uk. Anders queried the Russians several times, but Russian authorities claimed that the Polish prisoners had all been freed. On 3 December 1941, Sikorski flew to Moscow to ask Stalin personally about the missing prisoners of war. Stalin feigned ignorance. He ventured the opinion that they probably escaped into Manchuria.[2]

The Polish Government in London knew quite accurately the names of the 15,000 prisoners of war at the three camps. The Russians had allowed them to write family members in Poland. However, in late April 1940, letters from the prisoners of war ceased, and no one knew what had happened. General Anders was anxious to see these soldiers, especially since 8400 of these 15,000 were experienced officers whom Anders needed for his Second Army Corps. They formed about forty-five percent of the officer corps of the Polish Army in 1939. For a time, the whereabouts of 15,000 Polish prisoners of war remained a mystery.

General Anders never got his officers and soldiers from the three prisoner of war camps. The Russians had brutally murdered them. The diabolical executions were carried out by the ruthless secret police, the NKVD, on order of Stalin to Laverenti Beria, chief of the NKVD. Prior to the mass executions, the Russian secret police repeatedly and intensively interrogated the prisoners, trying to determine those individuals who could be converted to Communists. The secret police identified 483 candidates. They were removed from the three internment camps and assembled at Grazovec. Thus, the 483 who escaped death were moved for a final interrogation to Moscow where the Russians selected a total of seventy-four Poles who seemed to be willing to serve as Communists.

The mass execution of the Polish prisoners of war took place in the Katyn Forest, ten miles west of Smolensk. The prisoners at the Kozelsk camp were transported to the Katyn Forest that served as a secret and exclusive area of the NKVD. Everyone but the NKVD was denied entry. The Russians concluded this restricted area was suitable for the mass murders without fear of detection. The Poles were bused from a railroad stop to the Katyn Forest in groups of thirty to forty at a time. The NKVD fired Russian-built hand guns with German-manufactured bullets. The executions were methodical. An agent fired a bullet through the back of the head of the Pole as another agent reloaded the guns. The dead bodies were buried in shallow mass graves, and young pine and spruce trees were planted over them. The dastardly crime remained hidden for two and a half years.

On 22 June 1941, Germany launched a massive attack on Russia that penetrated deep into the country, including the area of Smolensk. A German unit was billeted in the NKVD villa at Katyn where the Germans discovered the mass graves in February 1943. Josef Goebbels, German Propaganda Minister, seized upon this discovery as an opportunity to sever the unity of the Allies. On 13 April 1943, German radio blasted the world with the announcement that Russia murdered thousands of Polish officers at Katyn Forest. Russia angrily countered the German broadcast. Two days later it accused the Germans of the crime. Moscow radio put out a false story that Polish prisoners of war in 1941 were carrying out construction work for Russia and were captured by the German Army. Subsequently, the Germans executed the Poles.[3]

Public opinion in the United States and Great Britain believed that the Germans were the perpetrators of the crime, knowing the brutality of German occupation. The Germans, therefore, felt it necessary to conduct an open and complete investigation of the mass murder in the Katyn Forest. Another reason for the need of a thorough investigation stemmed from the Russian use of German bullets. From the propaganda point of view, a finding of Russian guilt would assuredly bring an end to diplomatic relations between Russia and the Polish Government in Exile. The Germans established an independent International Commission composed of thirteen scholars and specialists in forensic medicine from twelve countries (none from Germany). They were not knowingly pro-Nazi and did not join the Commission under pressure. The members elected Dr. Ferenc Orsov of the University of Budapest chairman of the International Commission. In addition, the Polish Red Cross from German-occupied Poland was invited. It sent a medical team of twelve persons who were given a free hand at Katyn. Germany also added its own Special-Medical Judiciary Committee. Unknown to the Germans and the other commissions, the Polish Red Cross had several members of the Polish Underground State whose purpose was to determine the identity of the murderers and dispatch this data via the Underground radio to the Polish Government in Exile.[4]

Members of the three commissions acted independently and reached their own conclusions, but they agreed on many important details. Eight mass graves were found, located at six to eleven feet below the surface. The corpses were lying face down, hands alongside their bodies or tied behind them, one upon another in ten or twelve layers. All had been shot in the back of the head. The rope for tying their hands was Russian-made. Some of the prisoners struggled to survive but were bayoneted by the Russian executioners. An examination of the wounds and holes in the material disclosed the use of a four-corner bayonet, a type used by the Russian Army.

The murdered prisoners of war were identified from the personal data in the pockets of their clothing, such as letters, photos, diaries, or military identification tags. The members of the Polish Red Cross concluded that the data were authentic and could not have been inserted before the discovery of the graves. The Polish Red Cross identified from among the dead more than 300 doctors and journalists, several hundred lawyers, twenty-one university professors, and hundreds of high school and elementary school teachers. They were reserve officers who had sprung to the defense of their country.

39

The key objective of the investigating commissions was the date of the executions. This determination would lead to the guilt of Germany or Russia. The three commissions agreed that the prisoners were killed about *three* years before they were exhumed, thus placing the executions in the spring of 1940 and a year before German armies attacked Russia and advanced into the area of Smolensk. The commissions based their conclusion on the medical examination of the corpses—the decalcification of the skulls and brains and the saponification of muscles, and the documentation on the bodies: diaries and papers issued them by Russian authorities. Another fact was the age of the young spruce trees that the Russians had planted on the mass graves. These trees were about three years old. Once in the area, the members of the commissions had no difficulty in locating the graves. They dug where the young trees grew.[5]

The Polish Red Cross tabulated the names of 4,483 corpses of Polish prisoners of war; the majority of them were officers. All had come from Camp Kozelsk. The list corresponded with the names of the missing Polish officers that the Polish government repeatedly had asked the Russian government about, and Russia repeatedly denied any knowledge. Because the Germans had broadcast the number of Polish dead at 10,000 to 12,000, the Germans now insisted that the Polish Red Cross announce the figure of 12,000 exhumed bodies, with the threat of retaliation for refusal. Notwithstanding, the Polish Red Cross refused to falsify its findings. An additional 10,000 Polish prisoners of war at Camps Ostoshkov and Starobelsk were evacuated and transported to Kiev, a stopping point, and further transported to an unknown destination where they disappeared. No doubt, the Russians mercilessly killed these Poles, as well.[6]

The Polish Red Cross was overwhelmed with pleas from family members who sought to have the bodies brought to Poland for burial, and they also inquired anxiously about their loved ones held in the other two camps at Starobelsk and Ostashkov. In German-occupied Poland, the Germans in their controlled *Kurier Warszawski* (Warsaw Courier) kept up a propaganda barrage about Katyn for four months—from 14 April to August 1943. Compelled to do something, the Polish Government in Exile asked the International Red Cross in Geneva to investigate the Katyn Massacre. Geneva was willing but only if it received a similar request from Russia which did not make a request. Although the Polish request to the International Red Cross was made independently, the Germans cleverly timed a similar request to that body and gave the impression that the Germans and Poles were collaborating. Stalin now found his alibi for breaking off diplomatic relations with the Polish Government in London. In identical messages to Roosevelt and Churchill, Stalin denounced the Poles as German collaborators and demonized Sikorski. The two Allied leaders rejected Stalin's charge of collaboration. Roosevelt, however, added that the Poles were wrong in contacting the International Red Cross. Under Secretary of State Sumner Welles expressed the indignation of the United States to Ambassador Jan Ciechanowski for the "audacity" of Poland to ask the International Red Cross for an investigation. Churchill also was clearly annoyed by the deep Polish anger over the Katyn Massacre. He silenced the Polish press in England, and told Stalin so, and also forbade Sikorski to make any further inquiries about Katyn. Meanwhile, the majority of the British press kept on publishing Russian lies. The Poles were frustrated by the grossly unfair treatment. As one example, the British *Daily Worker*, shamelessly pro-Russian, maintained its anti-Polish barrage week after week until the British Minister of Information denounced it for vilification of the Polish Government. However, the Katyn Massacre could not be silenced among the general public. Dr. Zawodny writes that 55,138 Communist Party members in Great Britain assailed the Poles and carried out Stalin's dirty work. Likewise, there were some 100,000 Poles in Great Britain at the time, mostly Polish Army soldiers. With their firm belief in human rights and yearning for independence, the Poles had no use for the despicable British Communists.[7]

In America, officials found dealing with the Katyn Massacre difficult. The tragedy had escalated into a political problem. The

Office of War Information (Elmer Davis) could not silence adverse public opinion. In 1943, there were more than six million Americans of Polish descent in a population of 132 million (according to the Census of 1940). However, there was a larger element of public opinion that favored and praised Russia. *Life* magazine, for example, kept selling Communist leaders to the Americans. Its issue of 29 March 1943 was dedicated to Russia and sported a front cover with Josef Stalin's photo. This issue also carried a full-page photo of the Bolshevik Nicolai Lenin whom *Life* praised as "perhaps the greatest man of modern times." The magazine also benevolently portrayed the ruthless NKVD agency, calling it "a national police force similar to the FBI." Indeed, *Life* editors exhibited utter ignorance and naivete, or engaged in deliberate propaganda. Perhaps *Life* was simply toeing the slavish pro-Russian policy of the Roosevelt Administration. On 18 November 1943, Secretary of State Cordell Hull told a joint session of Congress that Josef Stalin "was one of the great statesmen and leaders of the age." With a long-serving and experienced Secretary of State gushing forth with nonsense about a mass murderer, it is not surprising that *Life* published Russian propaganda.[8]

President Franklin Roosevelt seemed fascinated with Stalin from the very beginning of the coalition of the United States, Great Britain, and Russia in their common battle against Germany. The American tried to charm the Russian with his broad smile and fancy cigarette holder. Roosevelt's charm in politics worked at home but not with Stalin who was too savvy to be deceived. While the heated controversy over the Katyn Forest Massacre raged on and Churchill worked feverishly to keep the coalition from splitting, Roosevelt proposed a secret meeting with Stalin somewhere in the area of the Bering Straits. In a letter dated 5 May 1943, Roosevelt suggested a meeting *without the presence and knowledge of Churchill*. The President kept the proposed meeting so close to his chest that he had his letter hand-carried to Moscow by an "old friend," Joseph E. Davies. The "old friend" bypassed the American Ambassador to Moscow, Averell H. Harriman, telling him that he would not be needed at the meeting with Stalin. Roosevelt wrote Stalin that only he and his close adviser, Harry Hopkins, would attend the meeting. (Knowing just how much Hopkins advised the President to be nice to the Russian dictator would be revealing.) It appears that the secret meeting did not take place. However, Roosevelt's proposed meeting reveals a condescending and superior attitude for a close friend and staunch ally, Churchill.[9]

AUTHOR'S NOTE: For a long time this author held Eleanor Roosevelt in high esteem until his research revealed her incomprehensible fascination with Communism. During the Great Depression in the 1930 decade, when the author was growing up, President Roosevelt tried to improve the difficult life of Americans as the unemployment rate reached twenty-five percent (and few women were employed). The series of programs Roosevelt introduced had only a slight effect on the economy, but people appreciated his effort. During the war years this author served in the Pacific Theater of Operations. He was far removed from the events in the United States. Notwithstanding, he did learn of Mrs. Roosevelt's work in humanitarian projects as reported in the press. A favorable image was implanted in the author's mind. When the author began his research for *American Betrayal*, however, he discovered a vastly different Eleanor Roosevelt from the image he had carried for some seventy years. He was shocked and disappointed. She associated with numerous American Communists. She served as honorary chair for Communist front organizations such as the National Council of American-Soviet Friendship and Russian War Relief. The President and First Lady invited known Communists to the White House (where they slept in the Lincoln bedroom). She seemed to be more pro-Russian than the President. Eleanor Roosevelt must bear some of the responsibility for the President's contemptuous treatment of the Polish nation, not only because of its loss of freedom for forty-five years but also for the stifling of normal progress during this same period.

. . .

German Propaganda Minister Josef Goebbels was amused by the reaction in the British and American newspapers over the Katyn Forest Massacre. Zawodny writes that Goebbels noted in his diary: "The Poles are given a brush-off by the English and the Americans as though they were enemies." Meanwhile, Russian armies were driving the Germans back to the west. When the Russians regained the Smolensk area, they came prepared with a Special Commission that would "prove" the Germans to be guilty of the Katyn Forest Massacre.

The Russian mind was made up: the Germans massacred the Polish prisoners of war. The Russians set out to "prove" it their way. They did not invite a single foreign medical representative. The Russians knew exactly what they wanted to do and did not wish to contend with contrary findings of foreign medical personnel. The three previous commissions had established the time of the executions as early spring of 1940. The Russians, however, "found" the massacre to have occurred later, in the fall of 1941.[10]

During the presence of German troops in the Smolensk area, German Communications Regiment 537 under the command of Colonel Friederick Ahrens occupied the former lodge of the NKVD in the Katyn Forest. The Russians, therefore, rounded up a number of natives from the area who had come into contact with Ahrens. The Russians coached the selected witnesses, told them exactly what to say, and threatened them with death if they failed to comply.

In its report, the Russian Special Commission concluded that the slain Polish prisoners of war were buried about *two* years prior, between September and December 1941 (when the German Army occupied the area). The report reads that, after murdering and burying the slain Poles, the Germans prepared to announce the mass murder to the world. With this objective in mind, the Russian report says, the Germans now exhumed all 11,000 bodies (the number previously announced by the

Germans). Further, the Germans removed from the clothing all documents dated later than April 1940. The corpses were then returned to the mass graves. The Russians claimed that the preparation of the corpses took place in March 1943 when 500 Russian prisoners of war were employed for this purpose. Once completed, the Germans shot all 500 Russians soldiers. Notwithstanding, the previous commissions—International, Polish Red Cross, and German—did not find the graves of these 500 Russian soldiers supposedly shot by the Germans. And more remarkably, the Russian Commission did not claim to have found them. Had the Russians been able to point out the graves of the 500 slain Russian soldiers, their report would have gained much credibility.[11]

Although the Russians produced a spurious report, they gave the pro-Russian U.S. State Department a useful propaganda tool that the Roosevelt Administration dusted off repeatedly. The Russians steered clear of foreign medical experts, but they welcomed foreign journalists. American Ambassador to Moscow, Averell H. Harriman, sent his daughter, Kathleen Harriman, age twenty-five, to join the foreign journalists. He explained that as a journalist his daughter would more likely be able to go than as a member of the diplomatic corps. Despite the Ambassador's explanation, John Melby, third secretary of the American Embassy, went also. The foreign journalists were escorted into a tent where a Russian doctor was dissecting a corpse and explaining how well the flesh had been preserved. At the end of the tour, the Russians conducted a briefing. The journalists began asking penetrating questions which the Russians felt increasingly awkward answering. Suddenly, the briefing came to an end with the announcement that the train for Moscow was waiting. Kathleen Harriman wrote a report in which she accepted the Russian claim, placing all the blame on the Germans. The Ambassador immediately dispatched it to the State Department where officials repeatedly quoted the Kathleen Harriman report as proof of German guilt for the Katyn Forest Massacre. It appears that Ambassador Harriman's sole purpose in sending his daughter to join the foreign journalists was to provide a convenient cover-up for the State Department.[12]

Knowing that the trial of German war criminals (Nuremberg) would reverberate around the world, Russia insisted on adding the Katyn Forest Massacre to court proceedings. Great Britain, France, and the United States were reluctant to do so, but ceased to object when Russia persisted. The outcome at the Nuremberg Trial of the Katyn charge made Russia look ridiculously embarrassed (Chapter 10).

THE POLISH
UNDERGROUND STATE,
1939-1945

*A*UTHOR'S COMMENT: This chapter is based on Stefan Korbonski's book *The Polish Underground State: A Guide to the Underground, 1939-1945*. Korbonski served as a lieutenant in the Polish Army in 1939. The Russians captured him in the invasion of Poland on 17 September 1939. He escaped to Warsaw in German-occupied Poland where he became one of the leading organizers of the Polish Underground State. It was more than an ordinary resistance movement against the enemy like the French and Norwegian Resistance Movements. In Korbonski's words: "It was the merging of the activities of the civil and military underground that produced that phenomenon—unique in the history of Poland and of World War II—the Polish Underground State, which had all the attributes of statehood—government, parliament, courts, and a military force known as the Home Army."

.   .   .

The development of the Polish Underground State faced the territorial conditions that Germany and Russia had imposed on their halves of occupied Poland. Immediately after the September 1939 Campaign, Germany incorporated large areas of Poland into the Reich—the provinces of Poznan, Pomerania, Silesia, most of the Lodz district, the area north of Warsaw, and parts of the Krakow and Kielce districts. Poznan and land along the Baltic Sea had been seized once before by Prussia during the infamous Partitions of the late eighteenth century and incorporated into Prussia, including the province of Warmia with its main city of Olsztyn and the town of Frombork where Polish astronomer Nicholas Copernicus studied the heavens. In 1918, when Poland regained its independence, after 123 years of subjugation by Germany, Austria, and Russia, the Polish nation regained Poznan, fought the defeated Germans for Silesia, and gained access to the Baltic Sea. But Poland did not recover Warmia nor the city of Gdansk. The two Allied leaders of World War I, Lloyd George of Great Britain and Eduoard Daladier of France, were hostile to Poland. Rather than give Poland the seaport it needed, they set up the Free City of Danzig peopled mainly with Germans. Other Germans living in the new Poland of 1918 became citizens of Poland, but most of them changed allegiance when Adolf Hitler arrived.

In the Polish land incorporated into Germany in 1939, the Poles and Jews were denied all rights. The Germans began an intensive program of Germanizing the land. Thousands of German settlers arrived from the Reich and Russia (through population exchanges). Some 750,000 Polish peasants were expelled from their farms to make room for Baltic Germans from Latvia and Estonia. Blond-haired orphans were kidnapped from orphanages by agents of the blood stock organization, the *SS Lebensboom* (Fountain of Life). Heinrich Himmler, chief of the *SS* (*Schutzstaffel*), the military arm of the German Nazi Party, observed that these Polish children were closer to his Teutonic ideal than his own.[1]

The Germans imposed strict separation of the Germans and

Poles. Public transportation, park benches, and quality shops were marked with signs "For Germans Only." Non-Germans were restricted to their homes. Jews were forbidden to leave the ghetto or face execution.

Polish farms, businesses, and homes were confiscated for the benefit of the German settlers. The Polish inhabitants were forced into serfdom (like that in previous centuries) and forbidden to leave their assigned places of work. All pension payments and health insurance were abolished. The Poles suffered from the rationing of food of the worst quality and were paid starvation wages. In 1942, Germany forcibly drafted Polish men between the ages of twenty and thirty-two into the German Army.

Germany suppressed the use of the Polish language, history, and culture. All schools, secondary and higher, were closed. In the primary schools only the German language and arithmetic could be taught. The Polish language was forbidden outside the home. The Polish press was abolished. Libraries and book stores were burned down. Archives and museums were either moved to the Reich or destroyed. Wayside chapels with crosses (symbols of Polish culture) and tombstones in the cemeteries were destroyed. All markers and sign posts in Polish were removed, and the names of towns and villages were changed to German names. Only one church was allowed in each county; all others were either closed or destroyed. Sermons, prayers, and hymns in Polish were forbidden in the few remaining churches. Most of the priests were arrested and banished to concentration camps. Two million intelligentsia were transferred to the larger, central zone of occupation, the so-called *General Gouvernement*. Allowed to take only personal belongings, these Poles were loaded into cattle cars and transported to the General Gouvernement where they were dumped (frequently in the middle of the night) at some small railroad station.

The Poles in the annexed areas were subjected to a reign of terror and the most severe restriction on individual freedom. All Poles in position of some leadership were publicly executed—political leaders, mayors, landowners, local officials, priests, teachers, lawyers, doctors. The city of Bydgoszcz was cruelly punished and some 20,000 residents killed as a reprisal for an earlier attack and destruction of a German guerilla band by the Polish Army in the very beginning of the September Campaign. Any German, whether a civilian or wearing the uniform of the police, Nazi Party, or military unit, became the absolute master over the life and death of any Pole. In other words, any German could kill a Pole with impunity. Stefan Korbonski writes of the ridiculous case of a Polish woman in the city of Plock where she was fined 1000 German marks or three months in jail for the "effrontery" of her muzzled dog barking at the dog of a German inspector.

Poles felt the ban on travel most keenly. To travel by train, Poles had to obtain a pass that prescribed the route and duration of travel. Even bicycles were confiscated, except for the few Poles who needed the bicycles to reach their place of work. The German Government encouraged Germans to spy on Poles at work and elsewhere and report their observations to the authorities. Despite the reign of terror and severe restriction on freedom, Korbonski says, the Underground Movement was successfully organized in the lands incorporated into the Reich.

In the eastern half of Poland, the Russians achieved the same degree of subjugation but by treacherous methods. On 22 October 1939, Russia held an election of candidates, handpicked by the NKVD and selected mainly from the newly-arrived Russians and totally unknown to the local people. These selected delegates then petitioned the Supreme Council in Moscow for the admission of the "liberated" land into Russia. Of course, Russia graciously granted their request. The whole process was a big lie. The northern districts of the newly-incorporated territory were made a part of the Byelorussian Socialist Soviet Republic, and the southern districts, the Ukrainian Socialist Soviet Republic. To complete the process, Russia conferred citizenship on all inhabitants of eastern Poland. As a result, young men were eligible for service in the Russian Army.

Just as in the German zone, the Russians carried out destructive economic "reforms" that brought utter devastation. The

Russians seized all prewar state property, but the "reforms" did not stop at this stage. The Russians also confiscated private estates, factories, sugar refineries, distilleries, saw mills, and other industrial activities, plus banks and savings institutions. They then hauled this wealth to Russia. The countries around Russia were so far advanced over that country that Russians looted both friend and foe. (This author is aware of the case of Korea in 1946, when Russia occupied North Korea and the United States, South Korea. Travelers coming from North Korea to Seoul were debriefed by U.S. Army Intelligence officers. These Koreans reported the wholesale looting of industries and factories built by the Japanese during their forty years of occupation. Although Russia was grooming North Korea to become a Communist puppet, the Russians did not hesitate to strip that country of its wealth.)

In the Russian zone of occupation, Polish currency (*zloty*) was removed from circulation; banks and savings accounts were blocked. The Russian military units imposed massive requisitions for food and feed, causing food shortages. In place of the Polish language, the Byelorussian and Ukrainian languages were made official. In practice, however, the change meant the Russian language. The Russians closed down several thousand churches, convents, and monasteries. Roadside chapels and crosses were torn down. As for the policy of getting rid of Poles, the Russians and the Germans saw eye to eye. From the western lands annexed to Germany, the Germans deported some two million Poles to the General Gouvernement, established by Hitler's decree of 12 October 1939. These two million were allowed to drift by themselves. The Russians, on the other hand, conducted four massive deportations, some 1,700,000 people, deep into European Russia and Siberia. Like the Germans, the Russians were ruthless. Men, women, and children were grabbled by crude Russian soldiers without warning and permitted to take with them the barest personal items. At the prison camps, the Poles were worked under cruel conditions and starved to death.

The conduct of education by the Germans and Russians was different. The Russians retained the Polish structure of education but converted all programs along Russian methods and introduced variations based on nationality. The teaching of the Russian language was mandatory as well as the Russian interpretation of history and political-ideological indoctrination. Schools were divided into Byelorussian, Ukrainian, Jewish, and Polish where the Polish language was tolerated. The objective of all schools was to indoctrinate the students into Communism.

The Russians conducted a reign of terror from the very beginning. Thousands of Poles discharging official duties under Polish rule were murdered outright. The slaughter increased after Germany attacked Russia on 22 June 1941. The total number of murdered Poles is estimated at 100,000 individuals, including the 15,000 Polish Army officers.

The *General Gouvernement* comprised the Lublin district, part of the Lwow district, and most of the Warsaw, Krakow, and Kielce districts and contained some twelve million people. The Poles in the General Gouvernement were not exempt from the German master plan for the eventual extermination of the Polish race. They were too numerous to eliminate immediately. Meanwhile, the Poles would become a nation of serfs and a source of labor. Later, massive German colonization of the General Gouvernement would take place, as the Poles were to be deported to Siberia and death in the gulags. Only the Jews received immediate and harsher treatment than the Poles.

Both the Germans and the Russians initially directed their murderous onslaught against the Polish intelligentsia. They made massive arrests of political and social leaders, senators, deputies, professors, scholars, industrialists, doctors, attorneys, reserve officers, and others. These Poles were transported to German extermination camps in Germany and Poland. When the Germans opened the Auschwitz extermination camp on 14 June 1940, the first prisoners were Polish intellectuals, and not Jews nor Russian prisoners of war as some American Jews maintain. The German drive to exterminate Polish intellectuals began on 6 November 1939 with the "invitation" to 115 professors of the Jagiellonian University in Krakow to participate in an impor-

DESTRUCTION OF POLAND 1939

BALTIC SEA

LITHUANIA

EAST PRUSSIA

GERMANY

ANNEXED TO GERMANY

OCCUPIED BY RUSSIA

RUSSIA

● Stettin

● Gdansk

● Wilno

Vistula

● Poznan

● Warsaw

● Brzesc

● Pinsk

GENERAL GOUVERNEMENT

Oder River

Vistula River

● Lublin

● Krakow

● Lwow

CZECHOSLOVAKIA

HUNGARY

ROMANIA

Map by Vicki Trego Hill

Annexed to Germany   General Governement (German)

Russian-Occupied (Until 22 June 1941, when Germany attacked Russia)

tant study in Germany. The Germans perpetrated a cruel hoax. The professors were transported to Germany and disappeared in extermination camps.

Hans Frank, appointed by Hitler to be Governor of the General Gouvernement, ordered the execution of Polish civilians for the flimsiest reasons. Between 15 October 1943 and 1 August 1944, some 9400 individuals were rounded up on the streets of

Warsaw and executed. His purpose was to terrorize the rebellious Poles and force them into submission. German demands extended to the countryside, as well. The farmers were levied for huge quantities of food to be transported to Germany, leaving them denuded of food. The Poles, however, sought escape in sabotage (punishable by death). The farmers hid food for themselves and their fellow Poles in the cities. Germany seized men for forced labor not only in Poland but throughout occupied Europe. Some two million Poles were shipped to Germany as forced laborers.

The Germans made a massive effort to destroy Polish history and culture in the General Governement. All secondary schools and institutions of higher learning were closed. The teaching of history and geography in primary schools was forbidden. Museums, archives, and libraries were abolished and their holdings were either destroyed or removed to Germany. Historical monuments and markers were destroyed. Germany seized all Polish state property as well as private enterprise, large estates, and farms.

In many ways life for the Poles was easier in the General Gouvenement than in the Polish land annexed to Germany or in Russian-controlled Poland. A key difference was the absence of forced deportation of Poles from their homes. There was one exception, however, that the Germans later abandoned. In the region of the city of Zamosc, 100,000 Polish farmers from 297 communities were expelled so that German colonists could take their land. The Polish Underground destroyed the colonizing scheme by violent activities against the German colonists such as burning down the villages. Then, as the German Armies suffered defeat after defeat on the Eastern front, Germany abandoned the colonizing effort.

Another difference in the General Gouvernement was the retention of the Polish language as well as the administrative bureaucracy at the lower echelon that allowed the regulation of daily life, such as the lower courts, city and county governments, and the police. The methodical Germans simply used the existing administration for their purposes. The control of the General Gouvernemeent was exercised at the top not only by Governor Hans Frank but also by the German Army of Occupation. Members of the Underground were able to move about more freely here than in the Poznan province or in the Russian-occupied zone of Poland. Governor Frank, however, brought in a larger number of Gestapo agents than in any other occupied country of Europe. In addition, there were German SS units consisting of Ukrainians, Latvians, Estonians, and Lithuanian volunteers, and toward the end of the occupation, even Russian volunteers called Vlasovites.

Still, members of the Underground had to be alert. The Germans targeted specific individuals for seizure and investigation. In fact, any Pole saying goodbye to his family in the morning was never sure that he would return at night. During the first two years of occupation, the Gestapo and the NKVD shared information on the clandestine activities of the Poles. Their common goal was to suppress opposition. The Underground fought back, assassinating the more vicious Gestapo agents and attacking the gendarmerie posts. They became masters at creating near-perfect forgeries of identity cards, birth certificates, work permits, and passes.

Meeting places and living quarters were camouflaged and changed frequently. Meeting places, print shops, and broadcasting stations were guarded by posted security agents and armed personnel. First and foremost was the oath to protect the secrets of the Underground. Hundreds that inevitably were captured suffered torture and death to deny the enemy any secret. Despite great odds, the Polish Underground grew stronger with each passing month, and it developed into the Polish Underground State with its own government, parliament, jurisdiction, education, welfare, press, and army. It became the leading underground movement of World War II.

The Polish spirit of resistance continued unabated. Secret underground organizations emerged spontaneously throughout Poland. The Poles firmly believed that, with the help of the Allies, they would regain their freedom. These small groups trusted each other. They were based, in large measure, on prewar associations, such as the Veterans groups, sports clubs, and Boy Scouts. General Michael Tokarzewski-Karasiewicz, corps commander in General Tadeusz Kutrzeba's army in the September Campaign, took the lead in creating a central command of the Underground Resistance. When battered Warsaw surrendered to the Germans on 28 September 1939, General Tokarzewski already had outlined the underground organization. He formed a general staff of fifteen officers to whom he assigned staff functions and commands in central districts. They set out immediately to print false identity documents, gathered money, weapons, ammunition, and explosives.

General Tokarzewski's nascent Underground Resistance had an opportunity to take immediate action against Adolf Hitler himself. Hitler came to Warsaw to gloat over the capture of the city on 5 October 1939. The conspirators planned to kill him. They placed explosives at the crossing of two main streets—*Nowy Swiat* and *Aleje Jerozolimskie.* The explosives were to be detonated when Hitler's car passed this spot. Unfortunately, the coup failed. On the day of Hitler's visit to Warsaw, the German military cleared all streets of people, including the observers who were to signal to another compatriot positioned in nearby ruins. Without the prearranged signal, and unable to see his target, the conspirator did not detonate the charge.[2]

General Tokarzewski reached out for political support. Prior to the war, he had maintained friendly relations with the opposition parties of the prewar government. He bypassed the pro-government parties which had become discredited by the mistakes committed by the government in preparing for war, among them, the delay in mobilizing the reserves. (Foreign Minister Jozef Beck listened to the cowardly pleas of the French not to mobilize for fear of offending Hitler. And then the French shamefully abandoned their long-standing alliance with Poland that called for the opening of a second front in the West within two weeks of a German attack on Poland.)

Tokarzewski held a series of meetings with leaders of the opposition parties shortly after the fall of Warsaw. They formed a
secret society called the "Service for Poland's Victory," which
included the Central Political Committee. Becoming a unified
political-military organization, it had three stated goals—first,
to struggle for Poland's independence within the prewar boundaries; second, to rebuild the armed forces within Poland; and,
third, to set up a temporary government structure within the
country. The Service for Poland's Victory was led by a Commander-in-Chief who let the Central Political Committee handle
political affairs. At the district and county levels the local commanders worked closely with the Central Political Committee,
also known as the "Council for National Defense." The smallest
unit in the network was the "post" headed by a post commander.
Women assisted ably in liaison work and medical matters.
Tokarzewski informed the Polish Government-in-Exile, located
at the time in Angers, France, of the organization of the Service
for Poland's Victory. Disguised as a medical doctor, Tokarzewski
toured the more important units of his organization to insure
a common effort. In Krakow, he established liaison with the
underground organization commanded by Colonel Tadeusz
Komorowski who later led the Warsaw Rising of 1944.

The Service for Poland's Victory was short-lived. General
Wladyslaw Sikorski disapproved of Tokazewski's contact with the
prewar Commander-in-Chief of Poland's Armed Forces, Marshal
Rydz-Smigly, who had been discredited for his inept leadership
during the German invasion. General Sikorski abolished the Service for Poland's Victory and replaced it with the "Union for
Armed Struggle (UAS)." He placed General Stefan Rowecki in
charge and demoted Tokarzewski to the regional command of
Lwow, Poland. Because many patriots in Poland objected to
Tokarzewski's demotion, Sikorski set up two commands of underground forces—Rowecki in German-occupied Poland and
Tokarzewski in Russian-occupied Poland. The two top commanders were ordered to prepare for an armed uprising that would
be launched at the moment when regular Polish armed forces

entered the country. The political parties pledged to support the Union for Armed Struggle. A Political Coordinating Committee drafted a "Code of Rights and Obligations of a Pole," a set of rules between Poles and Germans in every sector of national life.

The Political Coordinating Committee requested from the Government-in-Exile information about the military and international situation. At the same time, the Committee sent its own recommendations relating to foreign policy to the Government-in-Exile. The Underground Government maintained that the Government-in-Exile should behave as Poland's ambassador to the world. Nevertheless, decisions affecting matters in Poland should be the responsibility and decision of the Underground Government. The Political Coordinating Committee necessarily had changes in membership because of arrests and transfers, but it functioned the same throughout the war.

The solidarity of the political parties within the Political Co-ordinating Committee suffered a break when the Polish Socialist Party withdrew from the Committee on 10 September 1941. The withdrawal followed the German attack on Russia on 22 June 1941. The Allies promptly pledged their support to Russia, and General Sikorski concluded the favorable Sikorski-Maisky Agreement that led to the release of Polish prisoners in Russia. The Socialists opposed the establishment of diplomatic relations with Russia because the Agreement avoided the question of Poland's eastern boundaries. Sikorski, a man of vision, did right to take advantage of the rapprochement with Russia. Sikorski's decision saved thousands of Polish lives and led to the organization of General Wladyslaw Anders' Second Army Corps that fought gallantly at Monte Cassino, Italy.

All political parties in occupied Poland supported General Sikorski's Government-in-Exile. They approved its foreign policy and its decision to carry on the struggle to final victory. They often jockeyed for power as to who could better carry on the struggle against the enemy in Poland. But they deferred to London. In Poland, the resident delegate of Sikorski's government established fifteen subordinate offices throughout the country charged with executing directives from the central office and to solve local problems.

The Polish Underground established the prewar governmental structure, propelled by the conviction that not only the military but also every sector of national life should be organized and carried on by the government. Consequently, the Underground Government set up various departments:

The Department of Internal Affairs carried out tasks of a current and future nature. Among its "tasks of the future," the Department prepared for the takeover of the country following the defeat of Germany. In 1942, the Bureau of New Territories was established. It was assumed that East Prussia, West Pomerania, and the Opole region of Silesia would become part of Poland after the war.

Department of Information and Press rendered great service during the five years of the war. The German propaganda machine sought to destroy the nation's faith in itself and in eventual victory. The Germans published Polish language newspapers daily in the General Governement where this "reptile" press slandered Polish history and culture and ridiculed the Polish Government-in-Exile. The reptile (Nazi) press also tried to convince the Poles that survival depended on blind obedience to the German master race.

The Department of Information and Press counteracted the German propaganda, and the Department succeeded beyond expectations. The Department monitored the Polish language broadcasts of the British Broadcasting Corporation (BBC) and later the Voice of America (VOA). The Department then published daily news bulletins based on the BBC and VOA broadcasts. As the Department gained experience and resources, it extended its monitoring to programs broadcast by neutral countries and Allies in the English, French, and Italian languages. A summary of the week's news was next published in *The Weekly Review*, and finally a compilation of the most important news of the month capped the monthly activities. The daily, weekly, and monthly news of the world was delivered first to the underground leaders, followed by agencies under their supervision. The Department also published a biweekly called *The Republic of Poland* which informed the people of the activities of the Underground. Many Poles were able to listen secretly to broadcasts of the BBC and VOA because they refused to turn their radios in to the Germans and hid them at great personal risk. Despite the efforts of the Germans to suppress news from the outside world, the Poles were well informed.

Department of Education and Culture provided a framework and standard of instruction. Underground schools sprang up in nearly every locality where Germans had closed the Polish schools. According to the program of Heinrich Himmler, the Poles were a source of laborers. Therefore, all they should learn was "to count up to 500, to write their names, and to know that by divine order they owed obedience to the Germans." As for the intelligentsia, this irreplaceable class was to be totally destroyed and never be allowed to regenerate.

Department of Industry and Commerce studied German agricultural methods and prepared reports for the Underground State. It also trained cadres of future personnel for the rapid reestablishment of the Ministry of Agriculture.

Department of Justice studied German policies and prepared reports and plans for future legislation. It also exerted pressure on the judges in the lower courts (permitted to operate by the Germans) to render decisions in the best interest of the nation.

Department of Public Works and Reconstruction compiled a register of destruction inflicted by the occupying powers in such sites as cities, ports, railroads, highways during the war or during the occupation. The Department also prepared a program of rehabilitation and reconstruction after the war.

Department of Liquidating the Effects of the War registered and compiled the losses suffered by occupation and war in every area of national life.

Department of National Defense was established in November 1944 to prevent any tendency of the military element from seizing the power of the government. A civilian headed this department.

The Underground State represented the implacable position of the people and their determination to continue the struggle against the enemy occupiers. It established the principles on which the struggle would be fought. Going beyond the former Polish penal code, the Underground State drew up new rules for civil resistance. It mandated boycott of all German orders and measures that were harmful or damaging to the nation, and encouraged all kinds of sabotage that injured or destroyed German capability. It reminded the Poles of their responsibility to obey the Underground State which represented the Government-in-Exile (London).

Detailed instructions were prepared for all segments of society. Among the first was the ban of registering as "Volks deutche" (citizens claiming German ancestry), boycott of forced labor in Germany, banning any social relations with Germans and forbidding attendance at movies, theaters, and concerts conducted by the Germans. Farmers were instructed to sabotage the delivery quotas of farm goods imposed by the Germans. The Underground Government told factory workers to remain on the job but to carry out sabotage within the bounds of personal safety. Civil resistance continued on all levels. Doctors issued false medical certificates to men being levied for forced labor in Germany. Priests were directed to issue false baptismal certificates for Jews hounded by the Gestapo. Judges were forbidden, as a rule, to transfer cases from a Polish court to a German court. Civil resistance proclamations were issued as they became necessary, such as helping homeless Jews and uprooted Poles and deserters from Hungarian, Italian, Romanian, or Slovak units.

The rules of civil disobedience were widely disseminated through many channels of communication such as the secret news bulletins and publications. Poles listened to the Polish language broadcasts of the BBC and the Polish radio station *Swit* (Dawn), even though listening was punishable by death. In reality, *Swit* was located in Great Britain and purported to be broadcasting somewhere in occupied Poland. *Swit* broadcast daily news items of events in Poland, thus seemingly confirming its location somewhere in Poland. To maintain this pretense, General Sikorski privately asked Stefan Korbonski to radio daily and secretly to London activities like German decrees and executions of Poles, attacks by the Home Army on German units. In turn, *Swit* broadcast the same news items on the same day. In the lands annexed to Germany, the rules of civil resistance could be followed admittedly only to a limited extent.[3]

The Chief of Civil Resistance, Stefan Korbonski, was appointed by the delegate of the London government and the commander of the Home Army to organize the Directorate of Civil Resistance and to carry out civil resistance. With his deputy Marian Gieysztor, he functioned in three areas of activities—first, Justice, Sabotage, and Diversion; second, Radio Communication; and, third, Registration of German Crimes. The Chief of Civil Resistance published biweekly *The Chronicle of Civil Resistance*, and his activities were carried out at the district and county level. To capitalize on the talents of the clergy, women, and young people, the chief appointed three special commissions composed of the three groups who then carried out social resistance.

THE POLISH UNDERGROUND SABOTAGES THE ENEMY

Sabotage against the Germans was carried out under the direction of the commander of the Home Army, and he succeeded well. Although no compilation of total results is available, a report for the period of three and a half years—1 January 1941 to 30 June 1944—covers twenty-one difference kinds of activities.

It lists some 7,000 locomotives damaged and 19,000 railroad cars damaged. The saboteurs blew up thirty-eight railroad bridges and destroyed some 4000 military vehicles. Polish workers in German-run factories produced 4,700 defective parts for aircraft engines, 92,000 defective artillery shells, and the astronomical total of 570,000 defective capacitors for the electronics industry. Although the sabotage was carried out secretly, as expected, the Polish Underground engaged in 5,700 instances of direct attacks on German soldiers. Poles also attacked Gestapo agents. On 26 March 1943, Underground fighters rescued twenty-five Polish prisoners in the clutches of the Gestapo on a street corner in Warsaw. Five Gestapo and two civilian agents were killed in the rescue.

The Underground especially targeted individual German leaders for their vicious and brutal treatment of Polish civilians. More than 300 Gestapo personnel were assassinated, among them SS General Franz Kutschera, chief of police of Warsaw, and Buerckel, commandant of the notorious Pawiak Prison in Warsaw. Shadowing Kutschera's movements, Polish intelligence agents learned his habits and planned his assassination on 1 February 1944. The action took only one minute and forty-four seconds. The Underground succeeded in destroying the large German colonizing effort near the city of Zamosc. The Poles attacked two villages of Germans and killed several colonists. The Poles burned the two villages to the ground. In reprisal for the execution of 280 Poles, the Underground destroyed the German colonized village of Siedliska and killed sixty-nine colonists. In Warsaw, the Poles carried out a reprisal attack after four soldiers of the Home Army had been betrayed to the Gestapo. The Polish attack killed twenty-two German colonists, seven German gendarmes, and three Polish collaborators.

The Poles pulled off a spectacular robbery of a German bank truck carrying 100,000 Polish *zlotys*. It was a brazen attack in broad daylight at a street corner in Warsaw. At the same time, the robbery was well-planned and executed. A member of the plot pushed a hand cart into the path of the moving bank truck, causing it to halt. Other "robbers" fired upon and killed the German guards. A Pole jumped into the driver's seat and drove the truck to a hideout. The Germans never caught the robbers, although they offered a huge reward of five million *zlotys*.

Polish saboteurs managed to operate successfully in Berlin itself. The work was often interrupted by arrests of members because they had no jobs to fall back on nor local addresses to tie them to Berlin. During the time the Poles operated in Berlin, they directed sabotage activities of Polish forced laborers in German industry and agriculture. In October–November 1941, the Poles derailed twelve trains and sixteen locomotives, followed by the burning of thirty-three loaded railroad cars during January–February 1942.

Poles in eastern Poland were forced to engage in partisan warfare against vicious Ukrainian bands who were encouraged by the Germans to attack Polish residents. The Ukrainians were joined by bands of Byelorussians and Lithuanians. The objective of these bands of Russian allies was to eliminate the Polish populations of Lwow and Wilno. Home Army units came to the rescue of the threatened Poles. They assembled these Poles into fortified bases surrounded by trenches and barbwire fences, and posted Home Army soldiers to guard the bases. Poles were constantly threatened by the vicious allies of Russia. Nevertheless, Home Army units always sprang to their defense.

NOTE: The above instances of sabotage activities describe only a part of what the Home Army had accomplished.

CHAPTER FIVE

POLAND'S HOME ARMY

*T*HE HOME ARMY (*Armia Krajowa*) was not simply a
band of civilian patriots joined in a common cause. On
the contrary, it was a planned organization, trained in a deliberate manner along military principles. It grew to a total strength
of some 380,000 soldiers when the Warsaw uprising struck the
German Army, 1 August 1944. General Stefan Rowecki was the
first commander of the Home Army. Unfortunately, the Gestapo
identified and seized him in Warsaw on 30 June 1943. Rowecki
was succeeded by General Tadeusz Komorowski (identified by
the code name *Bor*). The High Command operated with thirty-
three staff units. The commander involved himself mainly in
operations, liaison, quartermaster, communications, and the
Bureau of Information and Propaganda. The Home Army divided
the country into three regions, and each region was further sub-
divided into districts, sectors (counties), and posts (townships).
During the years the Home Army fought the Germans, it lost
some 62,000 men—5,000 officers, 29,000 non-commissioned
officers, and 28,000 soldiers. These figures exclude the severe
losses during the sixty-three days of the Warsaw Rising, when

the Home Army lost 10,200 soldiers and when some 150,000 to 200,000 civilians perished.

Initially the Home Army commander faced the task of consolidating some ten military forces that represented political parties. He successfully integrated these factions into the Home Army. Several fringe groups refused to join the Home Army. These were the radical leftist Polish People's Army, the Communist People's Army, and units on the right of the National Armed Forces that supported the continuation of the prewar National Radical Group.

The liaison with the Government-in-Exile and with the West in general, although fraught with great danger and difficulty, nevertheless, was maintained on an effective basis throughout the war. One of the most capable emissaries was Jan Kozielewski (pseudonym Karski). On his trips to the West, Karski carried eyewitness information about conditions in occupied Poland —the German terror inflicted on the population and the extermination of the Jews. He personally debriefed Foreign Secretary Anthony Eden in London and President Franklin Roosevelt in Washington. (After the war, Karski became a distinguished professor of history at Georgetown University.) Another successful courier was Jan Nowak who twice made the secret journey from the West to Poland and back. (After the war Nowak headed the Polish Section of the Voice of America and then became a member of the Polish American Congress.) Other daring couriers were Jerzy Lerski and Czeslaw Raczkowski. (Following the war, Lerski became a professor of history at San Francisco University. This author had professional contact with Lerski on historical matters.) Among military couriers the missions of Colonel Kazimierz Iranek-Osmecki stand out. He was a member of the High Command of the Home Army.

Precise planning and close contact had to be established and maintained in connection with three landings of allied aircraft in Poland. The planes set down on secret airfields, well hidden in the forests. These air missions were called "bridges," and they demanded great accuracy and the closest coordination with units of the Home Army in the area of the airfields. On the night of 15 April 1944, a British plane started from Brindisi, Italy, (in Allied hands), and landed on a secret airfield near Belzyce in the Lublin district. Aboard were two officers from the Polish Army head-quarters in London. On the return flight the plane carried two officials of the Underground State and three officers of the Home Army. The second flight to Poland also took off from Brindisi and landed at a pre-selected secret airfield in the vicinity of Zaborow near the city of Tarnow. The third flight occurred on 25 July 1944, taking off from Brindisi and landing at the airfield near Zaborow. The passengers on the third return flight were several high-ranking officials of the Underground State plus Captain Jerzy Chmielewski of the Home Army, who carried drawings and com-ponents of the new German V-2 rocket. Captain Chmielewski's trip was the culmination of the effort to capture a V-2 missile from a secret German testing center in German-occupied Poland.

The origin of the V-2 in Polish hands begins at the Peenemunde rocket development and testing center on the Baltic Sea. German scientists under the direction of Werner von Braun were devel-oping both the subsonic V-1 ramjet missile and the larger supersonic V-2 rocket. Earlier, British intelligence requested Polish intelligence agents to secretly survey the layout of the German center at Peenemunde, defining the land boundaries and location of key facilities. The Polish agents accomplished their important task. They undoubtedly were helped by Polish forced laborers at Peenemunde. After the Poles forwarded their report on Peenemunde to British intelligence, the Bomber Com-mand of the Royal Air Force (RAF) planned and practiced the mission to bomb the German rocket center. On the night of 17–18 August 1943, the Bomber Command staged a successful operation, making Peenemunde the only precision raid the RAF carried out by night.[1]

The German High Command became alarmed by the new and grave threat to its secret rocket program, which it believed would insure the defeat of the British nation. The Germans, therefore, decentralized the rocket program, and operations were set up at several different locations, one of which was in German-occupied Poland, at the village of Blizna near Mielec in southeastern Poland. The area was heavily forested and with few inhabitants. The villagers of Blizna were evicted. Under the supervision of the SS, Heinrich Himmler's men laid out a proving ground of about twenty kilometers square. On 28 September 1943, Himmler came to inspect the newly-established rocket testing center. Shortly, Home Army soldiers discovered the rocket facility and began to shadow it. The German rocket engineers conducted flights of the V-2 missile. Some failed during the initial stages of development. Other firings were successful. Most rockets were fired north and impacted in the vicinity of the Bug River. When a rocket crashed into the ground, the Poles rushed to the spot to pick up parts and disappear before German recovery crews came by. On 20 May 1944, a V-2 missile hit the ground without breaking up. The Poles decided to seize the entire missile, but the necessary time was too short for the purpose. The missile had landed on the bank of the Bug River near the village of Klimczyce, giving the Poles an opportunity to move the missile into a swamp along the river and hide it below the surface of the water. After the German recovery crews scoured the area and moved on, the Poles came back and hauled the V-2 to a secret hideaway. They pulled the missile out of the swamp with a team of three pairs of horses and then loaded the V-2 onto two wagons joined together and transported their precious cargo to a barn in a selected village. A group of Polish scientists and engineers dismantled the rocket into more than 25,000 parts. While engaged in this work, the Poles were acutely aware that the work of studying the missile and making numerous drawings took place in a region that was closely patrolled by German soldiers. Meanwhile, dispatches went back and forth between Warsaw and London on the progress of the examination.

The Home Army prepared Special Report 1/R, No. 242, that contained a text of 4,000 words, with eighty photographs, twelve drawings, sketch map of the rocket center at Blizna, and a record of firings. General Tadeusz Komorowski, Commander

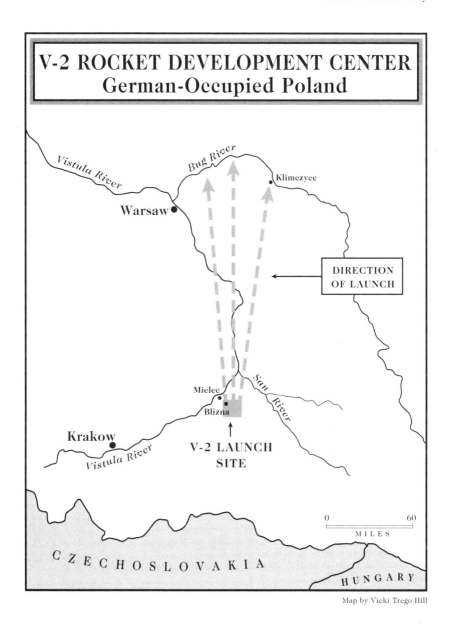

V-2 ROCKET DEVELOPMENT CENTER
German-Occupied Poland

Vistula River

Bug River

Klimczyce

Warsaw

DIRECTION
OF LAUNCH

San River

Mielec

Blizna

Krakow

Vistula River

V-2 LAUNCH
SITE

0   60

M I L E S

C Z E C H O S L O V A K I A

H U N G A R Y

Map by Vicki Trego Hill

of the Home Army, signed the report on 12 July 1944, and Captain Chmielewski was ready to fly the report and a bag of rocket components to London.

On the evening of 25 July 1944, a Dakota cargo plane took off for Poland from Brindisi, Italy. The crew was British, with a New Zealander for its pilot and a Pole as co-pilot and interpreter. The weather was favorable and the trip, uneventful. Local conditions in Poland, however, almost caused cancellation. The destination was an abandoned German airfield at Zaborow near the city of Tarnow in southern Poland. At this time, the German armies were retreating westward before a Russian counteroffensive so that movements of German units were occurring near Zaborow. A unit of German airmen rested not too far away, and two German reconnaissance planes landed on the airstrip but took off again shortly thereafter. Despite these activities, the Dakota came in for a landing. The first attempt was unsuccessful. When the plane climbed into the air for a second try, the roar of its motors shattered the silence of the night. The pilot landed the Dakota this time. A unit of the Home Army protected the landing site. After the landing, the soldiers quickly surrounded the plane, as well as boys from the surrounding villages, some barefooted, friendly but noisy. Departing passengers included Tomasz Arciszewsli of the Polish Government-in-Exile and Captain Chmielewski with his report and bag of V-2 parts.

Although the engines roared at take-off, the plane did not move. The wheels had sunk into the wet ground. The passengers left the plane as the pilot and co-pilot examined the problem. They asked the soldiers to dig small trenches in front of the wheels and fill them with straw. The second attempt to become airborne also failed. The soldiers now placed boards under the wheels and outwardly, and everyone got aboard. This time the pilot managed to take off with engines roaring. The Poles feared the noise of the engines would awaken every German soldier in the area, but the escapade succeeded.

The flight to Brindisi was uneventful. After some minor repairs to the plane and refueling, the Dakota flew on to London, arriving there on 28 July 1945. British officers immediately tried to claim Chmielewski's report. The Pole, however, had specific orders to hand the data to a representative of the Polish government. Shortly, it was turned over to the Crossbow Committee, a secret group of experts that gathered data on the German rocket program. (The capture of the German V-2 rocket could be the subject of a suspenseful, historical film.)[2]

The achievement of the Home Army in providing detailed analysis, rocket components, and drawings of the German V-2 missile to the Allies was a tribute to Polish ingenuity and competence of clandestine operations. Nevertheless, the crowning accomplishment of Poland's contribution to victory over Germany occurred earlier when Polish mathematicians broke the German Enigma code prior to the outbreak of World War II. They not only were able to read secret German communications but also constructed several Enigma machines. The code breaking team was headed by the brilliant mathematician Marian Rejewski. In July 1939 Polish intelligence personnel handed over to French and British crypto-analysts in Poland two working models of the Enigma machine, with complete instructions on how to decipher the code. With Enigma as the cornerstone, the British established an outstanding code breaking organization at Blechley Park near London. The Germans never learned that the Poles had broken their code, and all through the war years the Allies read the secret plans of the German Army, Navy, Air Force, and the diplomatic letters of the government.[3]

Enigma was a closely guarded secret during the war and for many years after. Because of its sensitivity, the whole story of Enigma was not known, except for the work at Blechley Park. In 1974, E. W. Winterbotham wrote the book *The Ultra Secret* in which he stated the British were the first to break the Enigma code. Winterbotham made a false claim, and since the publication of his book the claim has been totally discredited.[4]

The Home Army prepared for the day when it would rise up against the Germans as Polish forces from the outside were about to enter Poland. Organizing and equipping itself with arms for this momentous occasion became the main effort of the Home Army. Weapons were acquired from four different sources:

weapons buried by the Polish soldiers as the September Campaign ended in 1939, weapons captured or purchased from the Germans, arms produced by the Home Army, and those obtained from Allied air drops. Because of the lack of proper material to conserve the arms, the buried items became mostly unserviceable when they were dug up in 1944. Only about thirty percent were salvaged. Units of the Home Army and even individuals could purchase arms from German soldiers. These occasions were dangerous because the Gestapo tried to stamp out this practice. Buying weapons from Italian and Hungarian units located in Poland was simpler and safer. Despite the danger, raids by the Home Army on German sources of arms proved successful. The Poles attacked transport trains hauling arms to the German front lines in Russia. Guard houses and sentry posts were likewise attacked by surprise and arms obtained.

The Underground manufactured arms in three different kinds of shops: those operated by the Germans, those that were German-controlled, and those that were operated wholly by the Home Army. The secret arms production took place in five locations: two shops manufactured barrels for pistols, two assembly shops for automatic pistols, two testing ranges, two development shops, and four shops manufacturing explosives. The Poles badly needed anti-tank weapons, and some were air-dropped into Poland. In total, the Allies made 485 air drops to include 346 parachutists, twenty-eight couriers, some 4800 containers, 3000 packages, and forty-eight receptacles for a total of 600 tons. At the same time, the air drops were costly. Seventy planes were lost as well as sixty-two air crews of which twenty-eight were Polish.

AUTHOR'S NOTE: In the Hollywood movie *Schindler's List*, director Stephen Spielberg shows a scene during the Jewish Ghetto Uprising of 1942. Meeting secretly in the ghetto, a Polish soldier of the Home Army hands one pistol to a Jewish leader who looks at the Pole questioningly as if to ask, "Is this all?" And the Pole simply shrugs his shoulders. Certainly Poles were sympathetic to the Jewish uprising. However, it was doomed to fail, erupting from Jewish desperation. The Poles had their own master plan for a national rising at a time when the fortunes of war were favorable and regular Polish forces were about to enter Poland. The Home Army never acquired a sufficient number of weapons. In the Warsaw Rising of 1944, many soldiers had no weapons at all. The unarmed soldiers obtained weapons from a fallen comrade or a dead German soldier. Spielberg gratuitously smears the Polish nation.

The high-ranking member of the Polish Government-in-Exile residing in Poland as vice-premier ran the Department of Information and Press which served the entire country. In the Home Army, the commander relied on his own Bureau of Information and Propaganda for the rank and file of his army. The Poles considered the use of propaganda a very valuable weapon against the enemy. It was waged on three different levels. *Positive* propaganda—directed at the rank and file as well as a the prisoner of war camps. *Diversionary* propaganda—aimed at the enemy. *Counter* propaganda sought to counteract German propaganda. The purpose of positive propaganda was to inspire citizenship and patriotism in the ranks of the Home Army. The means of dissemination were massive. The press of the Home Army enjoyed a circulation of more than 200,000 based on some fifty publications (counting only the more substantial ones). The Bureau also published books and two songbooks containing melodies composed during the occupation. Hundreds of contact-girls and carriers were involved in the distribution of the underground publications. Regrettably hundreds of distributors were seized by the Gestapo and executed. As an "in your face" gesture, a copy of the Information Bulletin was sent by mail regularly to Dr. Ludwig Fischer, German Governor of the Warsaw district.[5]

The Underground State and its Home Army sought to prepare themselves for the day when the national uprising erupted. Therefore, the civilian population also had to be prepared. General Rowecki decided to carry out this function, which the Resident

Vice Prime Minister maintained was already being implemented. The Vice Prime Minister and the Political Coordinating Committee both believed that Rowecki was aiming for the military to take over the government. They opposed Rowecki. Nevertheless, the bureaus of the Home Army and the Vice Prime Minister began to be consolidated, since one was a duplication of the other. Finally, the President of the Republic of Poland (in exile) brought about consolidation by decree on 26 April 1944.

AUTHOR'S NOTE: The Warsaw Rising occurred on 1 August 1944. The conditions that led to the uprising and the sixty-three days of heroic fighting by the Home Army, while a Russian Army on the east bank of the Vistula River stood idly by, is fully described in Norman Davies' excellent book *Rising '44: The Battle for Warsaw* (2003).

CHAPTER SIX

TEHRAN AND YALTA CONFERENCES: THE ALLIES BETRAY POLAND

THE UNITED STATES and Great Britain immediately declared their support for Russia when Germany attacked its former ally on 22 June 1941. Powerful German Armies swept into Russia almost to the gates of Moscow. Russia was on the verge of collapse. The two Allies concluded that Russia must be kept in the war. The United States, especially, began a massive military aid program. President Roosevelt dispatched a military mission to Russia, led by Major General John R. Deane, which expedited and supervised the delivery of war materiel. Roosevelt asked for nothing in return, only that Russia stay in the war. Great Britain could offer limited aid because of the needs of its own armed forces as well as those of the Polish Army under the Government-in-Exile (London). Consequently, America now played the dominant role in the war, and Roosevelt began to pay more attention to Communist dictator Josef Stalin than to Churchill. In fact, he told the Briton that he could deal with Stalin more effectively than his friend. Roosevelt boasted: "I know that you will not mind my being brutally frank when I tell you that I

think I can personally handle Stalin better than either your Foreign Office or my State Department."[1]

President Roosevelt was anxious to meet with Stalin who kept
putting off the American. (After all, Stalin said he had a war to
run.) Stalin was not ready to have a face-to-face meeting with
Roosevelt and Churchill. He was not prepared to spring his demands on the two Western leaders, such as the Anglo/American
recognition of Russia's possession of the eastern half of Poland.
In addition, he needed time to organize a take-over of the government of Poland with his hand-picked Polish Communists. He
ordered several of his minions to parachute into Poland so they
could acquire some "residency" status and at the proper time
clamor for a government friendly to Russia. Meanwhile, Stalin
also needed time to study Roosevelt's weaknesses and convert
them to his advantage. Among Roosevelt's faults was his fascination with Stalin. The President felt that he could charm the mass-
murderer into a responsible statesman, who, with America, would
keep the peace after the war. Roosevelt made a tragic mistake.

After keeping Roosevelt waiting for two and half years, Stalin
suggested a meeting in Tehran, Iran. Stalin was very demanding.
He expected the invalid President to journey halfway around the
world. Despite the difficult travel, Roosevelt agreed. Prime Minister Churchill and he stopped in Cairo, Egypt, to confer with
Chinese Nationalist leader Chiang Kai-Sheik. The two Western
leaders then continued to Tehran where they conferred with
Stalin during the period of 28 November–1 December 1943. The
Russian now demanded that Roosevelt and Churchill recognize
Russia's seizure of eastern Poland. Stalin actually defined the
boundaries of the centuries-old Polish land he demanded (along
the old Curzon Line, a boundary proposed by English Lord Curzon
during World War I, which the Poles rejected). Stalin also included the Polish city of Lwow and the oil fields of Drohobycz in
his share of Poland. The two Western leaders conceded Stalin's
demand and agreed to keep the understanding secret. Roosevelt
felt no guilt about giving away Poland's land even though he violated his own Atlantic Charter. The Big Three also agreed to the

planned invasion of northern France (Operation Overlord) and of southern France (Operation Anvil). Churchill had long advocated the Balkan strategy, an Allied campaign up "the soft underbelly of Europe." The Polish Government-in-Exile also strongly recommended a Balkan campaign through Yugoslavia, Bulgaria, Romania, and Poland, thereby keeping Poland and the Balkans in the Western orbit. However, Roosevelt and his Chairman of the Joint Chiefs of Staff, General George C. Marshall, were adamantly opposed to a Balkan strategy. Stalin quickly agreed with the Americans. He did not want Anglo/American forces in the Balkans which he had staked out for his own sphere of influence. Roosevelt laughingly ridiculed Churchill about the Balkan strategy. Roosevelt, however, lacked the vision of Churchill.

General Mark Clark, commander of the American Fifth Army in Italy, regretted Roosevelt's and Marshall's rejection of the Balkan strategy. General Clark wrote that throughout the Big Three Meeting and negotiations at Tehran, Stalin was one of the strongest boosters of the invasion of southern France. Clark saw through the clever political strategy of Stalin, but the misguided Roosevelt and Marshall did not. Clark concluded with a prophetic warning about the future relations with Russia: "A campaign that might have changed the whole history of relations between the Western world and Soviet Russia was permitted to fade away."[2]

The Polish Government-in-Exile strongly favored a Balkan campaign of the Allies. The Home Army could play a very effective supporting role in such a campaign as the Allies approached Poland from the south. The Polish Government formally asked the United States to include Poland in the Allied strategic planning, meanwhile airlifting supplies and equipment to the Home Army. On 17 September 1943, Poland's resident representative to the Combined Chiefs of Staff in Washington presented a memorandum in which the key point read: "The Polish General Staff, therefore, considers it essential that the entire Polish Armed Forces should be placed under a common allied Command, and the area of Poland should be considered one of joint strategic responsibility." The American response was immediate and negative. On 23 September 1943, the Combined Chiefs of Staff rejected Poland's memorandum. To President Roosevelt and his Administration, General Marshall and the Combined Chiefs of Staff, and America in general, Poland was of little concern, even though Poland first opposed Adolf Hitler and as a staunch ally kept fighting the Germans to the bitter end. The Communist influence that saturated America was too strong to overcome.[3]

The following year (1944) the Allies carried out the invasion of southern France in Operation Anvil. On 15 August 1944, American and French forces under the command of General Alexander M. Patch landed in southern France against limited resistance of the German Nineteenth Army. General Patch made rapid advances. The southern operation was of little help to General Eisenhower in the north, and it was not needed. Eisenhower overcame the enemy in the drive to Germany with his own powerful armies. In fact, Eisenhower helped Patch by threatening the rear of the Germans as they retreated up the Rhone River Valley. The invasion of southern France seemed a wasted effort.

President Roosevelt and Prime Minister Churchill kept their betrayal of Poland a secret not only from the Polish Government-in-Exile but also from their own people. Undoubtedly they felt guilt about selling out a fighting ally. Roosevelt's motive was his obsessive desire to please and charm Stalin. At the time of Tehran in late 1943, General Sikorski was no longer the Premier of Poland's Government. He had died in a plane crash at Gibraltar on 4 July 1943. He was replaced by Stanislaw Mikolajczyk, leader of the strong Polish Peasant Party. Although he was not a scion of the gentry class, Mikolajczyk was a great patriot and was well known and liked in Poland. He, too, was unaware of the Roosevelt-Churchill betrayal, but he found out in the most embarrassing and devastating manner. In August 1944, Mikolajczyk flew to Moscow to confer with Stalin about the strained relations between the two countries. The visit proved fruitless. While in Moscow, the Polish premier became dismayed to learn of the growing authority of the so-called Lublin Poles (Communists) whom Stalin was grooming to take over the future government of Poland. Upon his return to London, Mikolajczyk drew up a new plan for a government of Poland that he believed could solve the Russian-Polish impasse. He proposed a government based on equal representation of five political parties—the Peasant Party, National Party, Polish Socialist Party, Christian Labor Party, and Polish Workers Party (Communist). He also outlined the objectives of the proposed government. The Polish cabinet approved the plan. The British and Americans also indicated approval, but Russia remained silent. After waiting a month, Mikolajczyk asked Russian Ambassador Victor Lebedev who answered that the plan was turned over to the Lublin Poles, and they rejected it. Although British Foreign Secretary Anthony Eden informed Mikolajczyk of British approval, Mikolajczyk wanted to discuss with Churchill the proposed plan for a Polish Provisional Government. However, the Prime Minister was in the act of departing for Moscow and unavailable.

Once in Moscow, however, Churchill urged Mikolajczyk to fly to Russia immediately, and together they would try to repair Polish-Russian relations. Mikolajczyk reached Moscow on 12 October 1944. The next day a momentous conference took place, attended by Churchill, Eden, Averell H. Harriman as observer for the United States, Mikolajczyk, Stalin, and Molotov who acted as chairman. Molotov seated the party around an oval table and called on the Pole to speak first. Quickly the conversation focused on the Curzon Line. Mikolajczyk told Stalin he had no authority to give up forty-eight percent of Poland. Stalin insisted that, if the Polish government wants good relations with Russia, it must recognize the Curzon Line as an actuality. He added that the land to the east of the line was, in fact, parts of White Russia and the Ukraine. Stalin was wrong. The land in question had been for centuries an integral part of the Commonwealth of Poland.

At this point, Molotov suddenly stopped Mikolajczyk: "But all this was settled at Tehran," Molotov cried out. He looked from Churchill to Harriman. The American remained silent. Stunned, Mikolajczyk asked for details of the Tehran Conference. Molotov,

STANISLAW MIKOLAJCZYK
Prime Minister of the Polish Government-in-Exile (London)

with his eyes on Churchill and the American Ambassador, explained:

> If your memories fail you, let me recall the facts to you. We all agreed at Tehran that the Curzon line must divide Poland. You will recall that President Roosevelt agreed to the solution and strongly endorsed the line. And then we agreed that it would be best not to issue any public declaration about our agreement.

Mikolajczyk could not believe Molotov's words. In Washington in June 1944, Roosevelt had assured him that Poland would emerge from the war strong and independent. Mikolajczyk looked at Churchill and Harriman, pleading with his eyes that they expose Molotov's explanation as a lie. Harriman looked down at the rug. Churchill then looked at Mikolajczyk and said quietly, "I confirm this." The admission made Churchill angry. He demanded that Mikolajczyk agree to the Russian demand at once in the presence of the Russians. The Pole shouted back, "I didn't expect to be brought here to participate in a new partition of my country!" Churchill tried to soften the blow by suggesting that the Curzon Line could be considered a temporary frontier. Now Stalin jumped in and asserted that Russia would not change frontiers from time to time. Silently, all conferees filed out of the room.[4]

In a follow-up meeting without the Russians, Churchill and Mikolajczyk in the presence of Eden continued to debate hotly the fate of Poland, punctuated with emotional outbursts. Churchill

---

LEFT: *Stanislaw Mikolajczyk became the Prime Minister after the death of General Wladyslaw Sikorski in an aircraft accident at Gibraltar on 4 July 1943. A man of intellectual and moral force, Mikolajczyk personified the strength of the Polish peasantry. In Poland, he led the strong and well-organized Polish Peasant Party in direct opposition to the Moscow-trained Polish Communists. The Prime Minister's slow and deliberate manner of speech made one feel his tenacity and stability. He spoke in good English, punctuated with a characteristic Polish accent. (Photo from* The Rape of Poland *by Stanislaw Mikolajczyk)*

MEETING WITH PRESIDENT ROOSEVELT

President Franklin Roosevelt greets Stanislaw Mikolajczyk, Prime Minister of the Polish Government-in-Exile (London), in the Oval Office, Washington, D.C., 7 June 1944. Mikolajczyk sought American support for Poland in its struggle to overcome the machinations of Russia. The President spoke in generalities and did not reveal that he had already agreed to give Russia the eastern half of Poland at the Tehran Conference six months earlier (December 1943). (Photo from The Rape of Poland *by Stanislaw Mikolajczyk)*

promised the Pole that if he agreed to let go of eastern Poland, Churchill would personally guarantee that the remaining Polish state would be free of Russian interference. And for emphasis, Churchill added that his ambassador to Poland would see to that. Mikolajczyk knew the treacherous Russians too well to believe

Churchill's pledge. He answered the Prime Minister with a cutting remark: "I prefer to die fighting for the independence of my country than to be hanged later by the Russians in full view of your ambassador!" Taken aback by the contemptuous remark, Churchill stomped out of the room. Calming down, Churchill returned, and Mikolajczyk and he apologized to each other for their emotional language. Mikolajczyk returned to London with no options to defend Poland's future. The majority of the Polish cabinet lost confidence in Mikolajczyk, and he believed he had no other recourse but to resign as premier, 24 November 1944.[5]

On 27 October 1944, Churchill gave a report of the Tehran Conference to the House of Commons. He spoke at some length about Poland and offered a promise of a bright and peaceful future:

> Speaking more particularly for His Majesty's Government, it is our constant aim that the Polish people, after their suffering and vicissitudes, shall find in Europe an abiding home and resting place which will nevertheless be adequate for the needs of the Polish nation and will not interfere in character and quality to what they had previously possessed.[6] (Generous words but devoid of reality.)

The Tehran Conference was followed by the final conference of the Big Three at Yalta in Russia's Crimean Peninsula, 3–11 February 1945. The three countries met to confirm the agreements made at Tehran and to coordinate policy and strategy as the fighting began to draw to a close. Roosevelt considered places such as Malta, Egypt, and Jerusalem, but Stalin chose the site of Yalta. He forced the invalid and sick President to cross the Atlantic and Europe to the Black Sea. Indeed, President Roosevelt was ill physically and mentally. On 19 January 1945, the day before his inauguration for his fourth term, Labor Secretary Frances Perkins was shocked to observe his pallor. "Don't tell a soul," she begged of her secretary. "I can't stand it, the President looks horrible. I'm afraid he is ill." Four days later, on 23 January 1945, Roosevelt boarded the heavy cruiser U.S.S. *Quincy* for Yalta.[7]

At the conference site, the American party occupied quarters at Livadia Palace where the deliberations took place. The British were housed at Vorontsov Villa at Alupka, a half hour's drive from Livadia Palace, while the Russian delegation stayed at Prince Yusupov's Koreis Villa, halfway between the Americans and the British. Ambassador Averill Harriman was a member of the American delegation. His daughter Kathleen Harriman was at Yalta, too. (No doubt, to prop up the Russian position.)

The Americans sent secret messages daily to Washington by means of a cable ship, U.S.S. *Catoctin*, anchored at Sevastopol some eighty miles from Yalta. Stalin "thoughtfully" provided Russian women to guard the delivery of the messages to the American cable ship. (Undoubtedly the Russians read the messages before they reached the *Catoctin*.)[8]

The relevant part of the Yalta Conference pertaining to Poland reads:

> We came to the Crimea Conference resolved to settle our differences about Poland. We discussed fully all aspects of the question. We reaffirmed our common desire to see a strong, free, independent, and democratic Poland. As a result of our discussion we have agreed on the conditions in which a new Polish Provisional Government of National Unity may be formed in such a manner as to command recognition by the three major Powers. The agreement reached is as follows:
>
> A new situation has been created in Poland as a result of her liberation by the Red Army. This calls for the establishment of a Polish Provisional Government which can be more broadly based than was possible before the liberation of Western Poland. The Provisional Government now functioning in Poland should, therefore, be reorganized on a broader democratic basis with the inclusion of democratic leaders from Poland itself and from Poles abroad. This new Government then should be called the Polish Provisional Government of National Unity. Mr. Molotov, Mr. Harriman, and Sir A. Clark Kerr are authorized as a Commission to consult in the first instance in Moscow with members of the present Provisional Government and with other Polish democratic leaders from within Poland and abroad, with a view to the reorga-

nization of the present Government along the above lines. The Polish Provisional Government of National unity shall be pledged to the holding of free and unfettered elections as soon as possible on the basis of universal suffrage and the secret ballot. In these elections all democratic and anti-Nazi parties shall have the right to take part and to put forward candidates.

When the conditions of the Yalta declaration are met, the Big Three would take the following action:

> When a Polish Provisional Government of National Unity has been properly formed in conformity with the above, the Government of the U.S.S.R., which now maintains diplomatic relations with the present Provisional Government of Poland. And the Governments of the United Kingdom and the United States will establish diplomatic relations with the new Polish Provisional Government of National Unity and will exchange Ambassadors by whose reports the respective Governments will be kept informed about the situation in Poland.
>
> The three heads of Government consider that the eastern frontier of Poland should follow the Curzon Line, with digressions from it in some regions of 5–8 kilometers in favor of Poland. They recognize that Poland must receive substantial accessions of territory in the north and west. They feel that the opinion of the new Polish Provisional Government of National Unity should be sought in due course on the extent of these accessions, and the final delimitations of the western frontier of Poland should thereafter await the Peace Conference.[9]

Perhaps no other group of individuals was more upset and confused by the Yalta Agreement than the Communist Lublin Committee, pre-ordained by Stalin to constitute the future government of Poland. The Committee demanded an explanation from Nikolai Bulganin, Stalin's personal representative in Lublin. The Lublin Communists wanted to know how Stalin could promise Roosevelt and Churchill that free and democratic elections would be held in Poland after assuring the members of the Lublin Committee that they would be the government. Bulganin was stumped for an answer, and he flew to Moscow to confer with Stalin. Returning on 17 February 1945, Bulganin explained to the Committee: "The Yalta Agreement is a scrap of paper. It was necessary to satisfy Roosevelt and Churchill—but we will not abide by it. We will go ahead with our plans as stated to you by the Great Stalin." Bulganin emphasized again that the Lublin Poles will be the government of Poland no matter how the future elections might turn out and whatever might happen in the meantime.[10]

The Big Three made decisions on Poland not only without the participation and authorization of the Polish Government (London) but also without its knowledge. The behavior of the Big Three leaders is reminiscent of the treacherous and coarse behavior of the ambassadors of Prussia, Austria, and Russia who met secretly in Warsaw to plot the destruction of Poland in the late eighteenth century. Historian William Henry Chamberlin writes: "There was not one positive, worthwhile contribution to European revival and stability in the sordid deal at Yalta, only imperialist power politics at its worst."[11] A severe critic of President Roosevelt's foreign policy, author Felix Wittmer, condemns the President: "Our concessions of territory which did not even belong to us, besides being immoral and illegal, were based on ignorance and stupidity."[12] The Polish Government-in-Exile believed the worst was yet to come.

President Roosevelt returned to Washington from Yalta on 24 February 1945. In need of medical help, he flew three days later to the Mayo Clinic in Minnesota where he remained for two weeks. The nation eagerly awaited the President's report on the Yalta Conference which he delivered on 2 March. Too exhausted to stand, the President sat in his wheelchair. "Speaking in all frankness," he said, "the question of whether it is entirely fruitful or not lies to a great extent in your hands." He explained that the matter of lasting results depended on the concurrence and support of Congress and the American people. The nation, however, became disillusioned quickly. Opinions in the press were divided. Many Americans believed that Yalta was a sellout to Stalin. By mid-March 1945, an incident occurred in Romania that indicated

Russia's meaning of a "friendly government." King Michael was forced to replace a number of ministers with pro-Russian sympathizers. Romania, however, did not arouse much interest, for it had been a German satellite during the war. Poland, however, was different. It was the first country to stand up to Germany and was brutalized for it. Poland was a constant reminder of the cynical Molotov-Ribbentrop Pact that precipitated World War II. Notwithstanding, the Yalta controversy remained. "It was to appear evident," historian Robert E. Sherwood writes, "that a complete deadlock had developed among the British, Russian, and American conferees in Moscow over the composition of the Provisional Polish Government."[13]

In Great Britain, Churchill's report on the Yalta Conference to the House of Commons received overwhelming support. Nevertheless, a group of about thirty Conservative members rejected Churchill's concessions to Stalin. They expressed an anguish that "we should have to face the enslavement of a heroic nation." These Englishmen were prophetic; they understood the evil of Communism.

AUTHOR'S COMMENTS: This author consulted the book *Yalta* (1975) by Diane Shaver Clemens. Following a period of twenty-five years after the Yalta Conference, Clemens set out "to learn what really did and did not happen at Yalta." Presumably, then, Clemens' purpose was to make an objective analysis of Yalta. Her book was published by the respected Oxford University Press.

Despite Clemens' stated purpose of a thorough review of Yalta and objective conclusions, I found Clemens to be biased negatively toward Poland, an unfortunate trait of most American historians. Clemens calls "extreme" Poland's reaction to the Russian mass murder of 11,000 Polish prisoners of war in the Katyn Forest in 1940. Would a massacre of a larger number of prisoners, say 20,000, make it seems less extreme to Clemens? At Malmedy, Belgium, 17 December 1944, the Germans viciously murdered ninety American prisoners of war. Based on the thinking of Clemens, the massacre of only ninety Americans should have been brushed off as inconsequential. Yet, Malmedy was one of the serious charges brought against the German war criminals at the Nuremberg Trial in 1945. Furthermore, Clemens rebuts Polish accusation of Russian crimes with statements of Stalin and lets them stand without challenge, as if Stalin spoke the gospel truth. In the case of Great Britain, the history of Polish and British relations during World War II reveals a continual British pressure on Poland's Government-in-Exile to accede to Russian demands in order to maintain so-called friendly relations with Russia. Clemens calls the British pressure "reasonable" and the British position "a realistic stance." (How could the Poles be so obstinate! After all, giving up one-half of their country seems to Clemens like a minor concession. What would Clemens say if Stalin had demanded from Roosevelt the American Northwest?)

Clemens correctly states that Roosevelt conducted a devious foreign policy with respect to Poland. "To keep the Polish government in line," Clemens writes, "the United States dropped hints that the United States supported the Poles' refusal to negotiate on frontiers." Roosevelt did more than conceal the agreements reached at Tehran. At a meeting with eleven leaders of the Polish American Congress at the White House on 11 October 1944, Roosevelt pointed to a large map of Poland placed behind his executive desk so as to allow the Polish Americans to believe that he supported a Poland with its 1938 boundaries. (No Curzon Line appeared on Roosevelt's map of Poland.)

Clemens writes of the patient and reasonable Russians, explaining that Russia "made a few more attempts to reach a settlement with the London Poles, but the Poles ignored these indications." Again the Poles were obdurate, Clemens implies. The Poles, however, understood the treacherous character of the Russians. Cooperation with Russia meant capitulation and surrender. Clemens does not admit the vile character of Russia. Twenty-five years after World War II Clemens still considered Russia capable of honest negotiations. "Churchill and Eden," Clemens also says, "became even more determined to save the

Polish government from its folly." To Clemens, Poland's fight for its international rights was folly. Poland also defended its territory courageously against the onslaught of German and Russian armies in September 1939. In contrast, Czechoslovakia gave up without a fight. Winston Churchill remarked about the Czech failure to stand up and fight. The timidity of the Czechs actually assisted Germany to build up its forces for the massive attack on Poland. Churchill said: "Had he [President Eduard Benes] told his cannons to fire at Munich time, the Second World War would have begun under conditions far less favorable to Hitler, who needed many months to make his army and his armour."

Relying on the lies of Stalin, Clemens falsely claims that units of the Home Army harassed the Russian Army advancing through Poland. Clemens writes:

> Their [Poland's] partisans and their official Army in Poland, the *Armia Krajowa*, were continually harassing Red Army units on Polish soil. Stalin complained to Roosevelt in his December 1944 letter that "terrorists," instigated by Polish émigrés, assassinated Red Army soldiers and officers in Poland, wage a criminal struggle against the Soviet forces engaged in liberating Poland, and directly aid our enemies, with whom they are virtually in league.[14]

Clemens, unfortunately and like Roosevelt, believes the explanations of Russian leaders. However, the Russians lied and deceived the world in order to advance their evil designs. Despite what Clemens believes and writes, units of the Home Army tried to cooperate and help the Russian commanders in Poland. The Polish soldiers of the Home Army knew the locations of German units in Poland and could lead the Russians to them. Stanislaw Mikolajczyk in his book *The Rape of Poland* (1947) calls attention to the program of cooperation with the advancing Russian Armies in Poland—code-named "Tempest"—the command given to Armia Krajowa units to rise and help the Red Army liberate each area. The British knew of Tempest. The Poles had earlier provided the British with complete instructions to the Underground for strengthening the fight against the Germans and offering full cooperation with the Russians. But what happened? Stalin considered the Home Army an enemy. The Russian commanders first accepted the Polish help and then turned on them. Mikolajczyk protested the deceitful and barbaric Russian behavior to Foreign Secretary Anthony Eden, 4 March 1944.[15]

On 4 April 1944, the Polish Government informed the British that Russian forces received assistance everywhere and praised the fighting spirit and leadership of the Polish Underground. Nevertheless, reports of hostile activities against the Polish Underground had been communicated to the London government and boded ill for future concerted action against the enemy. Despite the problems, the Polish government still wanted cooperation. The Polish Government said: "Instructions to come into the open and to cooperate with the Soviet Army in the fight against the Germans have not been revoked and still remain in effect."

Mikolajczyk concludes his explanation of Polish cooperation and Russian treacherous behavior:

> But the greatest of these efforts to collaborate with the advancing Russians, "Tempest," became a grim synonym for betrayal. The deliberately provoked uprising of the Warsaw underground army and its pitiless annihilation by the Germans while a considerable Red Army force looked on from the suburbs of the capital will forever hold its ugly place in the blackest of history's record.[16]

This author asks: Should author Clemens' pro-Russian attitude be considered objective American historiography. Twenty-five years after Yalta, Clemens set out to write "what really happened at Yalta." Instead, she wrote a book of Russian propaganda and the editors of Oxford University Press bought it.

[Clemens lists *The Rape of Poland* in her bibliography and mentions Mikolajczyk several times in her narrative, but she avoids mentioning Tempest.]

CHAPTER SEVEN

HARRY TRUMAN
BECOMES PRESIDENT

*A*FTER HIS EXHAUSTING TRIP to the Crimean Peninsula for the Yalta Conference, President Roosevelt sought rest and a chance to recuperate at the winter White House in Warm Springs, Georgia. On 12 April 1945, however, he died of a massive stroke. Vice President Harry S. Truman became the thirty-third President of the United States. He was thrust into the center of momentous world events—the end of World War II with its bourgeoning problems, the formation of the United Nations, and the execution of the decisions of the Yalta Conference in which the future of Poland was at stake.

Truman found himself at a great disadvantage when he assumed the Presidency. In Roosevelt's day and earlier, vice presidents did little, if anything, except to step up to the presidency when a presidential vacancy occurred. Vice Presidents were normally not invited to join the inner circle of Presidential advisors, especially in the case of President Roosevelt. In foreign policy, only a few of Roosevelt's advisors knew his activities and decisions with regard to Russia. Historian William Henry Chamberlin succinctly sums up President Truman's difficult position: "He [Roosevelt] left an unhappy legacy in foreign relations to his successor, who was without personal knowledge and experience in this field. So secretive and personal had been Roosevelt's diplomacy that for some time it was impossible for the Chief Executive to get a clear picture of what assurances had been given to foreign governments or what diplomatic IOUs were outstanding."[1] Nevertheless, Truman met his responsibilities squarely and quickly sought to become knowledgeable.

President Truman immediately asked Secretary of State Stettinius to give him an outline of the principal problems that faced the country. The next day, 13 April 1945, Stettinius submitted his report. On Poland, the Secretary wrote in part: "The present situation relating to Poland is highly unsatisfactory, with the Soviet authorities consistently sabotaging Ambassador Harriman's efforts in Moscow to hasten the implementation of the decisions at the Crimea Conference." Truman considered the so-called Lublin government, which Russia had unilaterally recognized, as "a puppet regime of Russia's own making." Despite his feelings, Truman believed it was his duty as President to carry out Roosevelt's agreement with Stalin and Churchill at Yalta: "That the Warsaw provisional government then functioning in Poland should be broadened by the inclusion of certain democratic leaders who were still in Poland and by others who were living abroad at the time. This new government would then be pledged to hold free and unfettered elections as soon as possible on the basis of universal suffrage and the secret ballot." Properly carried out, Truman believed, the agreed procedure would lead to a solution. It was now apparent, however, the Russians had no intention of allowing a new Provisional Government of National Unity organized according to the Yalta Agreement. "The reason for this attitude," Truman concluded, "was that they were in no doubt that such a government would mean the end of the Lublin group's Communist control in Poland."[2]

Prime Minister Churchill began to communicate with the new President. Churchill planned to dispatch a message to Stalin on the composition of a broadened Polish Provisional Government. Truman suggested that Churchill add four points to his message. The first suggested the names of three Poles from the London Government and four from Warsaw, with a fifth person from Warsaw selected by Moscow. His second point suggested that the group from Warsaw come first to Moscow for consultations. Third, the invited Polish representatives be allowed to recommend other Poles so that all major Polish groups might take part. Fourth, that the United States and Great Britain had no wish to commit themselves in advance to any formula for determining the new Polish government. President Truman knew, of course, that Great Britain and the United States had recognized the Polish Government-in-Exile for a long time. Nevertheless, he understood that the members of that government could not be forced on Russia as a group, and at Yalta Roosevelt and Churchill had made no attempt to do that.[3]

Truman continued to look for sources of information on foreign policy. He considered Harry Hopkins, who was ill and exhausted from his strenuous activities and long travels as personal representative of President Roosevelt. Still, he came to attend Roosevelt's funeral ceremony. Hopkins' presence in Washington gave Truman an opportunity to confer with him. Truman sought firsthand information about Stalin and other heads of state with whom he would be dealing. He also wanted to learn all he could about the relations between Russia and Poland. The two talked for more than two hours and did not take time out for lunch, but the President ordered trays of food brought to them from the White House kitchen. Truman found Hopkins a storehouse of information. Hopkins characterized many world leaders he had met, to include vivid descriptions of Stalin and other Russian officials.

Communications between Truman and Churchill dealt often with the formation of a representative Polish Government of National Unity. The Prime Minister told the President that the Lublin Communist government felt the backlash of the Polish nation which was not unfriendly to Russia but strongly independent-minded. The Poles regarded the Lublin government unfavorably because they knew it was a puppet of Russia. The Western Allies also wanted to have observers present when elections were held in Poland, but the Russians adamantly opposed the presence of observers. Ambassador Harriman reported that the Russians were reluctant to permit observers because of "a fear that observers might discover the small support actually possessed by the Warsaw government."[4]

On his way to attend the conference on the formation of the United Nations in San Francisco, British Foreign Secretary Anthony Eden stopped in Washington to see President Truman, 16 April 1945. Eden was accompanied by British Ambassador Lord Halifax. Eden delivered a draft message meant for Stalin for the consideration of Truman. The two reviewed the British and American versions and agreed on a final, joint message to be delivered to Stalin. The text concerned the selection of Poles who would then be called upon to form a Provisional Government of National Unity which would function until free elections were held. The joint message named three Communists from the Warsaw government: Bierut, Osubka-Morawski, Rolla-Zymierski, the Catholic Cardinal Adam Sapieha, and a Polish political party leader not associated with the present Warsaw government. The joint message also suggested an additional number agreeable to Russia. The message named them: Witos, Zulawski, Chacinski, Jasienkowicz; and from London Mikolajczyk, Grabski, and Stanczyk.[5]

On 16 April 1945, President Truman made his first address to the Congress. He pledged to carry out the war and peace policies of the late President Roosevelt. He called on all Americans to help him to keep the nation united in defense of American ideals. His speech was favorably received. The President's schedule continued to be full. He received a cable from Ambassador Harriman in Moscow that the Russians were preparing to conclude a Russian-Polish treaty of mutual assistance. Harriman cautioned Deputy Foreign Minister Andrei Vishinsky that the signing of such a treaty before the provisional government was formed would be interpreted by the world that Russia did not intend to carry out the Yalta agreements. The President became disturbed. He considered the mutual assistance treaty to be another Russian maneuver for getting their own way in Poland. He asserted he would bring out the matter in a meeting with Molotov. Meanwhile, he instructed the State Department to lodge a protest with Russia.

Returning to the United States, Ambassador Harriman reported to the President several problems that he had encountered in Moscow, pointing to the changing Russian attitude since the close of the Yalta Conference. He concluded that the United States was facing a "barbarian invasion of Europe." Russia's control of a country," Harriman explained, "meant not only control of its government but also control of its people by the secret NKVD and the subsequent destruction of the freedom of speech." How should the United States respond to this unpleasant fact? Harriman asked, especially since he believed Stalin had concluded that an honest execution of the Yalta Agreement would mean the end of the Russian-backed Lublin government. Truman replied that unless the Polish question was solved in accordance with the decision at Yalta, America's joining the United Nations would not pass the Senate. And he emphasized, "I intend to tell Molotov just that in words of one syllable." Because Roosevelt had abandoned Poland to the Russians, President Truman tried to salvage an element from Yalta—the conduct of free and unfettered elections that would reflect the will of the people. The Russians, however, gave lip service to Yalta while they did their dirty work in Poland to insure a totally subjugated people.[6]

On 22 April 1945, President Truman met with Russian Foreign Minister Vyacheslav M. Molotov at the Blair House in Washington. In preparation, Truman held a prior meeting with Secretary of State Stettinius, Ambassador Harriman, Assistant Secretary of State James Dunn, and Charles Bohlen, interpreter. Stettinius reminded the President that, despite opposition from the United States and Great Britain, Russia had unilaterally recognized the Moscow-imposed Communist government of Poland.

And would Truman bring up the matter with Molotov? Truman said he would not, but if Molotov did, the President would tell him frankly that a Russian-only recognition was not helpful toward a resolution of the Polish problem. Subsequently, Truman greeted Molotov at eight-thirty in the evening. Stettinius, Harriman, and Bohlen were present, too. Quickly the discussion turned to Poland. Truman told Molotov that "in its larger aspects the Polish question had become for our people the symbol of the future development of our international relations." Molotov responded that the discussions among the three heads of state led to satisfactory agreements. Truman agreed, and added that he intended to carry out all agreements made by President Roosevelt. Before ending the meeting, the President said he would like to meet with Stalin before too long. Molotov now joined Stettinius and Harriman for a discussion on Poland at the State Department.[7]

The next day, 23 April 1945, the President held an important conference with his diplomatic and military advisors. In attendance were Secretary of State Stettinius, Secretary of War Henry Stimson, Secretary of the Navy James Forrestal, Admiral William Leahy, Assistant Secretary of State James Dunn, Ambassador Averell Harriman, General George Marshall, Admiral Ernest King, General John Deane, and Charles Bohlen. Stettinius spoke of the meeting with Molotov the previous evening. Although Molotov had been pleasant with President Truman, his behavior changed into an uncompromising attitude. "In fact," Stettinius said, "a complete deadlock had been reached on the subject of carrying out the Yalta agreement on Poland." Stettinius emphasized once more that the Lublin or Warsaw government did not represent the Polish people. Furthermore, it had become evident that the Russians would try to force this puppet government upon the United States and England. Stettinius explained to Molotov that the United States regarded this matter very seriously and that public confidence would be undermined by a failure to carry out the Yalta agreement. The President responded: "It is clear that our agreements with the Soviet Union had so far been a one-way street and that this could not continue." Next, Truman asked each one present to state his views:

Secretary of the Army Stimson said that the diplomatic problems with Russia were new to him. In military matters, the Russians had kept their word. [It is evident that Stimson knew or pretended to know little of the evil design of Russia to subjugate Poland. The right of Poles to self-determination seems not to have entered his mind.]

Secretary of the Navy Forrestal emphasized that the difficulty over Poland could not be treated as an isolated incident. Russia had indicated its objective of dominating adjacent countries and disregarding the wishes of her Allies. He said the United States should have a showdown with Russia now rather than later. [Forrestal showed an excellent understanding of Russia's dirty politics, much more profoundly than Stimson. Forrestal was of the same conviction as General George Patton, Jr., who, likewise, believed that the United States should be prepared to fight Russia.]

Ambassador to Russia Harriman concluded that after Yalta, Stalin and Molotov realized that their Communist-imposed puppet government was very shaky. The introduction of any genuine Polish leaders like Stanislaw Mikolajczyk would probably mean the elimination of the Russian hand-picked minions. Harriman said the real issue was whether the United States was to be a party to a program of Russian domination of Poland.

Admiral William Leahy was present with Roosevelt at Yalta. In response to a question from Truman, Leahy said that upon departing Yalta he had the impression the Russians had no intention of permitting a free government to operate in Poland. Leahy believed the United States should tell the Russians that "we stood for a free and independent Poland." [Leahy expressed the proper and moral position of the United States. However, in January

1947 the Russians did not allow the conduct of free and unfettered election.]

General Marshall said he was not familiar with the political aspects of the Polish question. (As for military affairs, he did not mention that he had rejected out of hand the recommendation of the Polish General Staff to include Poland in the war strategy of the Allies.)

Admiral King asked whether the issue was the invitation of the Lublin government to San Francisco (for the conference on the United Nations). Truman answered with emphasis: "The issue was the execution of agreements entered into between this government and the Soviet Union."

General Deane, after mentioning matters relating to the war in the Pacific, was convinced from the time spent in Moscow that if the United States was afraid of the Russians we would get nowhere. He stated we should be firm when we were right.

The President thanked his advisors for their points of view and ended the session. He asked Stettinius, Harriman, and Bohlen to remain behind and review subjects to be brought up for the President's meeting with Molotov scheduled for late afternoon the same day.[8]

Molotov arrived for his meeting with President Truman, accompanied by Andrei Gromyko and an interpreter. Truman wasted no time on protocol but went straight to the point. He told Molotov that he "was deeply disappointed that the Soviet government had not held consultations with representatives of the Polish government other than the officials of the Warsaw regime." He cautioned Molotov about a possible breakdown in postwar collaboration due to the failure of the principal Allies to carry out the Crimean decision with regard to Poland. Truman handed Molotov a message for immediate transmission to Stalin, in which the United States earnestly requests that Russia accept the proposals set forth in the joint message of the United States and Great Britain to Stalin. Molotov answered that his government stood by the Crimean decisions and that "it was a matter of honor." Truman answered sharply that "an agreement had been reached on Poland and that there was only one thing to do, and that was for Marshal Stalin to carry out that agreement in accordance with his word." Surprised by the unexpected tough talk from an American, Molotov frankly revealed, "I have never been talked to like that in my life." And Truman shot back, "Carry out your agreements and you won't get talked to like that." [9]

Comment: Truman's strong stance on fulfilling the Yalta Agreement on Poland undoubtedly caused Stalin to back off a bit on his program of communizing Poland. Non-Communist leaders were invited to join in the consultations for a representative Polish government. However, the apparent cooperation with the United States and Great Britain was a sham. Stalin nullified the effort for free elections through murders, court trials, intimidation, and other treacherous means. To emphasize, the damage to Poland's independence occurred at Tehran where Roosevelt opened the flood gate of surging Communism that overwhelmed the Polish nation, and Truman now tried to repair some of the damage by insisting that the formation of the Polish government be based on a broad representation of Polish leaders, as agreed to at the Yalta Conference, 2–9 February 1945.

On 24 April 1945, President Truman received Stalin's disturbing answer to the joint message of the United States and Great Britain on the formation of the Polish Provisional Government. The American/Anglo position maintained that the formation should proceed from a broad representation of Polish leaders, with the Communist-imposed government in Warsaw as only one of the consulting groups. Stalin insisted on treating the current Communist government as the core to which other Polish leaders could have an input. Stalin wanted a "friendly" Poland for his neighbor, meaning a subservient Poland. Truman admitted that the United States and Great Britain "were making very little headway with Stalin over the explosive Polish question." Churchill now concluded that Russia's obstinacy would lead to the creation of two opposing and hostile camps, Western and Communist, and would tear the world apart. Churchill accurately predicted the coming Cold War.[10]

Truman believed strongly that a new relationship had to be established among Churchill, Stalin, and himself, and that an early meeting of the three was necessary. Because of Harry Hopkins' knowledge of Stalin and Russian affairs, the President chose Hopkins as his emissary to Moscow. On 19 May 1945, Truman telephoned Stalin that he was sending Hopkins and Harriman to meet with him for a discussion of outstanding problems. Truman instructed Hopkins to inform Stalin that the United States faithfully carried out all commitments, and we expected the Russians to do the same. The President told Hopkins bluntly that he could use diplomatic language with Stalin "or a baseball bat if he thought that was the proper approach." (Perhaps Truman would use baseball-bat language himself, but Hopkins was too circumspect to do so. In retrospect, Truman called on the wrong man to represent him. Undoubtedly, Truman did not understand Hopkins' strong pro-Russian bias that could undermine the President's position.) Truman further instructed Hopkins to inform Stalin that Truman would be glad to see Stalin personally. Truman felt that Stalin should come to the United States for the meeting because Roosevelt had gone to Russia. At the same time that Hopkins traveled to Moscow, Truman dispatched Joseph E. Davies to London to see Churchill.

Hopkins and Harriman met with Stalin and Molotov on 26 May 1945, and a series of conferences continued until 7 June. Hopkins informed Truman daily of the gist of the discussions. The first resulted in setting up a meeting of the Big Three. Stalin recommended the meeting be held in the suburbs of Berlin, and Truman accepted the site. All agreed to meet in Babelsberg, a suburb of Potsdam, on 15 July 1945. From the conference in Moscow, Harriman reported to Truman, too. Harriman seemed to be suggesting that the President soften his determined stance with respect to Stalin. Harriman praised Hopkins: "Hopkins did a first-class job in presenting your wishes to Stalin and in explaining the most important matter—particularly Poland—which was causing us concern." Harriman also tried to excuse Stalin's uncompromising attitude toward Poland. "I am afraid," Harriman cautioned, "that Stalin does not and never will fully understand our interest in a free Poland as a matter of principle."[11]

Hopkins and Stalin also discussed the names of Poles in London and in Poland who were not members of the Lublin government but who would be invited to Moscow for consultations on the organization of a provisional government. Hopkins proposed a list of three names from London and five from Poland. These eight names had been approved in advance by Great Britain and the United States. Stalin proposed four names from the existing Communist government of Poland. Hopkins cabled these Communist names to Truman who accepted them on 1 June 1945.[12]

In his *The Rape of Poland*, Stanislaw Mikolajczyk discloses a different version of Hopkins' agreement with Stalin. Mikolajczyk states that Hopkins bowed to Stalin's pressure in breaking the deadlock of the Committee of Three (Harriman, Clark Kerr, and Molotov) who were to compose the Polish Provisional Government of National Unity. Stalin refused to go forward with the formation of the new Polish government unless his Lublin Poles dominated the provisional government. Stalin insisted that one of the three Poles from London must be a Lublin Pole, and that three or four of the five from Poland must be sympathetic to the old Lublin Committee. Stalin and Hopkins finally agreed on the following line-up: From London—Mikolajczyk, Stanislaw Grabski or Jan Stanczyk, and the strongly pro-Communist Julian Zukowski; from Poland—Cardinal Adam Sapieha or Wincenty Witos, esteemed and elderly leader of the Polish Peasant Party; Professor Stanislaw Kutrzeba of the University of Krakow (independent); Zygmunt Zulawski, Socialist; and two pro-Communists, Professor Krzyzanowski and Dr. Henryk Kolodziejski; from the existing government—Communists Boleslaw Bierut, Edward Osubka-

Morawski, Wladyslaw Kowalski, and Wladyslaw Gomulka. Indeed, Stalin stacked the consultative body with Communists. Reporting the lopsided group of names to Truman, Hopkins claimed the make-up of Poles fulfilled the Yalta Decision, and he urged the President to approve it. Truman did, on 1 June 1945.[13] Ten days later the Commission of Harriman, Clark Kerr, and Molotov issued invitations to the selected Poles to come to Moscow by 15 June. The Commission had reached a satisfactory agreement among themselves for broadening the provisional government with the admission of Mikolajczyk, Grabski, Witos, and Stanczyk, and others who were not part of the Communist Warsaw government. The agreement on the Polish Provisional Government was only the first step in complying with the Yalta Decision. The vital second step of free and unfettered elections was yet to be carried out. Harriman asked for assurances that freedom of assembly would be granted prior to the election as well as amnesty for Poles accused of political offenses. President Bierut assured Harriman (privately) that eighty percent of all political prisoners in Poland would be released, an outright Communist lie. Following the formation of the Polish Provisional Government, the United States and Great Britain jointly announced the establishment of diplomatic relations with Poland's Provisional Government of National Unity, 5 July 1945. Thus, the United States and Great Britain abandoned their wartime ally, the Polish Government-in-Exile (London).[14]

Earlier, as the Commission of three foreign ministers began its work of organizing the Polish Provisional government in Moscow, the Russians suddenly announced the trial of sixteen Polish democratic leaders who had been previously arrested under treacherous circumstances. Outraged by the arrest and trial, Truman said: "The deliberate timing of events by the U.S.S.R. in order to confront the negotiators with a *fait accompli* at the very outset of the discussions was fast becoming part of the habitual pattern of Russian tactics." Truman was shocked to learn the treacherous character of Stalin and the country the United States was dealing with.

Foreign correspondent Sydney Gruson cabled a report from London to the *New York Times*, 5 May 1945, that British officials were "gloomy" over the news that "sixteen missing Poles about whom the British Government had made repeated inquiries in Moscow had been arrested." Gruson quoted the Russian news agency TASS which explained the reason for the arrest of sixteen Polish leaders, among whom TASS singled out General Okulicki, the commander of the Polish Home Army. TASS charged: "General Okulicki's group and especially he himself are accused of preparing diversionary acts in the rear of the Red Army as a result of which more than 100 officers and men of the Red Army lost their lives." The explanation of TASS was totally false.

British officials could, indeed, feel gloomy over the arrest of the sixteen leaders of the Polish Underground State. These men represented the will of the Polish nation. Their seizure by the Russians under treacherous conditions undermined a key proposal of Winston Churchill for the formation of the Polish Provisional Government. He had stated earlier: "It was essential that representatives from within Poland should comprise men who really carried weight and could speak on behalf of the Polish parties. We had to have the right to nominate Poles from inside Poland and could not leave the choice solely to the Russians." Although the Russians did not murder any of the convicted Poles, they were effectively removed from participating in their nation's future.[15]

Mikolajczyk explains how the sixteen leaders of the Polish Underground were seized by Russian treachery. On 27 March 1945, Vice-Premier Jan Jankowski, Kazimierz Puzak, speaker of the Parliament of the Underground State, and General Leopold Okulicki, who succeeded General Tadeusz Komorowski to the command of the Home Army, were invited by Colonel General Ivanov of the Russian Army to meet with him in the suburbs of Warsaw. The purpose was to invite them and others to Moscow to take part in the formation of the Polish Provisional Government. The Polish leaders were promised "on the word of honor" of General Ivanov that the Poles would have safe conduct in Russia and then be permitted to fly to London for talks with London Poles and finally to return home. The first three Poles did not return from their meeting with Ivanov. Presumably they had left for Moscow. The next day, as arranged, thirteen more Polish leaders met with Ivanov. The Polish party included the chairmen of the four major political parties of the Underground State. These thirteen likewise disappeared. On 6 April 1945, the Polish Government in-Exile (London) announced that the Russian promise of safe conduct had been violated. The sixteen had been arrested and disappeared. The following month on 4 May, when delegates from many countries were gathering in San Francisco and engaging in the formation of the United Nations, Molotov admitted that the Russians held the Poles who were accused of "diversionary tactics in the rear of the Red Army" and were now awaiting trial. The Americans and British strongly protested the underhanded Russian tactics but continued to do business with Stalin who ignored the protests. Having eliminated the genuine representatives of Poland, Russia and its puppet Polish government signed a treaty of friendship, mutual assistance, and cooperation. Russia held the fake trials and found twelve of the sixteen Polish patriots guilty on all or part of the charges against them. There was no appeal. Individual sentences were: General Okulicki sentenced to ten years imprisonment; Jankowski, eight years; Bien and Jasiukowicz, five years; Puzak, eighteen months; Baginski, one year; Zwierzynski, eight months; Czarnowski, six months; and Stypulkowski, Mierzwa, Chacinski, and Urbanski, four months each. These Polish patriots had fought the enemy for six years, since 1939, in the face of formidable odds, terror, grave danger, and with limited means. An emotionally-charged Mikolajczyk indignantly wrote: "The Russian court found them guilty in a trial for which there was no precedent in international law."[16]

THE POTSDAM CONFERENCE
16 JULY–2 AUGUST 1945

On the eve of the Potsdam Conference, Winston Churchill was plagued with pessimism. He doubted whether a truly democratic Poland would emerge from the ashes of war. He believed that all political parties, except for the Communist puppets, were a hopeless minority in the new Polish Provisional Government. "We were as far as ever," he said, "from any real and fair attempt to obtain the will of the Polish nation by free elections." He held out some hope that the impending meeting of the Big Three would lead to an honorable settlement. "So far only dust and ashes had been gathered," he concluded, "and these are all that remains to us today of Polish national freedom."

The Potsdam Conference of President Truman, Prime Minister Churchill, and Marshal Stalin was held in Potsdam in the Palace of the German Crown Prince. The three delegations were housed in Babelsberg, southwest of Potsdam in the Russian sector. Truman departed Washington on 6 July 1945, traveling to Europe aboard the U.S.S. *Augusta.* Truman chose the slower sea route to provide time to study the many documents assembled for him. (Roosevelt also had many documents and position papers on his long travel to Yalta, but it seems he never touched them. He was plagued with colds and headaches.) As the *Augusta* sailed out of Hampton Roads, Virginia, it was guarded by the cruiser U.S.S. *Philadelphia.* The President arrived at Antwerp, The Netherlands, nine days later on 15 July 1945. From Antwerp he motored to an airport in Brussels, Belgium, from where Truman and the Presidential delegation flew in three C-54 aircraft to Berlin. Next, an automobile caravan carried the President and the Americans to Babelsberg, which lies about twelve miles southwest of Berlin, between Berlin and Potsdam. Truman was lodged in a three-story stucco residence which the American party called the "Little White House," although it was painted yellow. Quartered with the President were his new Secretary of State James

R. Byrnes, Admiral Leahy, and several others. The Joint Chiefs of Staff and State Department personnel also stayed in Babelsberg as well as Churchill and Stalin. The sessions of the Potsdam Conference were held in Cecilienhof Palace in Potsdam.[17]

Truman met Stalin on 17 July 1945 when the Russian paid a visit to the Little White House. Molotov and an interpreter accompanied him. Secretary Byrnes and Charles Bohlen were at Truman's side. The President invited Stalin to lunch and continued the conversation with him. Truman said, "I was impressed by him and talked to him straight from the shoulder." Stalin, too, looked Truman in the eye when he spoke. Truman was surprised by Stalin's stature, being not more than five feet five or six in height. Truman felt encouraged by Stalin's visit: "I felt hopeful that we could reach an agreement that would be satisfactory to the world and to ourselves."[18]

The first meeting took place on the afternoon of 17 July. The three leaders were assisted by their staffs. With Churchill had come Clement Atlee, the leader of the British Labour Party. Only days before, on 5 July, Great Britain held national elections whose ballots had not been counted, as yet, but with the possibility that Labour might take control of the government. Stalin and Churchill asked Truman to be presiding officer. The general purpose of the day's meeting was to set the agenda. Truman placed several proposals on the table, one of which related to war criminals. Truman proposed that "war criminals and those who had participated in planning or carrying on Nazi enterprises involving or resulting in atrocities or war crimes should be arrested and brought to judgment." Truman also asked for the fulfillment of the Yalta Declaration on liberated Europe as it pertained to several countries. Churchill said Great Britain wished to add the Polish problem. [*Comment:* All during the war, European and American leaders consistently used the overworked term "the Polish problem." It was never a question of Polish independence, boundaries, human rights, crimes against civilians, and so forth. These leaders behaved like the European monarchs in the nineteenth century. Whenever the Poles rebelled against their

oppressors—Russia, Austria, and Prussia—they created a problem. Europe, it seems, could not live in peace unless those
troublesome Poles behaved.]

One of Stalin's proposals involved the determination of Poland's
western frontier and the liquidation of the Polish Government-
in-Exile (London). In this respect, Churchill brought up the
British responsibility for the thousands of Polish soldiers in their
midst. He said they cannot be released without making proper
provisions for them. He added that he attached great importance
to the Polish elections in order that the will of the Polish people
could be reflected. Before closing the session, Truman proposed
that the next day's session begin at 4 P.M. in order to provide
more time for arriving at decisions. Stalin and Churchill agreed.
Truman returned to Babelsberg with some confidence. "I hoped,"
he said, "that Stalin was a man who could keep his agreements."

At the second session on 18 July 1945, the Big Three first
addressed the question of what constituted the land of Germany
as it existed in July 1945. They agreed that the Germany of the
Versailles Treaty and its 1937 boundaries would be the basis for
discussion. Churchill called attention to a clause in a document
which dealt with the destruction of all arms and implements of
war in Germany. Many items should not be destroyed, he said,
such as wind tunnels and other technical facilities. Stalin immediately interjected that the Russians were not barbarians, and
they would not destroy research institutions. However, Truman
noted in his *Memoirs* that the Russians in Berlin demonstrated
evidence of a lack of appreciation for civilized facilities. They
robbed houses of such rare items as fine old grandfather clocks,
putting them in the bottom of wagons and throwing heavy objects on top of them. They smashed objects of art in the same
coarse manner. Truman also wrote about the Russian demand
for twenty billion dollars in reparations. He said that reparations
could not be paid by vanquished countries because they were
prostrate. "We would rather make grants for rehabilitation to
our allies and even to our former enemies," Truman said. In contrast, the Russians stripped the countries they occupied, whether

friends or enemies, of everything that could be carted off. Poland, Romania, and Czechoslovakia are stark examples of the rewards that come from helping the ungrateful Russians."[19]

Continuing with the second session, Stalin introduced a proposal about Poland that recommended all governments of the United Nations to withdraw recognition of the Polish Government-in-Exile (London). Furthermore, Stalin proposed that all assets of that government be transferred to the provisional government in Warsaw. This proposal would place all Polish armed forces under the control of the Warsaw government. Truman immediately saw the thrust of Stalin's military proposal. The Russians wanted to lay their hands on all the property and equipment of the 150,000 soldiers in the Polish Army for the Warsaw regime. However, the equipment had originally been provided by Great Britain and the United States. Churchill pointed out that, if the Russian proposal were to be carried out, the burden would fall most heavily on Great Britain. There was no property of any kind that had belonged to the pre-war government of Poland. He disclosed that twenty million pounds of gold were frozen in London and Canada, and it was the ultimate property of the Polish national state. Churchill then spoke of the contribution of the Polish armed forces to Allied victory. He said he informed Parliament that if these soldiers, who had fought with the Allies, did not wish to return to Poland, Great Britain would receive them as British subjects. "We cannot cast adrift men who have been brothers in arms," Churchill declared. As for Truman, he was concerned with the holding of free elections in Poland, as assured by the Yalta agreement. Stalin replied that the Polish government (Communist-controlled) had never refused to hold elections [of the Communist kind]. The question of elections was referred to the three foreign secretaries for their recommendation. The second session ended after an hour and fifty-eight minutes of discussions. Truman believed that the three leaders made some progress. However, he wanted more action and fewer words.[20]

In the third session, 19 July, President Truman asked Anthony Eden to present the agenda of the foreign ministers on matters referred to them. This session did not take up any discussion of Polish matters.

In the evening Truman entertained the delegations in the Little White House. A special concert orchestra provided the music, including the performance of Sergeant Eugene List who played Chopin's great *Waltz in A Flat Major, Opus 42.* Learning that Stalin was a fan of Chopin music, the President had asked Sergeant List to rehearse several compositions of Chopin. List obtained the score of *Waltz in A Flat Major* and practiced it for a week before the dinner. Stalin was delighted by the Chopin waltz and nocturnes. He walked over to the Sergeant, shook his hand, drank a toast to him, and asked him to play more. Churchill also complimented List although Truman noted that the Prime Minister was not that interested in Chopin. Truman also got into the musical program. Requested to play the piano, he rendered one of his favorites, Paderewski's *Minuet in G.* Truman believed that social occasions promote a friendly atmosphere.[21]

The President called the fourth session to order at 4:05 P.M. on 20 July. He asked Molotov to report on the agenda of the foreign ministers. Molotov said that a long discussion on the supervision of elections in Bulgaria, Romania, and Greece came to no conclusion. Truman objected to the term "supervision of elections." He said that "observe" would be more accurate. Churchill said that Great Britain did not contemplate the control of elections nor want to have responsibility for them. The discussion next turned to reparations from Italy and the assignment and control of zones in Vienna. Truman then ended the session.

The fifth session on 21 July began with a statement on the Polish question. Secretary Byrnes reported that the three foreign ministers were unable to reach agreement and wished to refer the question to the Big Three for decision. Churchill and Truman were able without too much effort to get Stalin to accept two paragraphs in the declaration on Poland which Molotov had blocked in the meeting of the foreign ministers. One recognized the principle that the liabilities of the former Polish government should be considered when arriving at the total Polish assets abroad. Mainly found in Great Britain and the United States, the assets were to be turned over to the Warsaw government. The second of Stalin's concessions would allow press observers to be present at the Polish elections. [To move a discussion along, Stalin would make concessions which he never intended to carry out. In retrospect, negotiations with Russia were useless. Western diplomats acted in good faith while the Russians behaved with treachery hidden behind disarming smiles.]

The next item was that of the Polish western frontier. Truman reminded Stalin that Yalta had set up four zones of occupation in Germany: American, British, Russian, and French. Russia, however, appeared to have set up a fifth Polish zone—the western extension of Poland to the Oder-Neisse Rivers. Truman charged that Russia created another zone of occupation without consultation with the United States. The American government wished to be consulted because the areas of occupation affected the matter of German reparations.

Stalin countered that as the Russian armies advanced westward, the German civilians fled, leaving only Poles in place. Anxious to provide stability in the rear of Russian forces, the Russians felt the need to establish a Polish administration of German land. German civilians everywhere hastily abandoned their homes and fled from the approaching Russians. The Germans dreaded the conduct of Russian soldiers. Admiral William Leahy in his book *I Was There* writes that the day before the opening session of the Potsdam Conference, President Truman, Secretary Byrnes, and he visited the ruins of Berlin. As they drove the thirteen miles from Potsdam to Berlin, they observed long lines of old men and women with children trudging along the country roads to somewhere where they could find food and shelter, "apparently to get out of the Soviet-occupied territory."[22]

Stalin acknowledged that the Oder-Neisse boundary was not final. Nevertheless, it was a de facto boundary. Stalin referred to Yalta that did allow Poland territory for the loss of eastern Poland to Russia. Truman answered that he could not agree to the separation of the eastern part of Germany, that is, not at the Potsdam

Conference. [*Comment:* Truman's argument was technical; Stalin's, practical in this situation. The Germans had thoroughly destroyed Warsaw and heavily damaged other areas in Poland. Three million Christian Poles and three million Polish Jews had been killed by the Germans and Russians. The Polish civilian population had suffered greatly during the enemy occupation.] Stalin opined that it was better to make difficulties for the Germans than for the Poles. The three heads of state, not being able to agree on establishing a Polish zone of occupation, referred the matter back to the foreign ministers.

On Sunday 22 July, the Potsdam Conference continued with the subject of Poland's western frontier. Truman objected to Russia's unilateral assignment of a Polish zone of occupation without consultation among the three powers. Truman explained: "While I did not object to Poland being assigned a zone, I did not like the manner in which it had been done." [*Comment:* Truman was right to challenge Russia's unilateral action and its pattern of behavior. Stalin and his Foreign Minister Molotov would agree to a proposal one day and change it the next.]

Stalin handed over to Poland the German territory east of the Oder-Neisse River line to placate the Poles for his seizure of the eastern half of Poland. However, he had a practical reason, too. He planned to expel millions of Poles from eastern Poland and resettle them in the German territory granted the Poles. This part of Germany had largely become denuded when the German residents abandoned their homes and fled to the West to escape the advancing and dreaded Russian armies.

The resettlement of Poles occurred in East Prussia and Gdansk except for the region around Koenigsberg which Russia seized for itself. Poland now regained the old Province of Warmia with its principal city of Olsztyn (Allenstein) which Prussia had seized in the infamous Partition of 1772. [This author visited the former East Prussia in 1979 when he was the guest of first cousin Helena and her two daughters in the village of Waplewo (*Wapleitz*). She referred to the region as the "Recovered Lands." East Prussia today is completely Polonized.]

Because the session seemed deadlocked over the matter of a separate Polish zone, Truman ended the discussions for the day. That evening Stalin gave a gala state dinner of an expansive nature in food, vodka, and entertainment. Sitting next to Stalin, Truman noticed that Stalin frequently replenished a small glass from a bottle he kept handy. Truman wondered how Stalin could drink so much vodka. He asked the Russian who looked at Truman and grinned. Leaning over to his interpreter, he said, "Tell the President it is French wine, because since my heart attack I can't drink the way I used to."

The sixth meeting took place on Sunday 22 July at 5 P.M. Earlier, Truman attended a Protestant service, followed by a Catholic Mass said by Truman's old friend Colonel Curtis L. Terman. He had been a chaplain in the 35th Infantry Division in World War I (Truman's Division) and currently served as Chief of Chaplains in the European Theater.

Because of the impasse over the Polish zone and the western boundary of Poland, Stalin proposed that representatives of the Polish government be invited to Potsdam for their views. Churchill concurred, and Truman as presiding officer issued invitations to these representatives. The discussion of the Big Three now turned to the subject of trusteeships and other matters.

The seventh meeting on 23 July involved the territories of Turkey, Koenigsberg, Syria, Lebanon, and Iran.

The eighth session on 25 July considered the western frontier of Poland. Churchill said he had a talk with President Bierut of the Polish Provisional Government and that Eden had seen the Polish delegation for two hours the previous evening. The Poles reported that about one and one-half million Germans remained in the western land under discussion. Truman said that Secretary Byrnes also had talked with the Poles and expected to have more talks.

Churchill complained that the Poles were driving the Germans out of their occupied area. The result was, he said, that the Poles, having little food and fuel, were forcing the Germans onto the British Zone. Stalin remarked that the Poles were taking revenge on the Germans for the injuries the Germans had caused them for centuries. Churchill responded that the revenge of the Poles took the form of throwing the Germans into the American and British zones to be fed.

Churchill, Atlee, and Eden left for England at the end of the ninth session to learn the results of the British general election. The sessions were adjourned until the return of the British delegation.

The British delegates returned to Potsdam on the afternoon of 28 July 1945. Churchill and Eden, however, did not return. The Conservative Party lost the election to Labour, and now Clement Atlee became Prime Minister with his new Foreign Minister Ernest Bevin. Due to the late arrival of the British party, Truman called for the first night meeting at 10:15 P.M., 28 July. The session considered the drafting of an agreement relating to the recognition of Italy, Bulgaria, Romania, and Hungary as well as the subject of reparations. The meeting was adjourned at five minutes past midnight.

On Sunday 29 July, Stalin remained in his quarters because of a cold. However, Molotov came to see Truman about several issues. Truman agreed to meet with Molotov. The President called for Secretary Byrnes, Admiral Leahy, and interpreter Bohlen. Byrnes handed Molotov a copy of the United States proposal for establishing the western boundary of Poland. The American proposal was a significant concession to Russia, in that it recognized the geographical region from the 1938 boundary of Poland westward to the Oder-Eastern Neisse River line, as being under the administration of Poland and that the Polish-administered area should not be considered a part of the Russian zone of occupation of Germany. The American note defined the extent of the Polish zone—the demarcation line ran from the Baltic Sea through the Swinemunde channel, to the west of Stettin and to the Oder River, and thence along the Oder to the confluence of the Eastern Neisse River, and along the Eastern Neisse to the Czechoslovak border. The Polish zone of administration included the port city of Gdansk and East Prussia except for the Russian-

Potsdam Conference Places German Land Under Polish Administration

BALTIC SEA

GDANSK

EAST PRUSSIA

GERMANY

Oder River

Polish Administration Zone

Western Neisse R.

1938 BOUNDARY OF POLAND

Poznan

Warsaw

POLAND

Eastern Neisse River

CZECHOSLOVAKIA

AUSTRIA

HUNGARY

Map by Vicki Trego Hill

occupied enclave around the port of Koenigsberg. Molotov objected to the American proposal because it did not include the area between the Eastern Neisse River and the Western Neisse. He said he would refer the American proposal to Stalin.[23]

No meeting was held on 30 July. Stalin was still sick, and Truman spent most of the day with his military advisors.

The eleventh meeting was held on 31 July. The three heads of state met twice. The major issues that remained unresolved were reparations, Poland's western frontier, and membership of satellite countries in the United Nations. Coming to agreement on reparations, Truman brought up the subject of the western boundary of Poland, and Byrnes read the revised American proposal— the Poles would have provisional administration of the area bounded by the Oder and the Western Neisse Rivers (again a concession to Russia). Foreign Minister Bevin objected. Truman explained the area would be under Polish administration, but the determination of the western boundary would be a matter for the peace treaty. After considering other matters, Truman adjourned the session.[24]

The twelfth meeting of the Potsdam conference convened at 4 P.M. on 1 August 1945, the last day for Truman. The first item was the unsettled subject of German reparations. Next, Byrnes introduced the subject of German war criminals. Stalin insisted on naming them publicly. Truman objected, relying on the advice of the Chief American prosecutor he had appointed, Justice Robert H. Jackson, who advised Truman that it would be a handicap to him if the war criminals were named before the War Crimes Commission was ready to bring them to trial. The three heads of state, however, agreed to have a public list of war criminals in one month.

The final meeting, thirteenth, convened at 9 P.M. on the same day. Two major documents were prepared—the protocol and the communique. There were no secrets at Potsdam. Truman stated: "I had made up my mind from the beginning that I would enter into no secret agreements, and there were none." Some changes were made in the texts of the two documents. Molotov suggested an amendment to the text relating to the western boundary of Poland. As stated, the line ran from the Baltic Sea through Swinemunde. He recommended substituting the word for "through" with "west of." Truman asked, "How far west?" Stalin suggested the words "immediately west of," and it was approved. (The Swinemunde channel controls the movement of commerce from the port of Szczecin to the Baltic Sea. To prevent possible misunderstanding with Germany in the future, Swinemunde [Swinoujscie] was placed entirely in Poland.)

The Potsdam Conference formally adjourned at 3 A.M., 2 August 1945. After saying their goodbyes, the American delegation returned to the Little White House. Shortly thereafter President Truman was on his way to the airport in Berlin. He flew to Plymouth, England, where the U.S.S. *Augusta* waited for him. In Plymouth, King George VI welcomed him to the United Kingdom, and after pleasant exchanges of visits, Truman sailed for America. Secretary Byrnes maintained that "the agreements did make the conference a success, but the violation of those agreements have turned success into failure." The President also reflected on the Potsdam Conference and his impressions of Stalin. Truman came to a prophetic conclusion: "The Russians were planning world conquest."[25]

CHAPTER EIGHT

A VALIANT TRY
FOR POLAND

ARTHUR BLISS LANE and Stanislaw Mikolajczyk were
two distinguished diplomats who sought to insure the
conduct of free and unfettered elections in Poland. The national
elections would establish a permanent government to replace
the provisional government which was formed in accordance with
the decisions of the Yalta and Potsdam Conferences. Appointed
by President Roosevelt in September 1944, Lane was the first
American ambassador to the provisional government. In Poland,
Mikolajczyk led the strong and well-organized Polish Peasant
Party. He has been mentioned prominently in his position as
Prime Minister of the Polish Government-in-Exile (London). As
Prime Minister, he strongly defended the territorial integrity of
Poland. Nevertheless, the acceptance by the two Western Allies
of the Curzon Line as the boundary between Poland and Russia
forced Mikolajczyk to bow to the inevitable. With the strong back-
ing of the United States and Great Britain, Mikolajczyk became
a member of the Provisional Government. Prior to departing
for Poland, Mikolajczyk met with Winston Churchill who urged

ARTHUR BLISS LANE
(1925 Photo)

the Pole: "So go, for the sake of Poland. The Lublin Poles have no real authority among the Polish people. They need you." Then, too, Mikolajczyk had received repeated appeals to return from Poland itself. He was sorely missed because most of the political leaders had been treacherously seized by the Russians and jailed. Mikolajczyk decided to make one final try to save Poland from Communism.[1]

Lane was serving as American ambassador to Columbia when he was notified of his selection as Ambassador to Poland. While still in Bogota in August 1944, he received some meager reports of the Warsaw Rising against the German occupation. The reasons for the uprising seemed strange to him, as he later acknowledged:

> If I had been told, at that moment, that Soviet intrigue had encouraged this result deliberately, and then made sure it was quelled by Germany, with the sole intent of imposing a Soviet-controlled government on Poland when the time was ripe, I would have thought it utter fantasy. I did not know what I know now.[2]

LEFT: *Arthur Bliss Lane became the first American Ambassador to the Polish Provisional Government of National United, 1945–1947. Appointed by President Franklin Roosevelt in September 1944, Lane was not able to assume his duties until July 1945, as the United States drifted from the support of the Polish Government-in-Exile (London) to the recognition of the Polish Provisional Government.*

As Ambassador, Lane sought valiantly to carry out the commitment of the United States for the conduct of "free and unfettered" national elections that would establish a permanent government. However, Lane was thwarted at every step by the Communist-controlled Provisional Government. He became dismayed by the machinations of Russian and Polish Communists who forced the Polish nation into a police state and carried out fraudulent elections on 19 January 1947. Ambassador Lane reported the agony of the Polish nation in his revealing book I Saw Poland Betrayed *(1948). (Collections of the Library of Congress)*

Lane was an excellent choice for the post of Ambassador to Poland. He had acquired much experience in nearly thirty years of diplomatic service, including duty at the American Embassy in Warsaw in prewar Poland. He knew nothing of the agreements of the Big Three on Poland made at the Tehran Conference. Lane writes in *I Saw Poland Betrayed* that the decisions at Tehran remained a secret during his stay in Washington in late October 1944 through June 1945. He met with Charles E. Bohlen and Elbridge Durbrow who were respectively Chief and Assistant Chief of Eastern European Affairs at the State Department. He visited the State Department regularly to learn about American activities in foreign affairs, in so far as he could. President Roosevelt maintained a secret, personal conduct of foreign affairs, and the top officers of the State Department cooperated with their silence. Lane writes: "Neither the White House nor the State Department disclosed to me what had taken place at Tehran with respect to Poland." He obtained information, however, from Jan Ciechanowski, Poland's Ambassador to Washington. (Apparently Roosevelt sought to avoid disclosing the embarrassing concessions to Stalin that violated Roosevelt's principles of freedom as stated in the Atlantic Charter, a document of his own creation.) Lane remained in Washington as the United States and Great Britain moved closer to Russia's position of forming a Polish provisional government independent of the Polish government in London. Meanwhile, Lane selected a staff for the Embassy that he would take with him.[3]

After the Senate confirmed Lane's appointment, the State Department continued to delay his departure due to the increasing possibility that the Polish Government-in-Exile might be replaced by another government. Lane used the time to expand his knowledge of Polish-Russian affairs.

Although Lane did not arrive in Washington from Columbia until 22 October 1944, he learned of the meeting of representatives of the Polish American Congress (PAC) with President Roosevelt at the White House, 11 October 1944. Earlier, in May 1944, the Polish American Congress requested an audience with the President who delayed answering for five months until the presidential elections. The PAC representatives met the President in the Oval Office. Charles Rozmarek, spokesman for the group of eleven, expressed the fear that America was abandoning the principles of the Atlantic Charter and the Declaration of the Four Freedoms. President Roosevelt answered in generalities but emphasized that he stood for a free and independent Poland. At the same time, he stooped to a stratagem to deceive his guests. Prior to the meeting, the President's aides placed in full view a large map of Poland behind the executive desk. The map showed Poland with prewar boundaries. (There was no Curzon Line on this map.) *The New York Times* published a report with a photograph of the meeting the next day, 12 October 1944. The Polish American community was led to believe that the President's purpose for displaying the map was to show his support for the territorial integrity of Poland. Yet, the President had already handed over to Russia the eastern half of Poland at Tehran almost a year earlier, December 1943.[4]

Lane keenly awaited the decisions of the Yalta Conference, for he feared that a spirit of appeasement prevailed at that conference. His fears were confirmed. The first report was released to the American press on 12 February 1945, and Lane received a copy at the State Department. Lane was appalled: "I glanced over it, I could not believe my eyes. To me, almost every line spoke of surrender to Stalin." Among Lane's reasons for disappointment was that no provisions were set up for the supervision of elections by the three Allies. The ambassadors would simply inform their governments of the situation in Poland. Thus, Yalta gave Russia an open invitation to meddle and influence the elections. Lane greatly regretted the irreconcilable decision to allow Russia to seize half of Poland, east of the Curzon Line. This surrender by President Roosevelt entailed great losses to the Polish nation. It deprived Poland of enormously rich timberlands, oil fields, and the beloved city of Lwow. The next day, Acting Secretary of State Joseph C. Grew announced to the press that Ambassador Lane would remain in the Department of State "pending devel-

DECEPTION AT THE WHITE HOUSE

President Franklin Roosevelt Meets Polish American Leaders in Washington, D.C., 11 October 1944

Charles Rozmarek, President of the Polish American Congress (PAC), and ten members of the PAC study a map of Poland (1938 boundaries) as President Roosevelt affirms his support for a strong and independent Poland.

The President said that Poland "must be reconstituted as a great nation" and "it is very important that the new Poland be one of the bulwarks of the structure upon which we hope to build a permanent peace."

The PAC had requested the meeting with the President in May 1944, but the President delayed it until October and the Presidential re-election campaign.

President Roosevelt deceived the Polish Americans who were unaware that the President had already handed over the eastern half of Poland to Russia at the Tehran Conference ten months earlier (December 1943).

Note that the ubiquitous Curzon Line that practically dominated all the discussions of the Big Three is not shown on the displayed map.

PAC members in the oval Office (left to right): Congressman John D. Dingell, Democrat-Michigan; Judge Thaddeus V. Adesko, Chicago; Dr. B. L. Smykowski, Bridgeport, Connecticut; Walter J. Pytko, Philadelphia; Stanislaw A. Gutowski, Newark, New Jersey; F. W. Dziob, Chicago; John J. Olejniczak, Chicago; John Mikuta, Scranton, Pennsylvania; Dr. Teofil Starzynski, Pittsburg; Mrs. Honorata Wolowska, Chicago; and Charles Rozmarek, Chicago. (Photo Courtesy of Associated Press, New York.)

opments." Lane understood what Grew's words meant: Lane would not be going to the Polish Government-in-Exile.[5]

AUTHOR'S COMMENTS: The Curzon Line, as applied to the boundary of Poland, became a ubiquitous term in the relations of Great Britain, Russia, and the United States. It was not a magical boundary that took preeminence in all the discussion of the Big Three, although one would gather that impression from the great amount of time spent in discussing the Curzon Line. The origin of the term is attributed to the Englishman Lord Curzon, British Foreign Secretary, who proposed it for Poland's eastern boundary in 1920. The thirteenth point of President Woodrow Wilson's Treaty of Versailles called for an independent Poland with access to the sea. However, no boundaries were defined. Poland had to fight Germany for Lower Silesia and the Russian Bolsheviks for the eastern boundary. Poland decisively defeated the Russian Army under General Tukhachevsky in the War of 1919–1920. Subsequently, the Treaty of Riga of 1921 established the eastern border. The Treaty returned only a part of the former Commonwealth of Poland.

Josef Stalin found the Curzon Line a useful gimmick with which to influence Winston Churchill because it had once been proposed by an Englishman. Lord Curzon based his boundary on ethnic distribution of people. To the west of the line, the population was overwhelmingly Polish; to the east of the line the majority consisted of White Russians to the north and Ukrainians in the south. Despite the distribution of populations, Marshal Jozef Pilsudski rejected the Curzon Line out of hand. It was unacceptable to Pilsudski because the Curzon Line violated Polish history. The region in question was historic and centuries-old Polish land. Pilsudski was a federalist. The origin of federalism goes back to the year 1386, when the young Queen Jadwiga of Poland married Grand Duke Jagiello of the Grand Duchy of Lithuania. The Jagiello dynasty ruled the two nations jointly for nearly two hundred years. During this period the two nations bonded to the degree that the gentry class of Lithuania became Polonized.[6]

The country developed into a commonwealth of three nations: Poland-Lithuania, White Russia, and Ruthenia (Ukraine). The Poles, Lithuanians, White Russians, Ukrainians, and Jews were all granted full and equal citizenship in the Commonwealth of Poland. An interesting incident reveals Pilsudski's thinking on achieving the status of a commonwealth. When Marshal Pilsudski took charge of the reborn Poland in 1918, he dreamed of restoring the historic Commonwealth. Immediately after World War I, Russia was wracked by revolutions that pitted one faction against another. The Russian Jews were victims of pogroms. They sought relief from oppression by fleeing into Poland where they gathered in temporary camps along the Polish border. As the number of Jews reached the large figure of 600,000, Poland's Minister of the Interior was overwhelmed. He sought advice from Pilsudski: "What can I do with the massive number of Russian Jews," he lamented. "They're not citizens." Pilsudski shot back, "Make them all citizens." Since then, Jews in Poland had a tender heart for Pilsudski.

In the United States, members of both political parties acclaimed the results of the Yalta Conference, and the people believed them. Lane wrote: "The American people hailed it as a definite milestone along the highway of international peace." In reality, President Roosevelt was swindled by Stalin, and the American people were deceived, as well. Lane called the Yalta agreement "a capitulation on the part of the United States and Great Britain to the demands of Russia."[7]

When President Roosevelt died on 12 April 1945, Harry S. Truman became President. The United States and Great Britain established diplomatic relations with the Polish Provisional Government of National Unity, 5 July 1945. Ambassador Lane and a nucleus of twelve members of the Embassy staff departed Washington by a special C-47 aircraft. He arrived in Paris the next day and telephoned Ambassador Robert D. Murphy, Political Advisor to General Eisenhower, at Frankfurt, Germany. Lane needed the permission of Russian officials (Marshal Georgi Zhukov) to

fly over the Russian Zone of Occupation. Not obtaining any reply from the Russians, Lane flew to Frankfurt where he personally
contacted General Eisenhower, 17 July 1945. A week later Robert
Murphy telephoned Lane in Frankfurt that he had received the
necessary permission. On 30 July 1945, Lane departed Paris for
Warsaw via Berlin, utilizing three aircraft for his personnel and
supplies. In Berlin, Lane and his staff stayed overnight in
Babelsberg where the Potsdam Conference was in session. Lane
had an opportunity to meet Averell Harriman, and he also called
on Zygmunt Modzelewski, Vice Minister for Foreign Affairs, who
had come to Potsdam with members of the Polish Provisional
Government in response to President Truman's invitation.
Modzelewski asked Lane's opinion of the appointment of Oscar
Lange as Poland's ambassador to Washington. Lange, a naturalized American citizen of Polish descent, had been a professor of
economics at the University of Chicago. Lane answered Modzelewski
that he was personally opposed to Lange's appointment as ambassador, calling it inadvisable because of his American citizenship;
and should Lange become a naturalized Polish citizen, his appointment would create an unfavorable opinion in the United
States, especially among the Polish American community which
was bitterly opposed to Lange, a confirmed Communist and a
traitor to the Polish spirit of independence. Lane attributed
Lange's acceptability as Polish ambassador to Communist sympathizers in the State Department.

While Lane waited in the room at Babelsberg, Modzelewski
left and returned with Boleslaw Bierut, the Communist President
of Poland, who greeted Lane in a friendly manner. Lane's description of Bierut is revealing. He stood about five feet seven
inches tall with a small, closely-cropped, brown mustache that
made him look like Adolf Hitler. His mouth was weak-looking,
and as he spoke through an interpreter he kept his eyes away
from the American. Bierut struck Lane as less than a dominating
personality.

As Lane spoke with Bierut, Stanislaw Mikolajczyk entered
the room. He now served as one of the two Vice Premiers of

the Provisional Government. He had come to Potsdam with the invited Polish officials. Lane met Mikolajczyk for the first time. Because of the presence of Bierut, Lane could not speak freely with Mikolajczyk. Lane had studied the Polish patriot's character from his statements, and he was deeply impressed. Lane described Mikolajczyk:

> Light-complexioned, with a broad forehead, of medium height, he personified the strength of the Polish peasantry. He struck me as a calm man, a man of intellectual and moral force. The direct gaze of his blue eyes, his slow, deliberate manner of speech made me feel his tenacity and stability. He spoke in good English, punctuated with a characteristic Polish accent.[9]

The next morning, 31 July 1945, Ambassador Lane, Mrs. Lane, and the Embassy staff departed Berlin in three C-47 aircraft on the two-hour flight to Warsaw. The planes landed at Okecie Airport, neglected, knee-deep in grass, and pitted with weed-filled holes. The runways and hangars had been destroyed. Only rain and wind greeted the passengers. Lane's telegram from Paris sent five days earlier had not arrived. Lane learned later that an honor guard had been ready to do honors for eight days but was canceled when Lane failed to arrive. Lane saw only a lone soldier. Saying little, the soldier looked over the strangers and walked off. About an hour later, an American jeep sped across the wet ground to the planes. The driver was U.S. Navy Lieutenant William Tonesk who was assigned to be the assistant naval attaché at the Embassy. Lane described him as a "tall and handsome young American." Tonesk was of Polish descent and spoke fluent Polish since childhood. Before the war he had attended the famous Jagiellonian University in Krakow and was very familiar with Polish history and culture. Tonesk had driven from Moscow in a jeep lent him by Ambassador Harriman. Tonesk had been sent to Moscow as an aide to the Ambassador during the deliberations of the three foreign ministers who selected the members of the Polish Provisional Government. Lane was delighted to have Tonesk in the coming year. As the Ambassador's aide and interpreter, Tonesk proved to be of inestimable value. Shortly, a green, dilapidated car maneuvered across the rain-swept field. The car had once been a Berlin taxicab, and it had been abandoned by the Germans in Warsaw. The stranger was Wincenty Rzymowski, Minister of Foreign Affairs. Although the season was early August, the Minister wore an overcoat to stay warm. The group was soon joined by Mr. Lebedev, Russian Ambassador to Poland, who welcomed Lane.[10]

Lane and the Embassy staff drove the seven miles from the airport to the city. Lane felt deeply depressed. He had known Warsaw before the war in 1919 when the Polish nation became free again, and in 1937, too, when Warsaw "was one of the most beautiful capitals of all Europe." Now, however, he saw only a few houses undamaged; all others were gutted by fire. He smelled the sickening sweet odor of burnt human flesh, a grim reminder that the Americans were entering a city of the dead. Part of the destruction of the city occurred in 1939 during the September military campaign. But a far greater destruction was due to the vicious answer of the Germans after the Warsaw Rising of 1944. Lane vividly describes the destruction that greeted his eyes:

> At the time the infuriated Germans acting under the Fuehrer's personal instructions drove all the inhabitants of Warsaw out of the city and herded them in a concentration camp at Pruszkow, a suburb some fifteen miles distant. They destroyed the city methodically, block by block and house by house. Almost every building was gutted by fire from incendiary bombs set off from the ground; a few were destroyed by explosive bombs. The only buildings left standing were those housing the Nazi High Command and the barracks of their troops.[11] [Roman Polanski's film *The Pianist* (2003) starkly portrays the destroyed Warsaw.]

Lane's party drove to the Polonia Hotel, spared destruction because it had been the headquarters of the German Army in Warsaw. The hotel was to house the American Embassy as well as the diplomatic staffs of other nations. The suite prepared for Ambassador and Mrs. Lane was comfortable and nicely furnished.

For the others, the rooms were adequate but cramped. On that first day in Warsaw, Lane recalled the assurances of President Roosevelt and others to the Polish people—that the Americans stood for a strong and free and independent Poland but that, because of the rigid control of the nation by the Russian and Polish Communists, Roosevelt's assurances would be difficult to carry out.[12]

The next day, 1 August 1945, Ambassador Lane traveled to the Polish Foreign Office located in the Praga section of Warsaw. Situated on the east bank of the Vistula River, Praga had largely escaped destruction. Lieutenant Tonesk drove Lane, Mrs. Lane, and counselor Gerald Keith in the jeep. On the way Lane asked Tonesk to go by the Count Maurice Zamoyski Palace which had housed the American legation in 1919 and where the Lanes had lived for four months. They found the Palace completely destroyed, although the walls still stood. Approaching the Vistula River, Lane saw the Poniatowski Bridge and the railroad bridge totally destroyed. A temporary wooden bridge and a small pontoon bridge had been erected. Tonesk drove the jeep across the wooden bridge. Large portraits of Stalin and Molotov dominated the entrance. At the other end were larger portraits of President Bierut, Prime Minister Osubka-Morawski, and Marshal Rola-Zymierski. The Lanes observed thousands of Russian soldiers marching east, along with horse-drawn German carts filled with goods of all types—sewing machines, bicycles, bedding, bath tubs, and other articles of plumbing. Lane noticed that business activities appeared normal, and shops were open for business. The Germans could not destroy Praga because it was occupied by Russian soldiers who, on orders of Stalin, remained fixed in position while the Germans and the soldiers of the Polish Home Army fought each other in the streets of Warsaw for sixty-three days.[13]

At the Office of Foreign Affairs Minister Wincenty Rzymowski, Lane presented the customary formal note reporting the arrival of the ambassador and a copy of the letter of credence. Lane inquired about the possibility of bringing an American military detachment to Warsaw for the purpose of selecting guards, drivers, and radio operators. Rzymowski answered that the protection of diplomatic missions was the responsibility of the Polish government. Still, Lane brought up the nightly firing audible from the Polonia Hotel by undisciplined Russian soldiers, attacks on pedestrians, and break-ins into private homes. Rzymowski, therefore, agreed in principle to allow the entry of American military personnel with the first convoy of automobiles from the American Zone of Occupation in Germany.[14]

The Polish Chief of Protocol suggested that Lane should be at the airport in the afternoon to greet President Bierut who was returning from Potsdam. Tonesk drove the Ambassador and the British Charge d'Affairs to the airport. In addition to the diplomatic representatives, Lane saw Prime Minister Osubka-Morawski who seemed pleasant but somewhat reserved in his comments that Tonesk translated. Lane described the prime minister: "A small unimpressive individual, he had a kindly smile, a nervous manner of speaking, and pale blue eyes which stared at me fitfully from beneath heavy eyebrows."

Although President Bierut had already met Lane at Babelsberg two days earlier, he broke protocol and greeted Lane first of the members of the diplomatic corps. Stanislaw Mikolajczyk, Vice Premier and Minister of Agriculture, arrived in the second plane. The next day Lane received disturbing information—all telegraphic and radio messages out of Poland, both official and private, must pass through Moscow. Not wanting to be at the mercy of the Russians, Lane instructed the communications officer, Major Lawrence Treece, to place a radio transmitter into operation for prompt contact with the outside world.[15]

Two Poles seeking employment came to Lane. Both had been employed at the American Embassy during the prewar period. They looked undernourished and discouraged. Lane would have liked to engage them, but he could not do so at the time. The Polish government had not, as yet, established a rate of exchange between the dollar and the Polish *zloty* for the diplomatic corps. Lane and several Americans dined at a restaurant where the meal cost them $100 each (in 1945). One of the work applicants commented that the soldiers of the German army in Warsaw had been fairly human in comparison to the Gestapo. He also said the German army had been strongly opposed to the destruction of Warsaw. The soldiers believed the destruction would serve no useful purpose except to create perpetual hatred of their nation.[16]

The Britisher Robin Hankey invited Lane to a luncheon where Lane met the Moscovite Communist Jakub Berman for the first time. Berman held the post of Undersecretary of State of the Council of Ministers, which ranked fourth in the government (behind the Premier and two Vice Premiers). Berman spoke a great deal about many problems so that Lane quickly concluded this man was a power in the government. Berman said with emphasis that Polish soldiers abroad should return to Poland as soon as possible. Lane suggested that Polish troops in Italy and elsewhere were afraid to come home because of the threat of being tried on political charges due to their service with General Wladyslaw Anders, commander of the Polish Second Army Corps. The Bierut government intensely disliked Anders for his support of the Polish Government-in-Exile and his condemnation of the Yalta Conference as a betrayal of Poland. Berman replied that sentences for political offenses could not be imposed *in absentia*, and therefore they could not apply to Polish troops abroad. Nevertheless, as Lane writes in his book *I Saw Poland Betrayed*, General Anders and seventy-five of his most senior officers were sentenced, while absent from Poland, to a loss of their citizenship in 1946. Lane mentions several other officers who likewise were deprived of their citizenship: General Stanislaw Kopanski, who became a hero of the fighting at Tobruk (Libya); General Antoni Chrusciel, Chief of Staff to General Bor-Komorowski during the Warsaw Rising of 1944; and General Stanislaw Maczek, commanding the Polish First Armored Division under General Eisenhower's command, who distinguished himself in the Normandy invasion in June 1944.

Berman seemed to be a highly intelligent man. "Quiet in demeanor and dignified in his bearing," Lane said, "he was elegant but forceful in speech." Berman's complexion was swarthy, and his nose revealed his Jewish origin. Lane was to learn that Berman was one of the Kremlin's principal agents in Poland. He directed the puppets.[17]

On 4 August 1945, Ambassador Lane and members of the Embassy were invited to the Belvedere Palace where the Ambassador was to present his credentials to President Bierut. Arriving in the courtyard of the Palace, Lane heard a military band render the *Star Spangled Banner*, and it performed the national anthem surprisingly well, considering the band played it publicly for the first time. After the formalities of presenting credentials and appropriate remarks, Bierut invited Lane, interpreter Tonesk, Foreign Minister Rzymowski, and Vice Premier Modzelewski to his study. There Lane introduced several activities that Poland should undertake to get on its feet economically. Lane told Bierut he hoped the Polish government would give permission to expand the American activities in Poland. In particular, Lane asked for:

1. Opening consulates in Poznan, Krakow, Lodz, and Gdansk.
2. Establishing a radio station in the Embassy so that Lane and staff could communicate rapidly with Washington through the American command in Frankfurt, Germany.
3. Establishing a weekly courier service between Warsaw and Berlin.
4. Admitting American newspaper correspondents in accordance with the terms of the Potsdam decision.
5. Permitting a U.S. Congressional delegation of four Congressmen to come to Poland in September 1945 to meet with members of the Polish government and to study existing conditions.

President Bierut replied that the Polish government would be glad to approve Lane's requests. Despite Bierut's assurances, Lane was not ready to believe the President. That Bierut's eyes rarely met his own irritated Lane. Bierut impressed Lane as a shifty and opportunistic individual who exercised little power in his own government. Bierut agreed too readily to Lane's requests. Lane explained: "I was soon to learn to my sorrow that the tactics of a Soviet-controlled government are to give sweeping praises which are rarely, if ever, implemented into action."[18]

The day after Lane's conversation with President Bierut, the Ambassador and Mrs. Lane, at the personal invitation of the President, attended a reception in honor of two leaders of the Russian Armies, Marshals Georgi K. Zhukov and Konstante K. Rokossovsky. The Lanes arrived at the Belvedere Palace with Lieutenant Tonesk. Bierut introduced the two marshals and, after a long speech, presented them with Poland's highest award, *virtuti militari*, for their part in the "liberation of Poland" by the Red Army. Radiating strength and good humor, Zhukov wore a white tunic of light wool and dark blue trousers. Rokossovsky was reserved and said little. He wore the regular Soviet gray field tunic. He appeared more massive than Zhukov and less outgoing. Rokossovsky was of Polish descent and spoke the language of the country. Reportedly for this reason, Stalin selected him to command the Russian Army in Poland.

During the luncheon that followed the presentation, Bierut invited Lane to sit at Zhukov's table. Through his interpreter Tonesk, Lane told the Marshal he hoped that better communications could be established with Berlin. Lane asked for blanket authority for the Embassy's weekly aircraft to fly over the Russian zone and for the American land convoy to travel to Poland. Zhukov advised Lane to submit his request to the American political advisor in Berlin for each request. Lane concluded that Zhukov had no authority to grant his request.

An informal concert followed the luncheon during which Michael Fogg, owner of a popular restaurant in Warsaw, sang Polish songs. For the first time Lane heard the song of nostalgia "*Warszawa*," composed during the German and Russian occupations of the country. Fogg sang with great feeling. Many of the Polish women in the audience were in tears. The song expresses the great longing of a Pole imprisoned in Siberia to be back in

Warsaw again and to see his country free. Lane said this song was later banned by the Communist government.[19]

At the reception, Lane spoke with Zygmunt Modzelewski, Vice Minister of Foreign Affairs, about the American offer to give Poland one thousand surplus trucks. Modzelewski surprised Lane with his answer that a Polish official had been sent for this purpose, but that he traveled to London rather than Paris. Modzelewski blandly told Lane to wire the American Embassy in Paris to send a representative to London to meet the Polish agent. Lane solved the problem by appealing directly to Jakub Berman who promised to send a representative to Paris with complete authority to conclude an agreement on the one thousand trucks. Lane became more convinced that Berman was Moscow's man in control of the Polish government.

In the early days of his ambassadorial duties, Lane sought to meet with various members of the government. He called on Marshal Rola-Zymierski, Minister of National Defense, and found the Marshal an affable individual. The Marshal had attended the *Ecole Militaire de Guerre* in Paris. Consequently, he spoke excellent French. But he was not the real directing force in the Polish Army. It was General Marian Spychalski, a Jew and Moscow-trained. Spychalski's job was to mask the Russian steps that would lead to the organization of the Polish Army and militia under the direction of Russian officers. Spychalski was the Polish counterpart of the political commissar in the Russian Army.[20]

Lane also visited a Dr. Dabrowski. Minister of Finance, a pleasant-mannered individual. Lane learned that Poland adopted the Russian policy of complete control of all commercial and financial transactions. Thus, the Minister of Foreign Trade would be the importer and exporter and would control all international trade through the issuance of licenses. Government control would likewise be expressed through the requirement that all accounts relative to foreign trade would be settled in *zlotys* through the National Bank of Poland. Lane cautioned Dabrowski that state controls would undermine confidence in Poland's recovery in economic and financial circles in the United States. The maintenance of multiple rates of exchange would lead to confusion and discourage the investment of American capital in Polish reconstruction.[21]

State control of the economy was contrary to the free enterprise spirit of Poles who believed in the capitalist system. State control stifled initiative to the detriment of the nation. President Roosevelt not only cast Poland into Communist captivity and loss of freedom but also his betrayal denied the Polish nation the opportunity to move forward over a period of forty years of Communist rule.

Lane took a day to visit Majdanek, the German concentration camp. His guide was Krzysztof Radziwill of the Polish Foreign Office and one who had suffered there as a prisoner of the Germans. At Majdanek, the guide led Lane's party from building to building clustered in an area a mile square. The guide trembled with emotion as he described the horrors he had witnessed. He led them to the shower rooms where the undressed victims, thinking they were getting a cleansing bath, were killed by cyanide gas flowing from jets in the ceiling of the room. The bodies of the dead were cremated in ovens, and the ashes were carted off to Germany as fertilizer. Radziwill related a terrible incident that occurred on Christmas Eve. The guards hustled all the prisoners outdoors before a decorated tree. Suddenly the guards grabbed several inmates, pinioned them to stakes in front of the tree, and then proceeded mercilessly to club them to death. "After this description," Lane wrote, "we did not feel like conversing. Silently in the dusk we drove back to Warsaw."[22]

Early on, Lane began to learn for himself the brutal behavior of the Russian secret police, NKVD. He had been warned by colleagues in the State Department that, as the Russian Armies advanced into Poland from the east, the secret police followed quickly behind and liquidated any individual deemed unfriendly or politically dangerous. The low mentality of the Russian considered that espionage is a duty of Russians and Communists. They assumed that all foreigners, even those having humanitarian functions, were secret agents, spying for a foreign country.

Poles who claimed American citizenship or who had contacts
in the United States were especially vulnerable, a condition
that affected the work of the American Embassy. In 1945, the
NKVD had not, as yet, intimidated the country to the extent
that developed later. Some Poles were willing to speak of events
that occurred since 1939 when the Russians occupied eastern
Poland. They spoke with the Embassy staff of the deportation
of one and a half million Poles to Siberia from 1939 to 1941.
Lane said that Americans saw for themselves convoys of the
Russian Army passing through Warsaw toward Russia. Horse-
drawn carts were filled with all kinds of loot. Undoubtedly some
had originated in the Russian-occupied zone in Germany. Other
contained Polish loot. The Russians took livestock, industrial
machinery, and other property. Undisciplined Russian soldiers
raped Polish women and even girls as these soldiers returned to
Russia through Poland.[23]

From the very opening of the American Embassy in the Polonia
Hotel, hundreds of Poles, growing into the thousands, besieged
the Embassy for visas and passports. For six years emigration
had been halted. Individuals claiming American citizenship by
birth and naturalization applied for passports. Those of Polish
nationality asked permission to visit the United States. The cruel
actions of the Russian secret police created an unbearable atmosphere from which Poles wished to escape. Many had relatives in
the United States.[24]

The physical facilities to accommodate the applicants was
practically non-existent at the Polonia Hotel. In the beginning
the "reception rooms" for visitors consisted of the bedrooms of
the Embassy staff. The hotel manager swore he had no more
space to offer, unless he could evict other diplomatic personnel.
Lane was fortunate to be able to employ some former Polish
members of the staff of the Consular General. These were women
who were familiar with American requirements for passports and
visas. The former employees appeared at the Embassy virtually
in rags, undernourished, and sickly. They had lost their homes
and all possessions as a result of the German occupation. But, as

Lane noted, "Their spirit was unconquerable." The Embassy opened its offices for business on 1 August 1945. The former Polish employees helped the Embassy officers to classify the various applications—visas, passports, employment, information about families in the United States, and the like. The staff gave friendly advice and support but little in a practical way. Applicants for visas had to obtain passports first, and the Polish government did not allow emigration of Polish nationals. Lane noted: "It was to escape the despair of ruined Poland that the poor people wished to join their relatives in the United States."[25]

Many applicants acted on behalf of fathers, husbands, brothers, or some who had been jailed when the Russian Army occupied Poland in 1939 and again in 1945. Because they were members of the Home Army, the Russian NKVD and the Polish Security Police UB (Urzad Bezpieczynstwa) seized and jailed them. The Russians labeled the Home Army a terrorist organization. A sizeable number of soldiers of the Home Army were native-born or naturalized Americans. Due to the destruction of Warsaw by the Germans and devastation throughout Poland, families of the arrested men could not provide proof of citizenship. Lane wished to see the imprisoned Americans. It was a normal diplomatic duty and provided for by the 1931 treaty between the United States and Poland. Lane had tried to gain access to the prisoners with President Bierut, the Prime Minister, and officers of the Foreign Ministry without success. Lane decided to see Stanislaw Radkiewicz, Minister of Public Safety, with whom even members of the Polish government had difficulty gaining access. Nevertheless, Lane tried and received an appointment for 27 September 1945. He traveled with Lieutenant Tonesk to the Praga district where the Security Ministry was located.

Radkiewicz greeted Lane cordially. Lane described him as a good-looking man with oily black hair, a keen and aesthetic face. The Security Minister was of Russian-Jewish origin. Radkiewicz told Lane blandly that no Americans were under arrest in Poland. He assured Lane that should an American be arrested, the Embassy would be notified at once. The promise was never kept. Lane tried to see Radkiewicz subsequently, but all attempts were rebuffed.[26]

Lane persisted in his attempts to see imprisoned American citizens. He took up the matter with Modzelewski, Vice-Minister of Foreign Affairs, on 10 October 1945. Modzelewski informed him all notes from the American Embassy had been turned over to the Ministry of Justice. Lane now saw Minister of Justice Swietkowski on 26 October. Lane described the Minister as a scholarly, benevolent, and serious-appearing official and a member of the Polish Socialist Party. When Lane asked about the Americans under arrest, Swietkowski calmly answered that the Foreign Office had not informed his Ministry of the arrests of any American citizens. Believing he was being deceived, Lane decided to force the truth out of Modzelewski. On the same day, 25 October, Lane called on him and presented a note that, of the thirteen American citizens under arrest, none had been allowed to contact the Embassy. Modzelewski did not answer Lane for five months. Finally, on 21 March 1946, the Foreign Office asked the Embassy to provide the basis for the claims to American citizenship of the arrested persons. Lane had already done so, but he forwarded the data again. Meanwhile, the United States granted Poland a credit of ninety million dollars, and on 27 April 1946 Modzelewski informed the Embassy in writing that each arrested person claiming American citizenship should submit answers to a questionnaire, on the basis of which his citizenship should be determined. At the same time, Modzelewski assured Lane that, if the Embassy wished to have contact with a person claiming to be an American, a meeting would be possible. Despite all the promises of the Communist government, no contacts were ever permitted during Lane's term of nineteen months as Ambassador. There was one exception, the case of Mrs. Irena Dmochowska, an employee of the Embassy, who was arrested in August 1946. Meanwhile, the number of arrested Americans increased to one hundred. Stanislaw Tupaj, born in the United States and confirmed as an American citizen by the State Department, was condemned to death and executed. He never was permitted to receive assistance from the American authorities. After the Embassy insisted for fifteen months, the Polish Foreign Office proposed in December 1946 that a joint commission be set up to determine citizenship of American prisoners and arrange for visits by Embassy personnel. Still, up to October 1947, when Lane had left Poland six months earlier, American citizens were unable to receive the protection to which they were entitled by treaty.[27]

The critical housing shortage in Warsaw greatly hindered the American Embassy to deal effectively with the thousands of applications for protection, passports, and visas. Foreign embassies and legations had to wait until buildings could be constructed. In contrast, Russia experienced no trouble. Its magnificent new building on *Aleja Sucha* (Dry Avenue, later renamed the Avenue of the Red Army) was erected and ready for occupancy in a few weeks. Finally, the Foreign Office assigned a small building at 17 Emilia Plater Street for the Embassy. The United States paid the rent to the Polish government, and the owners who lived in London got nothing. The Naval Attaché helped to provide additional office space. He brought to Warsaw four Nissen huts and had them assembled at the Embassy. When Lane permanently departed Warsaw in February 1947, he estimated that a time period of six to ten years would be required to dispose of pending applications.[28]

Ambassador Lane labored under the censorship of the Polish press controlled totally by the Communists. The press prevented Lane from accurately reporting to the State Department the true conditions in Poland. The Yalta Agreement clearly gave the American ambassador an international obligation to report to the American government. The Polish newspapers obtained all their news from the government-controlled Polpress. The leading Warsaw dailies were *Glos Ludu* (Voice of the People), organ of the Polish Workers Party; *Kurier Codzienny* (Daily Courier), organ of the Democratic Party; *Robotnik* (Worker), organ of the Polish Socialist Party; *Rzeczpospolita* (The Republic), allegedly independent but actually pro-government; and *Zycie Warszawy*

(Warsaw Life), dealing mainly with local events and also allegedly independent. Lane noted that the editorial policy of all newspapers favored Russia and reviled the Polish Government-in-Exile (London). Despite the withdrawal of recognition by the United States and Great Britain, the Polish London Government continued to function as a private body. In Poland, the newspaper of Stanislaw Mikolajczyk's Polish Peasant Party, *Gazeta Ludowa*, (People's Newspaper), was not granted permission to circulate until October 1945.

Ambassador Lane personally experienced the absence of freedom of the press in Poland. At the request of *Zycie Warszawy*, Lane gave an interview on 9 August 1945 to a reporter of this newspaper. He included a statement of America's keen interest in free elections. When the reporter returned with a draft of the interview, Lane noted that the key statement about free elections had been deleted. Lane let the matter go because he did not wish to make trouble for the reporter. The incident convinced Lane, however, that the stooge Polish government had no intention of holding free elections, unless it was certain of winning them. Lane became depressed by the editorials in the Warsaw press. In August 1945, the press deprecated the offer of financial and economic aid of the United States, alleging that the offer consisted of surplus goods that the United States had no use for and wished to dump on Poland. Russia's policy was to isolate Poland from the United States and force the Polish nation to become wholly dependent on Russia. The Communist-controlled press repeated the Russian propaganda line of Russia's "enormous contribution" to the victory over Japan (the Russians entered Manchuria for one week) and minimizing our effort in the South Pacific of more than three and a half years.[30]

Nothing troubled Lane more than the discovery that Russia was blocking his communication with Washington. He received a telegram from the State Department in September 1945 that only forty-three out of one hundred messages dispatched by radio had been received. The missing telegrams became evident because they were numbered serially. Lane confirmed that the missing telegrams had left the Warsaw post office for Moscow on the day of filing. The Russians blocked the American transmissions to Washington. These missing telegrams dispatched in the first months in Poland contained important data. Lane decided to fly to London and report personally to Secretary of State James Byrnes who was taking part in the first session of the Council of Foreign Ministers. On 12 September 1945, Colonel Edward J. York, Air Attaché, flew Lane to Berlin in a C-47 aircraft recently provided to the Embassy. York, an experienced combat pilot, had the distinction of piloting one of the B-25 Bombers of General James Doolittle that bombed Tokyo in April 1942. After the raid, he landed at Vladivostok, Siberia, where his crew and he were interned by the Russians. They later escaped. York was of Polish descent and spoke Polish and Russian fluently.[31]

York flew to Tempelhof Airport in Berlin. Although Lane had been in Poland for only six weeks, he felt a breath of freedom on landing in American-controlled territory. Lane and his secretary Iona McNulty were luncheon guests of Ambassador Robert A. Murphy who told Lane that the Warsaw government had invited General Eisenhower to visit Poland about 21 September 1945. Lane was elated. Eisenhower, like General Douglas McArthur, had been neglected in the Polish press. Departing Berlin, Lane continued his flight to London. Great Britain had suffered severely during the war, but it had not been controlled by an alien police force, the Gestapo, or the NKVD. The news of Lane's arrival in London spread quickly in Polish circles. That evening Lane met a group of Poles who overwhelmed him with questions about their families, conditions in Warsaw, the adequacy of food, and his estimate of a free Poland in the future. Lane found telling the truth painful. He gave his opinion that there was little hope of Polish independence until the Russian Army was withdrawn from the country. However, he did not express his private fear that the NKVD and the UB controlled Poland so tightly that no democracy in the American sense was possible for Poland for years to come.[32]

Secretary Byrnes received Lane the next morning at the

Claridge Hotel. Byrnes' eyes flashed indignation when Lane informed him of his inability to communicate regularly with the outside world. Byrnes asked Lane why he had allowed such a situation to develop. To Lane, the Secretary's question indicated that "Mr. Byrnes like all those Americans who had not lived in a Communist-controlled police state could not visualize the restrictive measures taken." Lane was hopeful that the lack of communications would no longer cause problems. The Embassy's radio station had finally been set up at Konstancin, twelve miles south of Warsaw. Lane reflected on his first few weeks in Poland—the economic needs, the lack of freedom of the press, terrorist activities of the Polish secret police, and the unconquerable spirit of Poles in adversity. Accepting Lane's suggestion, Byrnes authorized him to use the Secretary's name in urging the American press associations to send correspondents to Poland. Therefore, for the return flight to Poland, Larry Allen of the Associated Press and Charles Arnot of United Press came aboard Lane's C-47. Dr. J. H. Bauer and a Mr. Grady of the American Red Cross also joined Lane's party, although they had no visas. The next day, at Tempelhof, Lane received the news from Frankfurt that General Eisenhower would arrive in Warsaw for a one-day visit, 21 September 1945.[33]

Despite repeated and frantic calls to the Foreign Office, Lane was not informed of General Eisenhower's arrival time until the last minute. At eleven o'clock on a beautiful sunny morning, the door to Eisenhower's four-motor aircraft opened and a smiling General emerged, accompanied by General W. Bedell Smith, Chief of Staff, and Ambassador Murphy. Lane greeted the American guests and introduced them to General Spychalski. After the military band played the two national anthems, General Eisenhower reviewed the honor guard. On the motor trip to Warsaw, the lead vehicle carried General Eisenhower and Spychalski, Lane, and a Polish naval officer acting as interpreter. Lane suggested they drive to the Polonia Hotel so that Eisenhower could meet the Embassy staff. Spychalski agreed. Following the meeting indoors, Eisenhower walked out of the hotel onto the sidewalk where he was greeted by spontaneous cries of *Niech Zyje Nam!* (Long May You Live!) from a crowd of several hundred Poles who had suddenly gathered around the entrance to the hotel. No one told them of Eisenhower's presence, but the news spread quickly. Eisenhower made his way through the crowd without any police protection whatever. In contrast, Lane recalled the reception of the two Russian Marshals, Zhukov and Rokossovsky, on 5 August, who were flanked by armed guards as they walked through the gardens of *Lazienki* Palace. General Eisenhower paid honor to the Tomb of the Unknown Soldier, erected after World War I. The Tomb had been blown up by the Germans before they retreated from Warsaw. Eisenhower placed on the broken slab a bouquet of white and red roses, Polish national colors. An elderly woman at Okecie Airport had presented the bouquet to the General. Next, Eisenhower was escorted to *Stare Miasto* (Old Town), the oldest district in the city. When Hitler ordered the destruction of Warsaw, following the failed Rising of 1944, the German Army utterly destroyed the medieval buildings. The rubble caused the Eisenhower party to leave the automobiles and walk through the ruins of the *Rynek* (Market Square). Once of the most beautiful architectural gems in Europe, the *Rynek* was a mass of crumbled stones. It had been surrounded by houses of multi-faceted facades. Now nothing remained but rubble. Through an arch which was still standing, Lane pointed to an impressive view of the Vistula River below and Praga beyond. He explained to the General that during the Rising of 1944 this section of Warsaw was held initially by the Home Army which daily expected the Russians to cross the river and help the Poles. Scanning the river site and as an experienced soldier, Eisenhower exclaimed: "What a perfect bridgehead!" Eisenhower, too, wondered why the Russians had not joined the battle against the Germans. The tour included the ruins of the Jewish Ghetto, which extended over four square miles. Not even the walls of a single house remained. As Eisenhower continued to observe the destruction, his customary smile vanished. Lane commented on the visit: "Eisenhower observed grimly that of all the great cities of Europe that he had lately visited none had been so completely wiped out as Warsaw.[34]

At the Belvedere Palace, President Beirut, his cabinet, and high army officials cordially greeted Eisenhower. The President presented him with a high Polish decoration—the Order of Grunwald (Eisenhower had previously received the order of *Virtuti Militairi* but from the London Government). In his extemporaneous remarks, interpreted by Tonesk, Eisenhower said the award was a tribute to the United States and the American Army, which had fought with Polish soldiers. He spoke eloquently of the invaluable support which the Polish soldiers had rendered his command. Groups of cheering children in Polish national costumes paraded before the General as he stood at the entrance to the Palace. As Lane noted, however, "No regimented tribute could match the unbridled enthusiasm which the ragged men, women, and children had given Eisenhower in front of the Polonia Hotel that morning."[35]

General Eisenhower's visit to Warsaw may have reminded Lane of the difficult effort to re-supply the Home Army during the Warsaw Rising of 1944. The round-trip flights were made from Brindisi, Italy, by British, South African, American, and Polish crews. In Warsaw, the areas held by the Home Army were so small that the pilots flew the aircraft along the Vistula River at low altitude and on a steady course. The necessary flight pattern made the planes easy targets for German fighter planes and anti-aircraft fire. Many planes were shot down. The Poles made frantic pleas for air re-supply to President Roosevelt who ordered a limited number of planes for the effort. The stumbling block was Stalin who rejected Roosevelt's request for permission to land and refuel American planes in Russian-held Poland close to Warsaw. Nevertheless, American cargo planes joined the re-supply flights, and some were shot down.

Once in Poland, Lane heard that an American aircraft had crashed in Paderewski Park in Praga on the east side of the Vistula. With Colonel York and accompanied by several American reporters, Lane visited the Park. He found fragments of a plane scattered over an extended area near a lake. The remains of the aircraft were so badly damaged that neither Lane nor York could identify the nationality of the manufacturer. Lane placed a wreath on the wooden monument which the people of Warsaw had erected to the memory of the brave American fliers.

Polish spectators at the simple American tribute at the monument informed Lane that another plane had crashed in the Praga area, about two miles from Paderewski Park. A boy led Lane to a field near the center of Praga. Colonel York had no difficulty identifying the remnants of the plane as of United States manufacture. With his knowledge of Polish, York questioned residents of nearby houses and learned that the plane had crashed in flames on 15 September 1944, and Russian soldiers removed from the remains of the American aviators "dog tags" and all identifying documents. "Our blood boiled," Lane exclaimed, "as we heard of the treatment of our fliers who had been deprived of the assistance of fighter escort because Stalin desired the Warsaw insurrection to fail."[36]

The visit of General Eisenhower to Warsaw gave the Poles an opportunity to demonstrate their admiration and enthusiasm for Americans, which the puppet Polish government sought to turn against the United States and toward their "liberators." However, the Poles knew the real enemy, Russia. Meanwhile, Ambassador Lane's problems grew more difficult month by month, as the critically important national elections permeated every action of the Communist Polish government.

CHAPTER NINE

THE FRAUDULENT NATIONAL ELECTIONS

AMBASSADOR LANE became very concerned over the delaying tactics of the Polish Provisional Government with regard to national elections for a permanent government. The Yalta Conference called for free and unfettered elections "as soon as possible." The heads of state reiterated this commitment at the Potsdam Conference in July 1945. President Bierut told British Foreign Minister Ernst Bevin that elections would be held in early 1946. On 27 September 1945, President Bierut received Ambassador Lane and a delegation of four United States Congressmen at the Belvedere Palace. The representatives were Frances P. Bolton, Thomas S. Gordon, Karl E. Mundt, and Joseph P. Ryter. The Congressmen asked the President when the elections would be held. Bierut answered that probably not before late spring (May or June 1946) due to the severity of the Polish winters and the lack of transportation. He added that the thaws of early spring would make the roads impassable. At this meeting Lane was not aware of Molotov's reply to President Roosevelt's question at Yalta: "When would free elections be held?" Molotov answered, "Within one month." Lane was greatly disappointed that the State Department had denied him a key item of information. He did not learn Molotov's answer until he read it in James Byrnes' book *Speaking Frankly* published in 1947. Lane could have used Molotov's lying prediction effectively with President Bierut. As events unfolded, the national elections were finally conducted in January 1947, in the coldest month of the winter and when the deep snows in the countryside hindered travel. (Not one month as Molotov had stated but nearly nineteen months after the United States and Great Britain established diplomatic relations with the Polish Provisional Government on 5 July 1945.) The timing for the national elections was set by the Communists with obvious diabolical glee. They knew the severe weather and deep snowdrifts in January would reduce the vote of the independent farmers (not bound to the government for land or employment who formed the majority of Stanislaw Mikolajczyk's Polish Peasant Party). When President Bierut made excuses to the American Congressmen for delaying the elections, Lane came to the cynical conclusion that the real reason was to provide more time for the Polish Security Police (UB) to organize its machinery and prevent the electioneering activities of two opposition groups— the strong Polish Peasant Party and the Christian Labor Party. The means of intimidation by the police included censorship, arrests, murders, and other despicable tactics.[1]

On 24 September 1945, Lane called on Bierut to protest the government's censorship of the press, especially as it applied to the struggling publications of opposition groups. He cautioned the President that the lack of freedom of the press would create an unfavorable opinion in the United States. The same day the government notified the Embassy that correspondents of the Associated Press, United Press, and the *New York Times* were required to submit their dispatches to the Polish government for approval. Meanwhile, the Russian TASS agency sent its dispatches without the approval of Polish authorities.[2]

. . .

After being in Poland for two months, Ambassador Lane planned a short trip of Poland in order to see for himself conditions in other regions of the country. He decided to visit Krakow, the academic and cultural center of Poland; Katowice, the center of the mining industry; Wroclaw, located in the territory placed under Polish administration by the Potsdam Conference; and Lodz, heart of the textile industry. The population of Krakow was almost one million residents, outranking Warsaw at the time. Lane was accompanied by Lieutenant Colonel Andrew Wylie, USMC, the Embassy's Naval Attaché; Larry Allen, of the Associated Press; and Lieutenant William Tonesk, interpreter. They made a brief stop at Radomsko where a crowd of curious men, women, and children gathered about Lane's automobile. The Poles were attracted by the American flag and the military uniforms of Wylie and Tonesk. The spontaneous gathering of the Poles was a sign of friendship for the United States, and it was repeated daily during the Ambassador's trip. Lane continued to Czestochowa with its towering cathedral and shrine established in the thirteenth century. He asked a priest whether the government interferes with the freedom of worship. The priest answered in the negative but added that government agents took notes of the words of all sermons, indicating that repressive measures might be taken if the sermons were distrustful of the government.

At Zabrze, a large crowd surrounded the vehicle; they were not Poles but Germans. Formerly called Hindenburg, Zabrze had been a German city. One woman caught Lane's arm and begged him to use the influence of the United States to force the Polish government from obliging German children to attend Polish-speaking schools. She berated the Poles for their "inhumane" treatment of the Germans. Having seen the destruction of Warsaw leveled deliberately by the Germans and having noted the horrors of the German concentration camp at Majdanek, Lane believed the woman's attack on the Polish nation was most incongruous, and he forcefully answered her. The crowd slowly dispersed and some left sobbing.[3]

From Zabrze Lane journeyed to one of the most beautiful medieval cities of Europe, Krakow. Here he called on Archbishop, later Cardinal, Adam Sapieha. Although he was about eighty years old, the Archbishop exuded a sparkling personality and intense energy. Lane was the first American official whom he had seen since before the war. In fact, he had no contact with the outside world since 1939. The Archbishop had refused to call on German Governor Hans Frank at the medieval Wawel Castle where all the kings of Poland are buried. Archbishop Sapieha was greatly venerated throughout Poland for his strong moral resistance against the Germans. On this trip Lane met the elderly Wincenty Witos, respected leader of the Peasant Party. Through his interpreter Lane spoke with many Poles in the shops, restaurants, and on the street. They informed Lane that not more than five percent of the people supported the Communist Government, whereas the Peasant Party and the Christian Labor Party together represented more than eighty percent of eligible voters. The people of Krakow confirmed Lane's opinion that Poland was a police state governed by the Kremlin.[4]

From Krakow Lane traveled to Wroclaw, making a detour to stop at Auschwitz. He saw what was left of the German concentration camp, mainly parts of metal crematoriums. Most of the camp, including the barracks, asphyxiation chambers, and the quarters of the Germans, had been blown to bits by the Nazis before retreating.

AUTHOR'S COMMENTS: The German concentration camp at Auschwitz housed Poles as well as Jews. On one occasion several prisoners tried to escape. The German commandant decided to punish the inmates with a barbaric reprisal. He ordered the inmates out of the barracks and into the open and randomly selected ten for execution by a firing squad. One of the men in the crowd was a Catholic priest, Father Maximilian Kolbe, a dynamic individual who prior to the war had established a large religious center at Niepokolanow, Poland. Here he preached and published books and periodicals on the Gospel of Christ.

Father Kolbe was a natural target for the Germans who condemned him to Auschwitz.

One of the doomed men was Franciszek Gajowniczek, with wife and children. Father Kolbe knew the man and spoke up in his behalf. He asked the commandant that he take the place of Gajowniczek. The commandant agreed. Father Kolbe was executed along with the other nine men and Gajowniczek survived. Years later, when Pope John Paul II came to Auschwitz, he met Gajowniczek in the crowd of people. Knowing the life of the saintly Maximilian Kolbe, the Pope expedited Father Kolbe's sainthood.

Continuing his tour to Wroclaw, Lane found the city half-destroyed and in great confusion. Germans were being forcibly deported to German territory, and Poles were being brought into Wroclaw from other sections of Poland to replace the departing Germans. That the Polish government was not occupying Wroclaw temporarily while awaiting the peace treaty was obvious to Lane. Here the Polish residents confirmed what Lane had heard in Krakow: police-state methods were being enforced by the Communists.

In Lodz, Lane learned of the attempts of the government to force the people to join the two main government parties—the Workers and the Socialists. Those who joined were rewarded with ration cards entitling them to receive choice UNRRA supplies (United Nations Relief and Reconstruction Administration) and assuring them of their jobs. Following the tour of southern cities, Lane better understood why Molotov, at the meetings of the Moscow Commission, strongly objected to the presence of American observers in Poland where they could find out what the people actually thought of the Lublin government and its Kremlin masters. Clearly, as the security police solidified its methods of intimidation, the Poles would find it more difficult and more dangerous to speak to the members of the American Embassy.[5]

The Polish government tried to hide the fact of Moscow's control of Poland while denying it repeatedly. Vice Minister of Foreign Affairs Modzelewski sent for Lane on 26 October 1945 and complained that two press dispatches of American correspondents in Warsaw had indicated that Poland was under Russian control. Modzelewski threatened to expel the correspondents if such reporting continued. Reminding the official of the guarantee of the Potsdam agreement, Lane stressed that there was complete freedom of the press in the United States. Modzelewski heatedly denied a lack of freedom of the press in Poland. A few days later Lane spoke to Jakub Berman, the Communist authority in Poland. Berman wondered whether Lane got his impression of the lack of freedom of the press from the government's enemies. Lane rebutted with the evident and biased editorial policy of the Polish press. As an example, he cited President Truman's speech in honor of Navy Day, 27 October 1945, which the Polish press watered down considerably. The press eliminated Truman's statement of the American policy of not recognizing governments imposed by force and the glossing over of the powerful capability of the United States Navy and Air Force that Truman had emphasized. In his conversation with Lane, Berman actually contradicted his denial of censorship. Berman admitted that it would be suicide if the Polish government permitted its enemies to attack it. Such attacks would result in the fall of the Provisional government.[6]

In December 1944, the Provisional government introduced a scheme to deceive the opposition into joining the government parties on a single election list. The scheme was aimed principally at Mikolajczyk's Polish Peasant Party. The Russians employed the single list in all European countries which they dominated. The list grouped together on one ballot all parties not in opposition to the government. A vote for the single list would be a vote to keep the Communist-controlled government in power. Had Mikolajczyk agreed to join the bloc of parties, his political integrity would have been ruined, and he would have no assurance that the Communists would not eliminate his party and himself completely from the parliament and the government. Mikolajczyk rejected the offer.

The growing political tension between the Provisional government and the people erupted in a tragic incident in the town of Grojec, located about forty miles west of Krakow. On 1 December 1945, the residents stormed the local jail in an attempt to free a number of political prisoners. Although the attempt failed, UB police arrested four prominent residents, even though none was involved in the attempt. Two were members of the Polish Peasant Party. The UB took the four into the forest and shot them. One of the Polish Peasant Party members, who had some experience with the technique of the German Gestapo, dropped to the ground as the shots were fired and feigned death. After the security police had left the area, he dug himself out of the shallow grave and escaped to the Peasant Party office in Grojec. The Party demanded punishment of the guilty officials. The government refused. Nothing of the incident appeared in the press. However, the murders became common knowledge in the country.[7]

In his revealing book *The Rape of Poland*, Stanislaw Mikolajczyk lists endless persecutions of the people by the security police. In September 1945, the Polish Peasant Party held a provincial congress in Krakow. A member of the executive committee, Wladyslaw Kojder, was missing at the congress. At an earlier meeting he spoke eloquently against the presence of the Russian Army and the terror carried on by the security police. Kojder disappeared. Later, Mikolajczyk learned that his friend had been dragged from his home into a nearby woods and shot repeatedly with thirty bullets. The security police murdered another key member of the Polish Peasant Party, Boleslaw Scibiorek, who was killed in Lodz. The United States became very provoked by the political murders. The Provisional government flaunted the spirit of the Yalta decision, and Secretary of State James Byrnes denounced the outrages in a statement to the press. The Polish press, however, ignored Byrnes' statement. It would not permit any criticism of its Russian masters. When Winston Churchill delivered his historic speech in Fulton, Missouri, on 5 March 1946, the Polish press censored it extensively. There was no reference to the "Iron Curtain" in Eastern Europe nor to the police states east of the Elbe River, the Communist fifth column, the atomic bomb, the

Russian desire to gain the fruits of victory without fighting, and the Russian respect for strength and contempt for weakness.[5]

Amidst the murders committed by the Polish security police, tragedy struck the Polish Peasant Party. On 31 October 1945, the ailing Wincenty Witos died. The nation lost a tremendous force for democracy. Mikolajczyk was the natural choice to replace Witos. Mikolajczyk had to endure calumnies heaped on him and the Polish Peasant Party. He was accused of selling Poland to foreign capitalism because he had said that Poland needed foreign capital to rehabilitate itself. This despicable accusation was spread in Poznan through thousands of leaflets. Mikolajczyk rebutted the false charge: "If I indeed want to sell Poland to foreign capitalist interests, then I must be on the same side as Stalin and Minc [Hilary Minc, Minister of Industry] for they are both seeking foreign credits."

The members of the Polish Peasant Party from the National Council of the Homeland (Legislature) met on 2 April 1946 to set an early date for the national elections. Nine months had passed since the formation of the Provisional Government. The congress, therefore, resolved to hold elections without further delay. The Communist censor, however, forbade the publication of the resolution. At a following meeting of the entire National Council of the Homeland, the Socialist Party introduced a resolution to hold a national referendum on 30 June 1946, thus further delaying the elections. The two opposition parties protested in vain. The referendum would pose three questions—abolition of the senate, agrarian reform and nationalization of industry, and the western frontier. All political parties favored the frontier as decided at Potsdam, and that it should be made permanent. Lane asked himself why the government could not use the same machinery set up for the referendum for the national elections and therefore fulfill the obligation prescribed by the Potsdam Conference. Obvious to Lane was that the Provisional Government felt it did not possess sufficient control to risk the outcome of elections. Furthermore, the conduct of the referendum would determine how effectively the intimidating procedures of the security police worked and how much popular support it had in the country.[9]

To inform the State Department of the gravity of the political situation in Poland, Lane forwarded a lengthy letter on 1 March 1946 detailing the repressive measures executed by the Communist-controlled government. He wanted to be called home for consultations in June 1946 so that he, the President, Secretary of State, and others in the State Department would follow a coordinated policy. He also believed having confidential talks with the members of the Foreign Relations Committees of the Senate and House would be helpful. When the Polish Government advanced the date for the referendum to 1 June, Lane decided remaining in Poland for the conduct of the referendum would be best.

The American Embassy was well informed of the reign of terror on the population and so were American correspondents. By February 1946, eighty-four claimants to American citizenship were in jail, almost all for the "crime" of having once served in the underground Home Army. As acknowledged to Lane by Bierut and Berman, the policy of the government was clearly demonstrated by repressive measures against the Polish Peasant Party through arrests, beatings, and breaking up of political gatherings.[10]

Polish members of the Embassy staff had complained to Lane that they had been summoned individually and secretly to the headquarters of the security police who pressured them to sign forms that required them to spy on the Embassy. In some cases they were threatened with torture and death. Citizens of a country employed by American Embassies, it should be noted, are by law not permitted access to confidential documents. Their work is confined to the processing of passport and visa applications, translation of newspapers, and other routine duties. The sinister and suspicious Russians firmly believed that, like Russian organizations abroad, Americans and various agencies acted as spies for the United States government.

After some twelve threats to the Embassy's Polish employees had come to Lane's attention, and when the British and French Embassies had met the same problem, the Ambassador recommended to the State Department that he be instructed to lodge a vigorous protest against the systematic terrorization. If not stopped at once, it would seriously affect the work of the Embassy and make it increasingly difficult for the Embassy to employ Polish nationals. After receiving approval of the State Department, Lane delivered a note to the Polish Foreign Office on 25 June 1946, in which the United States protested the intimidation of its Embassy staff, an action which made a most unfavorable impression on the United States Government. The note also requested that this procedure be stopped at once. Lane delivered the protest note to Olszewski, Director of the Political Department of the Foreign Office. He responded that the Ministry of Security denied the charge, and he asked for names. Lane naturally refused, not wanting to single out the individuals for special intimidation. The Provisional government disregarded the American protest and continued the intimidation.[11]

The problem of harassment and intimidation escalated to an alarming level. The security police arrested Irena Dmochowska, an American citizen born in Chicago, Illinois, and a member of the Embassy staff. Her duties consisted solely of preparing a daily English summary of the local Polish press, and she worked under the direct supervision of Thomas P. Dillon, Third Secretary. When she did not report for work on 23 August 1946 and sent no word of explanation, Dillon called at her apartment where he heard that she had disappeared. The next day, however, Lane learned that Mrs. Dmochowska was being held by the Polish UB. A personal request to contact her with the Ministry of Security was rejected. The Ambassador appealed to the Foreign Office. After stating the facts, Lane's note concluded with a request for positive action: "I have the honor to request that she be released immediately and an explanation furnished to the Embassy as to the reason for the action taken against an American member of the Embassy."[12]

Lane called on Prime Minister Osobka-Morawski who said he could do nothing. He was actually a figurehead with no authority over the Minister of Security. About ten days after the arrest of Mrs. Dmochowska, Dillon was able to see her in the UB headquarters. He was permitted to give her food parcels and cigarettes. Then, on 12 September 1946, the Ambassador was permitted to visit the imprisoned employee. He was escorted to the room of a Captain Hummer, "an evil-looking official who advised me that I was not to question Mrs. Dmochowska about her case and that I was not to address her in English." Extremely nervous, hands trembling, and lips quivering, Mrs. Dmochowska was brought into Hummer's office. She spoke in a low, almost inaudible voice to Lane's questions which were translated into Polish by Stephen D. Zagorski of the Embassy staff (he succeeded Lieutenant Tonesk as Lane's interpreter). She told him she was well treated and begged him to tell her mother not to worry. During the hour-long session, Hummer's eyes flashed warning signals to Mrs. Dmochowska. Lane saw her once more on 5 October 1946.

Finally, she was tried in public court on 17 January 1947. She pleaded guilty to the charges of having in her possession a revolver without a permit, possessing knowledge of the murder of Boleslaw Scibiorek, prominent member of the Polish Peasant Party, and not reporting it to the police, and assisting persons associated with the murder to leave the country. On the basis of this confession—made under duress—she was sentenced to five years imprisonment. Fortunately, her sentence was suspended in a general amnesty in February 1947 (after the national elections). However, she did not resume her duties at the American Embassy. Lane concluded sadly that the staff and he were at the mercy of the Polish authorities who ignored precedent and the mutual recognition by nations of the laws and customs of others.[13]

The challenging problems for the Embassy continued. Lane was concerned with the large number of Russian troops in Poland. Their presence could hinder the conduct of free and unfettered elections. At Potsdam Stalin agreed to withdraw all troops except for a number sufficient to maintain two lanes of communication between the Russian zone of occupation in Germany and Russia. Lane had learned that Marshal Rokossovsky commanded a force of 300,000 soldiers at Legnica in western

Poland. Another 100,000 Russian soldiers were located at Wroclaw, only fifty miles away. The Russian ambassador admitted to Lane that misconduct by Russian soldiers was seriously hurting Russian and Polish relations. The Poles began to fear that the Russian Army would become a permanent occupying force. With the passing of time, however, the soldiers in Russian uniforms decreased and those in Polish uniforms increased. Curiously, many of the latter spoke with a Russian accent. The Polish Army, organized by cadres trained in Russia, grew to at least 100,000. The militia or ordinary police forces had grown to the same size. Yet another organization called the Volunteer Citizens Militia Reserve (ORMO) of 100,000 had been formed. This organization, composed of members of the Polish Workers Party, engaged in breaking up political meetings of opposition parties and damaging buildings of the opposition. Like the hoodlums of the German Brown Shirts, the ORMO made life disagreeable for all who opposed the government. They dressed in civilian clothes and were identified by red and white arm bands and rifles slung over their shoulders. Most dreaded of all, however, were the security police (UB). When Lane departed Poland in February 1947, the strength of the UB was estimated to be 100,000 agents.[14]

The hostility of the Russian and Polish governments toward the United States and Great Britain was vividly demonstrated on 7 March 1946. British Ambassador Victor Cavendish-Bentinck and Lane gave a joint showing of *The True Glory*, a film of the Normandy invasion in 1944. It was a magnificent portrayal of the solidarity of British and American forces as well as the overwhelming force launched against the Germans. The two Ambassadors invited the Polish government ministers, the senior officers of the Polish Army, and diplomats. Few ministers attended and only some army officers. The public, however, vigorously applauded the film. At another occasion the Ambassadors showed a film of the invasion and capture of Okinawa. Vice Premier Gomulka, apparently with entire honesty, asked why American aircraft had not been used in Europe during the war.[15]

The Polish secret police carried out physical measures against officials of the Embassy. Agents tried to enter the rooms of Howard A. Bowman in the Continental Hotel in Poznan in March 1946. Bowman served as American Consul there. Bowman managed to persuade the agents to leave. On another occasion agents tried to break in at two o'clock in the morning into the quarters of Alexander Radomski, an attaché of the Embassy temporarily at the Grand Hotel in Lodz. On one occasion a Russian general tried to remove tools from the automobile of Lieutenant Colonel York at the point of a gun. Lane's protests against these hostile actions were ignored. In 1946, Lane estimated that more than 100,000 Poles were being forcibly detained either by Polish or Russian police officials. The prisons in Krakow, Lublin, and Poznan were filled to capacity with political prisoners.

The visit of Marshal Tito of Yugoslavia on 14 March 1946 contrasted sharply with the earlier visit of General Eisenhower. All the chiefs of missions were invited to be present at Wlochy railroad station some ten miles from Warsaw. The road was lined with soldiers along the entire route from Wlochy to Warsaw. On the streets of the capital along which the caravan of some twenty-five automobiles passed, the soldiers were so closely lined up that no would-be assailant could come near. In the company of Marshal Rola-Zymierski, Tito traveled in a closed armored car and could not be recognized by the people. How different, Lane thought, was Tito's appearance to the spontaneous welcome which had been given to General Eisenhower for whom it was unnecessary to have military protection.[16]

Lane continued to observe how the Communist-controlled government used its power to subvert the will of the people. The first relief mission of the United Nations (UNRRA) headed by the Russian Menshikov sent a shipload of supplies to the port city of Gdynia, Poland. Earlier, Menshikov had signed an agreement with the Polish government, giving it total jurisdiction over the distribution of UNRRA goods. Lane and Jedrychowski, Minister of Navigation and Foreign Trade, traveled to Gdynia to see the arrival of the vessel. Gdynia, Lane observed, had been bombed during the German invasion in September 1939, mostly the harbor area. Much of the residential area escaped damage. Gdansk, ten miles away, was almost as severely damaged as Warsaw. Residents told Lane the Germans boasted before retreating that, if they could not have Gdansk, no other nation would have it. Accordingly, the Germans destroyed the city, house by house, not even sparing the beautiful Gothic St. Elizabeth's Cathedral. When the Russians arrived in Gdansk, full of vodka, they completed the destruction of the portion left by the Germans.[17]

The national referendum scheduled for 30 June 1946 became the leading issue between the government and the opposition parties. The vote would determine three issues: (1) whether Poland should have a unicameral or bicameral legislature, (2) whether the nationalization of industry and agrarian reform should be part of the constitution, and (3) whether Poland's permanent frontier should remain on the Oder and Western Neisse Rivers. The three issues were non-controversial for most Poles, possibly excepting the first which proposed to eliminate the senate. The two opposition parties were Mikolajczyk's Polish Peasant Party and Karol Popiel's Christian Labor Party. Popiel had been a member of the Polish Government-in-Exile (London). The two parties decided to oppose the first point, as being contrary to the Polish Constitution of 1921. The two parties also believed that a senate could serve as a brake on actions of the lower house, *Sejm* (parliament), especially if it were controlled by Communists. Therefore, the decision was to vote against the first point and for the other two. Wishing to obtain and record the voting procedure employed during the referendum, Lane urged the United States government to encourage extensive coverage by the American press. More than a dozen American correspondents reported the elections. In addition, the Embassy sent out teams to various districts of the country and invited correspondents to accompany them.

Before election day, the security police hindered the opposition parties in their campaigning against a unicameral legislature. Opposition posters were torn down, and the two opposition parties were given little, if any, time on the Communist-controlled radio. The government censor did not allow Mikolajczyk to publish his instructions to his members to vote No on Proposition 1. The Polish Peasant Party had to resort to word of mouth. Three thousand party members were arrested in Poznan and kept from voting. Other members throughout Poland were arrested. In contrast, the government campaign slogan "3 Razy Tak" (3 Times Yes) was posted or painted on thousands of buildings. Light trucks bearing signs "3 Razy Tak" paraded through cities and villages. During the morning of 30 June 1946, Lane drove about Warsaw to observe the crowds, orderly and good-natured, awaiting their turn to vote. Visiting several voting stations, Lane saw no evidence of intimidation. In the afternoon, Mrs. Lane and he visited several villages. The peaceful Sunday gave no sign that a heated political battle, with international implications, was being waged. Returning to the Hotel Polonia, Lane soon began receiving reports from his observers.[18]

The voting which reached ninety percent of the electorate was conducted in an orderly manner. From all reports the day passed quietly and without any disturbances. The voter could mark his ballot secretly. Nevertheless, the observers reported a suspicion of fear that fraudulent means could be used to count the ballots. Indeed, there was provision in the referendum law that could lead to collusion or dishonest practice. For one, a blank ballot was regarded as a Yes vote on all three questions. In addition, government organizations and government-controlled industries voted in blocs. Fearing loss of jobs, the workers of these controlled groups voted en masse for the policies of the government.

Some observers reported that practical means were used to impede impartial observation. Steven Zagorski, Administrative Assistant, and Edward R. Raymond, Agricultural Attaché, had driven to Kielce to observe the procedure and to note the attitude of the people. While they ate lunch at a restaurant, security police arrested them on the charge that they had distributed anti-government hand bills. Despite their protest of diplomatic immunity, they were held at headquarters for more than three hours and then released, but not until the voting was concluded. Lieutenant Colonel Frank Jessic, Assistant Military Attache, was arrested near Bialystok by Polish troops on the charge of traveling in a forbidden area and photographing Russian troops. John Scott, correspondent of *Time* magazine, was arrested near Poznan a few days before the election. He was held and questioned by two Russian officers. Knowing the Russian language fluently, he noted that the phone conversation between these officers and the Ministry of Public Safety (which resulted in his release) was carried on in Russian.

The counting of ballots led to serious suspicion of fraudulence. The law called for the counting of ballots at the polling places in the presence of representatives of all parties. Despite the clarity of the procedure, top government officials and the secret police gave illegal orders to the electoral authorities to remove the ballot boxes from the polls before the votes were tabulated and carry them to the headquarters of the district commission. At one polling place, the electoral commission seemed to be aware of the government's intentions. The commission counted the ballots and reported the results before instructions were received to move the ballots. The government was forced to admit that in Krakow the voting was eighty-four percent "No" on question one. With this exception, the government claimed a sweeping victory on all three questions. On the controversial question of doing away with the senate, the government claimed a victory by more than eighty-four percent. But, according to figures compiled by Embassy observers independently of one another, the opposition voted "No" in about the same percentage. The referendum served two purposes for the Communists: first, testing of the electoral machinery and the possibility of diverting it to fraudulent use; second, serving as an excuse for the postponement of the election for a permanent government and thereby allowing the security police an opportunity to impose stronger controls on the country. Lane reported the voting results to the State Department, summing them up as fraudulent beyond any doubt. The Associated Press interpreted the view held in Washington that relations between the United States and Poland would become more tense as the national elections drew nearer.[19]

On 6 September 1946, Secretary of State James Byrnes delivered a major speech at Stuttgart, Germany, in which he stated in part that the boundary between Poland and Germany would be determined by the peace treaty. Byrnes simply stated the decision of the Potsdam Conference. The speech, however, encouraged the Germans to hope that perhaps they might not lose territory to Poland. Nevertheless, the boundary along the Oder and Western Neisse Rivers had become a de facto boundary. At Potsdam, President Truman and Winston Churchill agreed to accept the Polish zone of occupation. In April 1946, the Polish government celebrated the first anniversary of the liberation of the city of Szczecin by the Russian Army. In his speech, Vice-Minister for Foreign Affairs Modzelewski stated that the presence of representatives of all the diplomatic missions in Poland confirmed the intention of their governments to support Poland's new western boundary. Then, too, the United States had requested permission to open consulates in Szczecin and Wroclaw which lay in the newly-acquired territory. Although the two consulates were never opened, the American request indicated concurrence with Polish claims to this territory. At Potsdam, also, Truman and Churchill agreed to allow Poland to transfer Germans out of this territory. Certainly it seemed inconceivable that the peace treaty would deny Poland the acquired western land and force it to engage in a reverse transfer of populations.

In his speech Secretary of State Byrnes simply repeated a provision of the Potsdam Agreement as it affected Poland and Germany, and the Communist-controlled Provisional Government understood this fact. Nevertheless, Byrnes gave the Communists an opportunity to vent their hostility toward the United States and, more importantly, to curry favor with the nation. On 7 September 1946, the entire Warsaw press, except Mikolajczyk's *Gazeta Ludowa*, bitterly attacked Byrnes' speech. The next day, Sunday 8 September, the government staged a massive meeting that stirred up the passion of the crowd. The diplomatic corps was not invited to the meeting, but French Ambassador Roger Garreau, on his own initiative, was conspicuously present and applauded the speeches hostile to the United States. Following the meeting, a crowd of about 1500 excited individuals surrounded the headquarters of the Polish Peasant Party on *Aleje Jerozolimskie* and broke all the windows. Then, fifteen to twenty ringleaders, armed with clubs and guns, beat up ten members of the Polish Peasant Party in the building and destroyed Party records, typewriters, and office furniture. The crowd moved on three blocks to the Polonia Hotel where they shouted insults against the United States and Byrnes. The Ambassador and Mrs. Lane were absent at the time. The attack on the headquarters of the Polish Peasant Party was carried out by hoodlums. The Communist newspaper, *Glos Ludu*, linked Mikolajczyk and the Polish Peasant Party with the alleged attempt to deprive Poland of its newly acquired territory. The stated reason was false. In fact, Mikolajczyk vigorously campaigned to retain the land of the Polish zone of occupation, and his Party voted for it.[20]

Ambassador Lane became increasingly apprehensive that the Provisional government, backed by Russia, would defy the United States in the upcoming elections. He reviewed the reasons: the falsification of the results of the referendum, denial of the right of assembly of the Christian Labor Party, and the repressive measures to destroy the Polish Peasant Party. He doubted the United States could do anything to salvage the last remnant of the Yalta Agreement—the conduct of free and unfettered elections. He asked the State Department to recall him for consultations in order to plan the next American move.

Lane arrived in Washington on 5 November 1946. He immediately held talks with Llewellyn E. Thompson, Chief of the Eastern European Division, who had succeeded Elbridge Durbrow. Secretary Byrnes was in New York for a meeting of the United Nations. The same day Lane saw Acting Secretary of State Dean Acheson to whom he recommended that the United States should withhold all further financial assistance to the Polish government until commitments for a free elections were fulfilled. Acheson's attitude, Lane said, was characteristically non-committal. On 13 November 1946, Lane received the news in Washington that Poland's National Council of the Homeland announced the date of 19 January 1947 for the conduct of national elections. The voters were to elect representatives to the *Sejm*, approve a new constitution, and elect a president. Therefore, Thompson and Lane prepared a note, approved by Byrnes, that Gerald Keith in Warsaw delivered to the Polish Foreign Office on 22 November 1946. In part, the note stated:

> The Government of the United States expects that equal rights and facilities in the forthcoming election campaign and in the elections themselves will be accorded to all democratic and anti-Nazi parties in accordance with the Potsdam Agreement. My Government could not otherwise regard the terms of the Yalta and Potsdam decisions as having been fulfilled.

In Warsaw, Keith telephoned Lane that repressive actions against the Polish Peasant Party were being intensified. Furthermore, the Party's meetings were being blocked, arrests were continuing, and the Party was declared illegal in twenty-five percent of the provinces. Keith urged the Ambassador to return, and Lane made plans to depart the United States on 28 November. Before leaving, Lane saw President Truman who indicated the United States no longer intended to appease the Polish government through financial means. Lane arrived in Warsaw on 12 December 1946. He found that Keith had not exaggerated the tense political situation. It was boiling.[21]

During Lane's absence, the Foreign Office of the Polish government allocated new offices for the American Embassy at *Aleje Ujazdowskie* 33, and Keith moved there promptly. Stanislaw Mikolajczyk called on Lane, as a representative of one of the Yalta powers, and delivered the official protest of the Party against the Provisional government for its many repressive measures leading up to the elections. The Party's document was supported by twenty-six annexes, giving names, dates, and places where the "State machinery" carried out its dirty work. Mikolajczyk reported that the provincial national councils at Olsztyn, Katowice, Lodz, Poznan, and Warsaw excluded the Peasant Party members from holding positions in the district and local election commissions. In the provinces of Krakow and Lublin, areas of electoral districts had been enlarged, contrary to the provisions of the electoral law. Therefore, even if the weather and road conditions were favorable, the added distance made voting difficult for many voters in the county districts during the twelve hours allotted. (The Provisional Government deliberately set the election for January, the time for the coldest and most severe weather in Poland. Recall that President Bierut told the four U.S. Congressmen in September 1945 that the election would be scheduled in May or June and not in the winter.)

Even the Polish Army campaigned for the Communist government. They distributed a booklet entitled *The Voice of the Soldier.* The publication charged that the United States and Great Britain were using Mikolajczyk and his Party to split Poland's national unity and weaken the country. In reviling the Polish Underground, the Army's publication linked the Polish Peasant Party with the "criminal underground." The illustrations of *The Voice of the Soldier* were in the crude Russian style. Cartoons of Mikolajczyk portrayed him as an American and British puppet, seizing money from the poor and giving it to the rich, and fraternizing with vicious-looking thugs labeled "underground."[22] In sum, the protest note of Mikolajczyk charged that the assurances and the rights of democratic parties had not been fulfilled with respect to the Polish Peasant Party.

The Communists suppressed the Polish Peasant Party's printed bulletin, the last chance of freely telling the views of its Central Committee to its members. Lane reflected sadly that, although Mikolajczyk's Party might number millions, not more than a handful could be told what was going on. Poles orally notified the Embassy staff during the last week of December 1946 that seventy-five out of 834 candidates of the Party for the *Sejm* had been arrested, and the names of forty more candidates had been stricken from the electoral list. Lane said that a foreign embassy in Warsaw with whom he maintained cordial relations had close contacts with the Communist members of the Polish government because of the strong Communist presence in its own country. This embassy told Lane the Communists of the Polish government admitted to close friends that the present government would fall if fair elections were held. The Communists also admitted to this foreign embassy that a deliberate policy had been adopted to reject as many candidates of the Polish Peasant Party as possible, on the false grounds that they were pro-Nazi. The police went from house to house in the cities and villages during the Christmas holidays, signing up voters in support of candidates on the government list, and threatening retaliation if they did not. The UB did more than threaten. Many cases of physical torture were reported to the Embassy. As one example of the means employed, individuals were forced to keep their feet in icy water for two or three days in attempts to drive them to sign the manifesto. An unfortunate man stood this torture for three days when gangrene set in. Both feet had to be amputated.[23]

Lane immediately cabled the State Department Mikolajczyk's arraignment of the repressive actions of the Polish government. Consequently, the United States sent a communication on 8 January 1947 to its co-partners in the Yalta agreement, Great Britain and Russia. In Moscow, Ambassador W. Bedell Smith delivered the American protest to Deputy Minister for Foreign Affairs, Andrei Vishinsky. The United States government said that it was "especially perturbed by the increasingly frequent reports of the repressive measures which the Polish Provisional Government had seen fit to employ against those democratic elements in Poland which had not aligned themselves with the bloc parties." The Russian reply on 10 January 1947 belittled the protest because it came from a single source, Mikolajczyk [Not true]. The Russians also decried the American attempt to meddle in the affairs of a sovereign nation, Poland.[24]

Under instructions of the Department of State, the Embassy in Warsaw delivered a note of protest to the Polish Foreign Office, 9 January 1947. Lane planned to deliver the note personally, but the principals there were too busy to see him. Therefore, Thomas P. Dillon left the note with a minor functionary of the Foreign Office. The reply of the Polish government was signed by Olszewski of the Foreign Office. The reply rejected the American objections to the repressive measures. They were based, the Foreign Office said, "on distorted facts and unfounded reproaches which are raised by the anti-democratic elements working in Poland." The elections would take place, the Foreign Office said, on 19 January 1947, "in accordance with the traditions of Polish democracy and with the will of the Polish nation." The American Embassy was totally rebuffed. As Lane explained the rejection: "In diplomatic language, we have been informed that the election was none of our business." The Polish government published its own response on 14 January but with none of the American notes, although the Department of State had released the notes to the press.[25]

Lane was gratified that at least fifteen American journalists were in Warsaw at election time, including well-known writers Dorothy Thompson, Ralph Ingersoll, family editor of *P.M.*, and Liston M. Oak, managing editor of *New Leader.* These were in addition to the correspondents regularly assigned to Warsaw. As he did for the vote on the referendum, Lane arranged to send out fifteen teams of observers from the Embassy staff, and he invited the correspondents to accompany them to whatever parts of Poland they considered most interesting. Lane gave general instruction to the Embassy teams on the nature of the information he desired—intimidation, if any, prior to the elections; procedures adopted in voting and counting ballots; general reaction to the elections in the different districts; and any other pertinent data. Interviews with officials and members of various parties should be sought, but with one restriction—contact with the underground should be scrupulously avoided (mostly for the protection of the persons interviewed).

Lane had good reason to be fearful because of a case involving the British Ambassador Victor Cavendish-Bentinck. The Ambassador's family had known the aristocratic Grocholski family in

Warsaw for more than thirty-five years. During Ambassador
Cavendish-Bentinck's first assignment to Warsaw in 1919, he and
Count Grocholski had become fast friends, and a cordial relationship continued over the years. Upon Bentinck's return to
Poland in 1945, it was natural that he should seek out his
old friend and invite him to the British Embassy from time to
time. One day when the Ambassador was paying a visit to Count
Grocholski's country home, the villa was surrounded by the security police, and the inmates, including Ambassador Bentinck,
were prevented from leaving. Bentinck insisted on his diplomatic
prerogative of immunity from arrest and finally was released.
On the other hand, Grocholski was arrested, charged with association with the Underground and with having given information
to a foreign ambassador. Like all patriotic Poles who had been
forced to remain in Poland as a result of the war, Grocholski had
been associated with the Home Army during the German occupation. At the public trial, Grocholski "confessed" to guilt on the
two charges. Five days before the elections, 14 January 1947, the
verdict was announced—death. The sentence was executed immediately. Lane concluded that the severity of the sentence was
the brutal way of the government of warning the people of the
risk they faced if they talked to foreign emissaries about conditions in Poland. The execution had a sinister connotation—the
danger to Poles for talking to the American and British Ambassadors about fraud and repressive measures in the election.[26]

On a bitterly cold Sunday, 19 January 1947, the long-awaited
national elections took place for a permanent government. The
Ambassador and Mrs. Lane, accompanied by several American
correspondents, visited polling sites on the outskirts of Warsaw.
At one site, Lane saw Lieutenant Rulski of the Foreign Office who
had acted as interpreter when Lane interviewed Mrs. Dmochowska
at UB headquarters. Rulski recognized the Lanes and courte-
ously invited them to seats in the building where the voting took
place. Voters picked up one of six ballots, a square piece of paper
marked only with the number on the list, from one to six. The
government bloc list was number three in all election districts

throughout the country. The Polish Peasant Party, by direction of the government, was listed with different numbers in the various districts. The shameful trick made it impossible for Mikolajczyk to give directions to his followers as to the list they should vote. This procedure made for confusion and was intended to diminish the total vote of the Polish Peasant Party.[27]

The electoral law provided for secrecy in the casting of ballots. At first, Lane was surprised to observe that many of the voters conspicuously showed their choices of the ballot which displayed the large black number 3 before placing it in the envelope. Lane also noted that the election officials made a special note against the names of all voters who placed their ballots secretly in the envelope.

Many of the Embassy observers returned to Warsaw that evening. They reported general calm throughout the country and considerable apathy toward the election. The story was the same as noted during the referendum six months earlier. The people had learned from experience that the results would be adjusted in favor of the Communists despite the wishes of the voters. The next day the results were announced. It was not surprising that the government bloc of parties scored an overwhelming victory over its only opponent—the Polish Peasant Party. In the estimate of unbiased observers, the Polish Peasant Party represented sixty percent of the electorate.

The Polish press, as expected, hailed the result as great blessing for Poland and a vote of confidence in the government. The government ordered a half holiday for the afternoon of 22 January, and all government employees were forced to be in the parade. The government failed in its objective. The marchers were unenthusiastic and so morose in their demeanor that passersby openly laughed at the spectacle. All realized that it was staged propaganda.

As Lane evaluated the situation the United States faced, he could see no difference between the objectives of Hitler and Stalin. Both craved world domination. The methods of the two tyrants were exactly the same—suppression of personal liberty, terrorism by the police, and the sickening propaganda that the totalitarian state is democratic. Lane's commitment to free and unfettered elections was definitely rejected by the Russian and Polish puppet governments. He now realized that his usefulness as Ambassador was over. Another ambassador should replace him, one not associated with the loss of political strategy which the United States had suffered. He believed strongly that from his experience in Poland, he might accomplish some good by bringing the facts before the American people. "My course was clear," Lane said. "I decided to resign."[28]

On 28 January 1947, Lane asked the State Department to relieve him as Ambassador to Poland. Mrs. Lane and the Ambassador motored to Krakow to learn what the people there thought of the elections. The Lanes found the Poles bitter, strongly believing that the outcome had been pre-arranged. While in Krakow, Lane received a telegram from Secretary of State George C. Marshall, who informed Lane that he would be recalled to Washington for consultation. In accordance to Lane's urgent recommendation, the State Department issued a statement, condemning the Polish elections as fraudulent and a clear violation of the terms of the Yalta and Potsdam agreements. At the same time, it said that the United States would maintain contact with the people of Poland. The text of the statement was suppressed in Poland. However, the Embassy passed out copies to all who wished to know the attitude of the United States.

The Ambassador and Mrs. Lane departed Warsaw for London on 24 February 1947. They continued to Washington arriving there on 6 March. Lane saw President Truman and informed him of his desire to retire from the foreign service. The President approved Lane's request and accepted his resignation on 25 March 1947. Lane was strongly affected by the machinations of the Communists in Poland. He called a press conference, 1 April 1947, in which he announced his intentions to publicize the events in Poland during his tenure as ambassador.[29]

CHAPTER TEN

U.S. CONGRESS FINDS RUSSIA GUILTY

The Katyn Forest Massacre

*T*HE GUILT for the massacre of 5,000 Polish prisoners of war in the Katyn Forest was first established by three independent commissions in 1943, namely, an International Commission of non-Nazi medical professionals and educators, Polish Red Cross from occupied-Poland, and a separate German commission. The three commissions concurred that some 5,000 Poles from the Russian prison camp of Kozelsk were shot to death methodically by a pistol shot to the head in the Katyn Forest near Smolensk, Russia, in the spring of 1940. The three commissions also concurred that the Russians perpetrated the crime. The German announcement of the crime struck the world like a bombshell. The West was disbelieving, since Germany had stooped to deception in the past. The Russians, on the other hand, responded with "righteous indignation." They denounced the accusation and blamed Germany.

In late 1943, the Russians stopped the German offensive into their country and began a relentless counteroffensive. When they retook the region around Smolensk, they were prepared to come up with their own version of the massacre in the typically crude Russian manner. Because the discovery of the graves occurred when the German 537 Signal Regiment occupied the Katyn Forest, the Russians placed the blame squarely on its commanding officer, Colonel Friederick Ahrens. The Russians rounded up several Russian civilians who had come in contact with Ahrens and forced them on the threat of death to testify against the Germans. The Special Russian Commission deliberately excluded outside medical professionals but invited the foreign press which could be manipulated. The Russians announced their findings: The Germans committed the crime. Although the report contained much data that could be proven false, many naive Americans believed the Russians, who enjoyed the favor of these Americans.

The United States Government became very knowledgeable about the Katyn Massacre. It obtained several reports that revealed the details of Katyn and which held Russia responsible. The United States Government, however, suppressed these reports because they undermined President Roosevelt's personal and secret diplomacy of maintaining friendly relations with Russia. Colonel Henry I. Szymanski, West Point Class of 1919, was one of the first to report the Russian crime of murdering Polish prisoners of war. When a Polish Army of former prisoners of war was organized on Russian soil, the U.S. Army appointed Szymanski Liaison Officer to the Polish force. Desperately in need of soldiers, the Western Allies were eager to assist the military force that became the Polish Second Army Corps of General Wladyslaw Anders. Born of Polish immigrant parents in Chicago on 4 July 1898, Szymanski spoke Polish from childhood. He was well suited for the role of liaison officer, possessing qualities of character and personality. His wife, Jean, described her husband as a man with a strong contagious zest for living, unbounded optimism, a faith and trust in fellow man, an integrity beyond reproach, and a never failing humor.[1]

Colonel Szymanski was not able to join General Anders' Corps. The Russians blocked his entry into Russia by denying him a visa. Frustrated by Russian obstruction, Szymanski complained to the War Department. Instead of insisting that Szymanski be allowed to carry out his military mission, the Chief of Army Intelligence dispatched a letter critical of Szymanski to his superiors in the Middle East Theater of Operations. Apparently Szymanski recommended action that could annoy President Roosevelt. The critical letter was uncalled for. Szymanski had shown excellent initiative, but he seemed to have been on the wrong side of the political fence. However, Szymanski was an outstanding officer. Upon completing his assignment in the Middle East, he was awarded the Distinguished Service Medal. For an earlier assignment, he was rewarded with the Legion of Merit. After the Polish Second Army Corps departed Russia for Persia, Szymanski finally joined the Poles. Szymanski now learned from the officers and soldiers the gruesome details of the Katyn Forest Massacre. He submitted a full report to the Army Staff in Washington. The Army, however, suppressed the report which was stamped "Top Secret" and buried in the bowels of the Pentagon. Meanwhile, Szymanski accompanied the Second Army Corps to Italy where it joined the British Eighth Army commanded by General Sir Oliver Leese. (Appendix B, Biographical Sketch, contains Szymanski's continuing liaison with the Polish Second Army Corps and the Italian campaign.)

Another American officer who submitted a report on the Katyn murders to the Pentagon was Lieutenant Colonel John H. Van Vliet, Jr., West Point Class of 1938. While fighting in the North African campaign in April 1943, he was captured by the Germans and imprisoned in *Oflag IX-A/Z*, in Rotenburg, Germany, until the end of the war in Europe. The camp housed mostly British officers, while Van Vliet was the senior officer of 125 American prisoners. He first learned of the Katyn Massacre by listening to radio news (although the Germans forbade the possession of radios in the prison camp). The Germans ordered Van Vliet, Captain Donald B. Stewart, West Point Class of 1940, and two British officers to journey under guard to Katyn Forest and observe for themselves the investigation of the crime by the three commis-

*AT THE SCENE OF THE CRIME
IN THE KATYN FOREST OF RUSSIA*

sions. They were a party of eight Allied prisoners of war. Van Vliet and Stewart protested their forced participation, but to no avail. At Katyn Forest they were well treated and dined in the German officers mess.

Van Vliet and the other officer-prisoners were transported to the burial site. "A sickly-sweet odor of decaying bodies was everywhere. At the graves it was nearly overpowering," Van Vliet said. Professor Herr Doktor Butz, a German forensic expert, was present together with other experts. Van Vliet noticed several Polish Red Cross workers. Each body was searched carefully, examined, identified, and reburied in a nearby mass grave. The articles removed from each body were placed in a large manila envelope for safekeeping. The examiners wore rubber aprons and rubber gloves. A typist recorded the findings on each body. Van Vliet and the other officers followed their guards right into each of the graves. They saw about three hundred bodies laid out beside one of the graves. All the bodies had their hands tied behind them. Van Vliet wrote in his report, "All bodies had a bullet hole in the back of the head, near the neck, with the exit wound of the bullet being in the forehead or front upper part of the skull." German photographers took both still and motion pictures of the Allied party while it inspected the graves. The Germans gave

---

LEFT: *Allied prisoners of war are brought to the scene of the crime to view the exhumed bodies of 5000 Polish prisoners of war in May 1943. Three independent commissions conducted the exhumation and examination—an International Commission, Polish Red Cross, and a Special German Commission. The three Commissions concurred that the Russians perpetrated the crime.*

(Left to right): German officer, German interpreter, Captain Stanley Gilder (British Army), Lieutenant Colonel Frank Stevenson (South African Army), Lieutenant Colonel John H. Van Vliet, Jr. (U.S. Army), Captain Donald B. Stewart (U.S. Army). In the background are three British soldiers and a British civilian. (German Photo, one of several given to each Allied officer)

copies of the photographs to Van Vliet and the others. Van Vliet mentioned a rustic lodge (the NKVD house) on the low bluff overlooking a small landing on the Dniepr River. He said the lodge allegedly was the scene of frequent torture, drinking parties, and various other orgies held by the Russian police as matters of amusement and recreation. Colonel Van Vliet and Captain Stewart were returned to the prison camp at Rotenburg.

At the end of the fighting in Europe, Van Vliet left the prison camp and reached the American 104th Infantry Division at Duben, Germany, on 5 May 1945. He showed the Division G-2 his report on Katyn. The G-2 concluded the report was of interest to both the State and War Departments, and he provided Van Vliet with transportation to Leipzig, Germany, headquarters of General J. Lawton Collins' VII Army Corps. General Collins, who knew Van Vliet from childhood, recognized the importance of the report and expedited Van Vliet's journey to Washington. Van Vliet, who resisted the pressure of being forced to see Katyn Forest and who believed strongly that the Germans were conducting a propaganda stunt, nevertheless, concluded his report, as follows: "I believe the Russians did it. The rest of the group that visited the site stated to me that they believe that the Russians did it."

In Washington, 22 May 1945, Van Vliet met with Major General Clayton Bissell in the Pentagon. General Bissell served as the Assistant Chief of Staff for Intelligence G-2 of the War Department. They were alone in the General's private office for twenty minutes. Undoubtedly, General Bissell was aghast to hear the words of Van Vliet, but he maintained a calm appearance. He said the report was important and directed his civilian secretary to go with Van Vliet to another closed room nearby and take dictation. Van Vliet dictated the report, the secretary typed it up, and Van Vliet added the photos as enclosures. General Bissell read the finished report and directed that it be stamped "Top Secret." The General dictated a letter directing Van Vliet to maintain silence. The Colonel signed the letter as the General explained the importance of keeping the report secret. Finally, General Bissell gave Van Vliet a copy of the letter and thanked him. If the

General thought he had neatly put Van Vliet's Katyn Report under wraps, he was badly mistaken. As for Van Vliet, he maintained that only four individuals saw his report: General Collins, General Bissell and his stenographer, and a Colonel Thomas D. Drake, senior officer at the prisoner of war camp at Rotenburg. Colonel Drake ridiculed the report as German propaganda. (Van Vliet also showed his report to Captain Stewart with whom he had discussed the Katyn Massacre.)[2]

To the growing list of documents on the Katyn Massacre and available to the United States Government were added British and Polish intelligence reports, as well as the report of John F. Carter's research group which was submitted to President Roosevelt. All were suppressed. A report by George H. Earle led to a confrontation with the President. Earle then served as Special Emissary for Balkan Affairs. In the period of 1936-1940, Earle was the Governor of Pennsylvania. In 1940, the President appointed him United States Minister to Bulgaria and commissioned him in the United States Navy where he advanced to the rank of commander. Sofia, Bulgaria, was an excellent listening post, and Earle gathered many facts on the Katyn Forest Massacre. When Earle saw Roosevelt, he reported the tragic massacre to the President, who scoffed at the report. He jokingly told Earle that he had been taken in by Goebbels' propaganda. Earle, however, was convinced of the Russian guilt. He confronted the President and told him he would publish his report. Roosevelt became greatly provoked by Earle's refusal to drop the Katyn matter, and he banished Earle to the far Pacific and American Samoa as assistant governor. Earle remained in Samoa until the death of President Roosevelt in April 1945.[3]

AUTHOR'S COMMENTS: The author had a short association with Governor Earle in August 1938. As a member of the Pennsylvania National Guard, the author competed with other young Guardsmen for one of four Gubernatorial appointments that would allow the four Pennsylvanians to compete in the finals. In March 1939, the author competed again with sixty other national finalists to

GEORGE HOWARD EARLE II

gain one of the twenty-three cadetships allocated each year at West Point to National Guardsmen. He entered the U.S. Military Academy on 1 July 1939, two months before the outbreak of World War II.

All reports of the Katyn Forest Massacre by experienced professionals were suppressed by the Roosevelt Administration except one—that of civilian-amateur Kathleen Harriman, daughter of Ambassador Harriman. When the newly-designated Ambassador to Poland, Arthur Bliss Lane, sought to prepare himself for his post, the only report on Katyn the State Department showed him was the pro-Russian Kathleen Harriman report.

In 1944, nine Polish American congressmen, fed up with the pro-Russian bias of the American press, requested the War Department for Colonel Szymanski's report. The War Department denied them the report on the basis that it was classified. The American Government's suppression of vital information extended into the civilian media, as well. In Detroit, Marian Kreutz on his Polish radio program condemned the Russian government for the Katyn Forest Massacre. Kreutz obtained data from the press agency of the Polish Government-in-Exile (London). At once, the Office of War Information silenced Kreutz's anti-Communist

---

LEFT: *Earle served as Governor of Pennsylvania, 1935–1939. President Franklin Roosevelt appointed Earle in 1940 to be Special Emissary for Balkan Affairs. From his listening post at Sofia, Bulgaria, Earle gathered data about the Russian massacre of 5,000 Polish prisoners of war in the Katyn Forest of Russia. Earle presented a report on the massacre to Roosevelt who scoffed at the report, telling Earle: "George, this is entirely German propaganda and a German plot. I am absolutely convinced the Russians did not do this." When Earle threatened to publish the report, the angry President banished him to the American Samoa in the far Pacific Ocean where Earle served as the Assistant Governor. (Collections of the Library of Congress)*

broadcasts. He was instructed to restrict his news to American wire services (pro-Russian) and avoid making "propaganda." At the same time, the Office of War Information allowed pro-Communist broadcasts of other radio stations. Poland, a fighting ally, had to suffer not only from the barbaric behavior of the Russians but also the discrimination of Americans.[4]

At the War Crimes Trial in Nuremberg in 1945-1946, the staff of American prosecutor, Judge Robert H. Jackson, received several secret documents from Military Intelligence relating to the Katyn Forest Massacre. Jackson's staff, however, deliberately kept the documents from Jackson (undoubtedly to allow Jackson to say honestly that he was not aware of the documents). The prosecution was carried out by four countries—United States, Great Britain, Russia, and France against some twenty German war criminals, with Hermann Goering the highest ranking. Why France was invited to join the prosecution team is questionable. In 1940, France gave up the fight pitifully after staging only a token resistance against the Germans. The quick surrender of the French placed at great risk of destruction a British Expeditionary Force of 325,000 soldiers and the capture of a Polish corps of 40,000 troops who eagerly had joined the French Army to fight the hated enemy. Earlier, France in 1939 had callously abandoned its long-standing military alliance with Poland. The Franco-Polish Alliance committed France to opening a Western front in two weeks upon the outbreak of hostilities. Instead, the French cowardly reneged on their commitment. In place of France on the War Crimes Commission the more suitable choice was Poland. But, unfortunately, Poland now was controlled by Communists as a result of the gullible policy of Franklin Roosevelt.

The Nuremberg Court, as constituted, was invalid. The United States, Great Britain, and France allowed Russia, a mass murderer, to sit in judgment on other mass murderers. This incredible condition struck at the very heart of moral decency. Nevertheless, the smelly atmosphere around the prosecution team was accepted by the Western countries because of power politics—Russia was too strong to oppose. But it was Roosevelt who allowed this diabolical condition to develop during the war. Professor Janusz K. Zawodny mockingly describes the composition of the court regarding the Katyn murders: "Here was a case where the murderer sat among the judges, and his democratic allies helped to hide his bloody hands with their own judicial robes." During the hearings of the Select Committee of the U.S. Congress, Alvin O'Konski, Republican from Wisconsin, expressed skepticism on the validity of the Nuremberg Trial. The Western Allies also allowed Russia to enter the Von Ribbentrop-Molotov Agreement of 25 August 1939 into the charges against the German war criminals. This infamous document made Russia equally guilty as Germany for starting World War II. The Western Allies, however, passed over this monstrous Russian crime. The German-Russian Agreement included a non-aggression pact which Germany violated when it attacked Russia on 22 June 1941. Historian Eugene Davidson writes in *The Trial of the Germans: Nuremberg*: "While accusing the Germans of having invaded Poland as part of a conspiracy, the prosecution and the tribunal ignored what had made the invasion a safe operation—namely, the non-aggression pact Hitler had made with the Soviet Union in August 1939, and the secret document that had accompanied it, under the terms of which the Red Army invaded Poland a few weeks later [sixteen days later]…and took up prearranged positions." Despite this damning evidence, the violation of the German-Russian non-aggression pact was allowed to be cited in the charges.[5]

At Nuremberg, Russia insisted on placing the charge of the Katyn Massacre on the court docket. The Western countries opposed this charge because of its very questionable validity. Notwithstanding, they agreed since the Katyn Massacre fell into the area of crimes to be prosecuted by Russia. During the trial, the Russian prosecutor introduced three witnesses: Dr. Markov, the Bulgarian professor who had served on the International Commission established by the Germans in 1943; a Russian doctor, and Professor Basilesky from Smolensk. Dr. Markov created a sensation. Earlier, as a member of the International Commission, he had concurred with the other members of the Commission that Russia was guilty. Now, at Nuremberg, he reversed his position, blaming the Germans. It should be noted that Bulgaria was occupied by the Russian Army, and the NKVD agents had time to prepare Dr. Markov for Nuremberg. The report of the Russian Commission placed the blame for Katyn on the German Signal Regiment commanded by Colonel Friederick Ahrens who was allegedly present in the area of Smolensk in the fall of 1941. To the surprise of the court, the German defense lawyers brought forth Colonel Ahrens himself, who testified and proved conclusively he was not at the Katyn Forest at the time of the massacre. The charge evaporated, and the Russian prosecutor sheepishly tried to forget the matter. At the summation of charges, he did not even mention Katyn.[6]

THE U.S. CONGRESS INVESTIGATES THE KATYN MASSACRE

Following the Nuremberg Trial, the guilty country of the crime of Katyn had not been officially determined. The several reports that had been submitted to the Roosevelt Administration were still kept secret. On the recommendation of Polish American congressmen, the House of Representatives unanimously adopted House Resolution 390 on 18 September 1951. It provided for the establishment of a Select Committee to conduct a full and complete investigation concerning the Katyn Massacre, an international crime committed against soldiers and citizens of Poland at the beginning of World War II. The Congress considered the Katyn Massacre one of the most barbarous international crimes in world history. Until the Congressional Committee completed its investigation, the massacre remained a mystery (officially). The Speaker of the House appointed the following members to the Select Committee:

Chairman, Ray J. Madden, Indiana
Daniel J. Flood, Pennsylvania

Thaddeus M. Machrowicz, Michigan
George A. Dondero, Michigan
Alvin E. O'Konski, Wisconsin
Timothy P. Sheehan, Illinois

They served on the Select Committee along with:

John J. Mitchell, Chief Counsel
Roman C. Pucinski, Chief Investigator

The Committee conducted the investigation in two phases:

1. To establish which nation was guilty of the massacre.
2. To establish whether any American official was responsible for suppressing the facts of the massacre with all of its ramifications from the American people.

The Congressional Committee got to work at once holding its first public hearing in Washington, D.C., on 11 October 1951. The Committee heard the testimony of Lieutenant Colonel Donald P. Stewart, U.S. Army. The next set of hearings was held in Washington on four days of February 1952. Seven witnesses testified about their knowledge of the Katyn Massacre. On 13 and 14 March 1952 in Chicago, seven witnesses gave testimony. In London, on 16–19 April 1952, twenty-nine witnesses testified. A subcommittee traveled to Frankfurt, Germany, where it heard testimony from members of the German Commission on Human Rights and obtained approximately 100 depositions. In Naples, Italy, 27 April, the sub-committee heard testimony of Dr. Vincenzo Mario Palmieri, a member of the International Commission that investigated the Katyn burial site in May 1943. In Washington again, the Committee took testimony from five witnesses on 2–4 June 1952. Up to this time, the Congressional Committee had obtained testimony from a total of eighty-one witnesses and studied 183 exhibits that were made part of the record.

The Committee was willing to listen to any individual, organization, or government having possession of factual evidence or information pertaining to the Katyn Massacre. Accordingly, the Committee invited the governments of Russia, Poland in Warsaw, the Polish Government-in-Exile in London, and the German Federal Republic. The Polish Government-in-Exile and the German Federal Republic accepted the invitation. However, Russia and the puppet Polish government rejected it. Russia's excuse was that it had already conducted its own investigation by the Special Soviet Commission which concluded that Germany was guilty of the crime. Russia added there was no need to reopen the issue. The Polish Communist government supported its Big Brother and grew belligerent. The Polish Embassy in Washington issued a vicious press release to newspaper correspondents. Outraged by the news release of the Polish Embassy, Chairman Madden published the release in the *Congressional Record* on 11 March 1952 and called on the Secretary of State to take action relative to the propaganda activities of the Polish Embassy in Washington. On 22 March 1952, the Secretary delivered a stern reprimand to the Polish Embassy and severely restricted its activities in this field.

The extensive evidence gathered by the Congressional Committee permitted it to announce its finding on the first phase of its investigation. The Committee announced that based on conclusive and irrevocable evidence, the Russian NKVD committed the massacre of Polish Army officers in the Katyn Forest in the spring of 1940. The Committee further concluded: "There can be no doubt this massacre was a calculated plot to eliminate all Polish leaders who subsequently would have opposed the Soviet's plan for communizing Poland."[7]

The Congressional Committee took up the second phase of its investigation: To determine why certain reports and files concerning the Katyn Massacre disappeared or were suppressed by the Departments of the United States Government. The Committee learned from the records and documents of the State and War Departments the tremendously important part the Katyn Massacre played in shaping the future of postwar Europe. From these hitherto secret documents the Committee learned that as early as the summer of 1942 authorities considered the Polish Army extremely vital to the Allied war effort. Documents introduced in the hearings describe conclusively the efforts made to create such an army on Russian soil as quickly as possible. The Committee learned that American authorities knew of Poland's desperate efforts to locate the missing officers who could lead the Polish Army being formed in Russia. These same documents show that, when high-level Polish officials failed to obtain a satisfactory reply from the Russians regarding the whereabouts of their missing officers, American emissaries intervened. In every instance, American officials received the same reply: the Russians had no knowledge of the whereabouts of the Polish prisoners of war.

Admiral William H. Standley, United States Ambassador to Moscow, advised the State Department on 10 September 1942 that Russian officials were opposed to United States intervention in Russian-Polish problems. Russian Foreign Minister Molotov made Russia's attitude clear to Standley when he inquired about the missing Polish officers. When Russia broke diplomatic relations with Poland, 26 April 1943, following the Polish request to the International Red Cross for an investigation of the Katyn Massacre, Admiral Standley warned the State Department that Russia had been seeking a pretext to break with Poland for some time. Standley also emphasized that the Russians were plotting to create a pro-Communist Polish government which would take over Poland after the war. Furthermore, he warned that Russia planned to establish a belt of Communist governments in Eastern Europe which would jeopardize the peace of Europe. The Congressional Committee concluded that American authorities knew of the growing tension between the Russians and the Poles during 1942–43, and they likewise knew about the hopeless search for the Polish officers. Nevertheless, all of these factors were brushed aside on the theory that pressing the search would irritate the Russians and hinder the prosecution of the war.[8]

The Congressional investigation disclosed that many individuals throughout the State Department, Army Intelligence (G-2), Office of War Information, and the Federal Communications Commission, as well as other U.S. Government agencies failed to evaluate properly the data being received from abroad. In many cases, the material was deliberately withheld from public attention and knowledge. The Army Intelligence (G-2) and the State Department failed to coordinate intelligence matters, as far as they pertained to the missing Polish officers and the Katyn Massacre. The Committee noted that many second-echelon personnel were overly sympathetic to the Russian cause, and being pro-Communist-minded, they attempted to cover up derogatory reports concerning the Russians. Former Ambassador Averell Harriman and former Under Secretary of State Sumner Welles testified before the Committee that consideration for a free Poland had to be disregarded on the grounds of military necessity and maintaining the alliance with Russia. The two diplomats admitted that the Allies feared Russia might make a separate treaty with Germany. (Harriman and Welles voiced a reasonable assumption about Russia's treachery, like the infamous Von Ribbentrop-Molotov secret agreement to carve up Poland in 1939, and the deliberate inaction of Russian troops on the east bank of the Vistula River during the Warsaw Rising of 1944 that gave Germany a free hand to destroy Poland's Home Army.)[9]

The investigation confirmed the attitude of some government officials toward American emissaries who reported conditions pertaining to the Russians. Their views and reports were disregarded if they were critical of the Russians. When some of these objective Americans expressed anti-Russian observations, President Roosevelt sent his personal representative to confer directly with Josef Stalin. For example, when Admiral Standley warned against Russia's post-war plans for setting up a pro-Russian belt of nations around Russia, President Roosevelt sent Wendell Wilkie to confer with Stalin. Also, when Roosevelt wanted to arrange a secret meeting with Stalin (without Churchill), the President sent his "old friend" Joseph E. Daniels to Moscow to meet privately with Stalin. Both Harriman and Welles testified that the United States officials had taken a gamble on Russia's pledges to work harmoniously with the Western democracies after the war and LOST. Harriman insisted that territorial concessions made to the Russians at the Big Three conferences were based on the military reality that the Russians were actually in physical control of these lands. To have resisted their demands, or to have tried to drive the Russians out by force, Harriman maintained, would have meant prolonging the war.

AUTHOR'S COMMENT: The presence of the Russian Army in Poland could have been neutralized by an Allied campaign northward through the Balkans. This strategy was advocated by the British and Polish general staffs. However, General Marshall rejected the Balkan campaign, much to the delight of Stalin. President Roosevelt and General Marshall insisted on the questionable invasion of southern France.

The Congressional Committee stated its belief that the tragic concessions at Yalta might not have taken place if the Polish officers corps had not been murdered by the Russians at Katyn. With proper leadership, the Polish Army could have relieved a great deal of the early reverses suffered by the Allies. The Kremlin's hand would not have been as strong at the Yalta Conference, and many of the concessions made because of "military necessity," as Harriman maintained, would have been obviated. This contention is borne out in a telegram sent to the State Department on 2 June 1942 by A. J. Drexel Biddle, Jr., Ambassador to the Polish Government-in-Exile (London). Ambassador Biddle reported in part:

> The absence of these officers is the principal reason for the shortage of officers in the Polish forces in Russia, whither officers from Scotland had to be sent lately. The possible death of these men, most of whom have superior education, would be a severe blow to the Polish national life.[10]

The Committee heard the testimony of George H. Earle, Jr., Special Emissary for President Roosevelt in the Balkans. Earle had tried to convince the President that the Russians were guilty of the Katyn Massacre. He showed the President secret documents and photographs of Katyn, but the President dismissed the evidence. Earle quoted the President's reply, as he recalled the words to the Committee: "George, this is entirely German propaganda and a German plot. I am absolutely convinced the Russians did not do this." The Committee concluded that the President and the State Department ignored numerous documents from Ambassadors Standley, Biddle, and Winant (Emissary to London) which reported information that strongly pointed to Russian perfidy. Throughout the war, however, Roosevelt acted from a strong desire for mutual cooperation with Russia. He believed in Russian "sincerity." The Committee noted: "It was equally obvious that this desire completely overshadowed the dictates of justice and equity to our loyal but weaker ally, Poland."

The Committee concluded that the Katyn Forest Massacre was a means to an end. The Russians had plotted to take over Poland as early as 1939. Their massacre of these Polish officers was designed to eliminate the intellectual leadership which subsequently would have attempted to block Russia's ultimate design for complete communization of Poland. This was but a step of the Russians toward the complete communization of Europe and eventually the entire world, including the United States. The investigation of the Congressional Committee found that the United States had been forewarned of Russia's treacherous designs on Poland and the rest of Europe. "Whatever the justification may be," the Committee concluded, "this committee is convinced the United States in its relations with the Soviets found itself in the tragic position of winning the war but losing the peace."[11]

.   .   .

The Testimony of
Major General Clayton Bissell
Assistant Chief of Staff for Intelligence,
G-2 Department of the Army

General Bissell testified before the Committee on two occasions that Lieutenant Colonel John H. Van Vliet, Jr. dictated the Katyn Forest Massacre to him in his Pentagon office in one copy, and that he (Bissell) had ordered Van Vliet to maintain absolute silence about the report. This Top Secret document disappeared from the files of Army Intelligence, G-2, and had not been found by 1951–52. The Committee set out to find the original Van Vliet report. An independent investigation conducted by the Army Inspector General in 1950 concluded the report had been "compromised and there is nothing to indicate it had ever left Army Intelligence." This finding was in response to General Bissell's allegation that he "believes" he had forwarded the Van Vliet report to the Department of State. General Bissell introduced into evidence a copy of a letter he said he had written to Assistant Secretary of State Julius Holmes on 25 May 1945. The letter bears no notation that an enclosure (Van Vliet Report) was attached. Also, there is no receipt for the "Top Secret" report to prove the document actually was received by the State Department. General Bissell introduced into evidence another letter he had written on 21 August 1945 to Frederick B. Lyon, Holmes' assistant in the Department of State. In this letter, the General included a report by a British officer who likewise was taken to Katyn Forest by the Germans. The General contended that the British report substantiated Van Vliet's report which was forwarded to Holmes on 25 May 1945.

Pursuing the matter of the missing Van Vliet report, the Committee summoned Holmes and Lyon who both testified under oath. They disavowed any knowledge of ever having received the Van Vliet report from General Bissell. They also stressed that if they had discussed this report with General Bissell they would have remembered it because of the political significance of the report at the time. On the basis of the testimony of General Bissell, Holmes, and Lyon, the Committee concluded that General Bissell was mistaken in his claim that he forwarded the Van Vliet report to the State Department. The Committee believed the Van Vliet report was either removed from or purposely destroyed in Army Intelligence, G-2. (Without doubt, General Bissell committed perjury.)

NOTE: The Department of the Army tried to right the wrong of the missing report. In 1950, the Army Chief of Information requested and received from Colonel Van Vliet a reconstructed report and released it to the public.

General Bissell told the Committee that he justified his action of stamping the Van Vliet report "Top Secret" on the basis of carrying out "the spirit of the Yalta Agreement."

His explanation did not sit well with the members of the Committee. The members were dismayed that the Assistant Chief of Staff for Intelligence, G-2, considered the political significance of the Van Vliet document. They contended that the document should have been evaluated objectively from a strictly military intelligence standpoint. The Committee was amazed to learn of the political atmosphere that permeated the Military Intelligence Division. The Committee heard evidence of three high-ranking American Army officers who were assigned to Army Intelligence during General Bissell's command of this Army Staff Agency. Testifying in executive session, all three agreed there was a band of pro-Russian civilian employees and some military officers in G-2. These pro-Moscovites found explanations for almost everything that Russia did. The pro-Communist sympathizers exerted tremendous pressure to suppress anti-Russian reports. The Committee also learned that high-ranking Army officers who were too critical of the Russians were bypassed in Army Intelligence.[12]

The Committee questioned Colonel Henry I. Szymanski, U.S. Army, with regard to the organization of the Polish Army in

Russia in 1941. The questioning dealt with the depth of knowledge of Army Intelligence with respect to the military potential of the nascent Polish forces in Russia. In March 1942, the Army assigned Colonel Szymanski as Liaison Officer to the Polish force in Russia. Szymanski testified that he was never able to carry out his mission because the Russians refused him permission to enter the country. Szymanski was recalled to Washington in November 1942 to give a full report of Russian obstruction to the organization of the much-needed Polish Army. The Committee uncovered evidence that Szymanski's highly critical report of Russia was buried in the basement of Army Intelligence, G-2, and subsequently moved to the "dead file" of that agency. The Committee concluded that Army Intelligence knew of the military potential of the Polish force composed of released prisoners of war and ignored it.[13]

The Roosevelt Administration practiced censorship at the highest levels of the Departments of State and War. These diplomats and generals supported the personal and naive policy of President Roosevelt who wanted to be nice to that murderous Stalin. Roosevelt infected his associates. Recall that the venerable Secretary of State Cordell Hull praised Stalin as one of the greatest men of history in a speech to Congress.

To insure that Russian lies were not revealed to the American public, the Roosevelt Administration suppressed the freedom of the press of civilian sources of information but propagated the Russian version of events. The Committee investigated the censorship of the Polish American press. When on 12 April 1943, Germany announced to the world the finding of the mass graves of the Polish officers at Katyn and accused the Russians, the Allies were stunned by the German action and called it propaganda. In the United States, Elmer Davis, head of the Office of War Information (OWI), broadcast the American response, on his own initiative and without any coordination with other government agencies, that the Germans were using the Katyn Massacre as propaganda. (The OWI was established by Executive Order, and Davis reported directly to the President.) Under questioning by the Committee, Davis admitted having frequent conferences with the State Department and other agencies. And on 22 April 1943, just nine days after the German announcement on Katyn, the State Department cautioned against making premature judgments because of the conflicting contentions on Katyn. Notwithstanding, on 3 May 1943, Davis used the OWI as a tool to spew his personal venom to the public. The Committee contended that Davis' unilateral action was another example of the failure to coordinate between government agencies. Further, the Committee stated that Davis bears responsibility for accepting the Russian propaganda version of the Katyn Massacre without a full investigation.[14]

The Roosevelt Administration blocked the right to freedom of the press of Polish American news media. The Federal Communications Commission (FCC) and the Office of War Information silenced Polish radio programs in Buffalo and Detroit when their news segments included press releases from the Polish Government-in-Exile (London) which condemned the cruel treatment of the subjugated Poles. As the Committee learned, members of the FCC carried out censorship indirectly through contacts in the Wartime Foreign Languages Radio Control Committee which endeavored to cooperate with the OWI and the FCC. Two members of the industry committee were specifically requested by OWI staff members to influence a Polish radio commentator in Detroit to restrict his comments to straight news items concerning Katyn and to limit them to those from the standard news services. In effect, the American position was to silence the Polish side and propagate the Russian position. The Committee was not impressed by testimony that publication of facts concerning the Katyn crime prior to 1951 would lead to an ill-fated uprising in Poland. Neither was it convinced by the statements of OWI officials that for the Polish Americans to hear or read about the Katyn Massacre in 1943 would have resulted in a lessening of their cooperation in the Allied war effort.[15]

The Congressional Committee questioned Judge Robert H. Jackson, Associate Justice of the U.S. Supreme Court and Chief

American Prosecutor at the Nuremberg War Crimes Trial. The Committee asked Judge Jackson how the Katyn Massacre happened to be listed on the agenda of the Nuremberg Trials under the indictment of Hermann Goering. He answered that the Russians were responsible for preparing indictments on war crimes in Eastern Europe. When asked if he had received the various reports then in the files of the State Department and Army Intelligence, G-2, Jackson testified that he had not. Before the Committee had been formed, there were many allegations that Americans on Jackson's staff at Nuremberg assisted the Russians in their preparation of the case on Katyn. The Committee specifically asked Jackson to clarify this point. He denied that any member of his staff participated in the preparation of the Katyn indictment.

During the testimony of Judge Jackson, a sharp exchange took place between the Judge and Congressman Alvin O'Konski, member of the Congressional Committee. O'Konski doubted the validity of the Nuremberg Court as well as the omission of the mass murderer Josef Stalin. In his book *Death in the Forest*, author Zawodny cannot resist lifting the exchange from the Committee hearings and neither can this author.

> *Justice Jackson:* I will make a bargain with you, Mr. Congressman. If you will capture Stalin, I will try him.
>
> *Mr. O'Konski:* I will ask for that job myself to be sure he hangs. I wouldn't trust another Nuremberg Trial.[16]

Conclusions

1. In submitting the final report to the House of Representatives, the Congressional Committee came to the conclusion that:

   a. In those fateful days nearing the end of the Second World War there unfortunately existed in high government and military circles a strange psychosis that military necessity required the

sacrifice of loyal allies and America's own principles in order
to keep Soviet Russia from making a separate peace treaty with
the Nazis (Germany).

b. For reasons less clear to the committee, this psychosis continued even after the conclusion of the war. Most of the witnesses
testified that had they known then what they know now about
Soviet Russia, they probably would not have pursued the course
they did. It is undoubtedly true that hindsight is much easier
to follow than foresight, but it is equally true that much of the
material which this Committee unearthed was or could have
been available to those responsible for our foreign policy as
early as 1942.

c. It is equally true that even before 1942 the Kremlin rulers gave
much evidence of a menace of Soviet imperialism paving the
way for world conquest. Through the disastrous failure to recognize the danger signs which then existed and in following
a policy of satisfying the Kremlin leaders, the United States
Government unwittingly strengthened Russia's hand and con-
tributed to a situation that has grown to be a menace to the
United States and the entire free world.

2. The Committee forwarded a copy of its report, and Volume 7 of
the published hearings, to the Department of Defense for such
action as may be proper with regard to General Bissell. The Committee did so because it believed that had the Van Vliet report
been made immediately available to the Department of State and
to the American public, the course of the American policy toward Russia might have been more realistic with more fortunate
postwar results.

[AUTHOR'S COMMENT: Apparently the Department of Defense
took no action against General Bissell for his political behavior as a military professional and, more importantly, for
his crime of perjury. General Bissell left the military service
in disgrace and cannot ever enter the ranks of "The Greatest
Generation."]

3. The Committee believes that the wartime policies of Army Intelligence, G-2, during 1944-45 should undergo a thorough investigation.

4. The Committee concluded that the staff members of the Office of War Information and Federal Communications Commission who participated in the program of silencing Polish radio commentators went beyond the scope of their duties as official government representatives. Actually they usurped the functions of the Office of Censorship and by indirect pressure accomplished domestic censorship which was not within the jurisdiction of either of these agencies.

5. The Committee believes that if the Voice of America is to justify its existence, it must utilize material more forcefully and effectively.

6. The Committee noted the striking similarly between crimes committed against the Poles at Katyn and those being inflicted against Americans and other United Nation troops in Korea. Communist tactics being used in Korea are identical to those followed at Katyn. Thus, the Committee believes Congress should undertake an immediate investigation of the Korean War atrocities.[17]

RECOMMENDATIONS

The final report of the Select Committee Investigating the Katyn Forest Massacre incorporates the recommendations of the interim report and recommends the House of Representatives approve the committee's findings and adopt a resolution:

1. Requesting the President of the United States forward the testimony, evidence, and findings of this committee to the United States delegates at the United Nations.

2. Requesting further that the President of the United States issue instructions to the United States delegates to present the Katyn case to the General Assembly of the United Nations.

3. Requesting that appropriate steps be taken by the General Assembly to seek action before the International World Court of Justice against the Union of Soviet Socialist Republics for committing a crime at Katyn which was in violation of the general principles of law recognized by civilized nations.

4. Requesting the President of the United States to instruct the United States delegation to seek the establishment of an international commission which would investigate other mass murders and crimes against humanity.

> Ray J. Madden, Chairman
> Daniel J. Flood
> Thaddeus M. Machrowicz
> George A. Dondero
> Alvin E. O'Konski
> Timothy P. Sheehan

This author is unaware of any recommendation and request to the President having been carried out. Nevertheless, the Select Committee of the U.S. House of Representatives performed a necessary task of world-wide importance when it placed the guilt for the mass murders of Polish prisoners of war squarely on Russia and exposed the pro-Communist and improper activities of high-ranking government officials of the Roosevelt Administration.

By 1993, Communism and the Soviet Empire crumbled, and Russia admitted to the world for the first time that it was responsible for the massive crime at Katyn. In addition, the Russian government submitted to the Polish government the letter from Stalin to NKVD Chief, Lavrenti Beria, to execute the 5,000 Polish officers held at the prison camp at Kozelsk. Two years earlier, 1991, other mass graves were discovered near Kharkov and Mednoye in the Ukraine. These graves contained the bodies of the murdered officers from the prison camps at Starobelsk and Ostashkov.

This author ends this chapter with the words of Dr. Janusz K. Zawodny, author of *Death in the Forest*, who cautions against the cynical attitude that prevailed during World War II: "I believe that democratic societies cannot afford callousness toward human life, through an amnesty of silence, without destroying the basic values which provide for the very reason for their existence."[18]

CHAPTER ELEVEN

DOCUMENTING POLAND'S TRAGIC BETRAYAL

*R*OBBED of the eastern half of their country by President Franklin Roosevelt, the Poles tried to salvage independence through "free and unfettered elections," as the Yalta and Potsdam declarations promised. The first American Ambassador to the Provisional Government of National Unity, Arthur Bliss Lane, worked valiantly to insure a free choice for the Poles, but in vain. Perhaps against his better judgment, Stanislaw Mikolajczyk returned to Poland from London to lead his Polish Peasant Party, the only real opposition to the Polish and Russian Communists. His tenacious efforts, however, were thwarted and nullified by Communist propaganda, intimidation, interference in the Party's political activities, torture, and outright murders. The fraudulent elections of 19 January 1947 dampened the spirit of the Polish nation and set it on the road to hardship and stagnation for the next forty years.

Ambassador Lane returned to the United States after the national elections. He believed he could not serve in his post against the backdrop of a failed American policy. Stanislaw Mikolajczyk also departed Poland after the elections, but he delayed his departure for six months. He had many responsibilities to discharge first. Mikolajczyk felt strongly, and he had received threats, that the Communists would eventually arrest him on trumped up charges, hold a mock trial, and execute him. Prior to the elections, the Communists tolerated Mikolajczyk as a cover for the seemingly democratic elections with opposition parties in the political campaign. After the elections, Mikolajczyk was no longer useful to the Communists. He himself felt no longer useful in Poland nor to his Polish Peasant Party (whatever remnant the Communists allowed to continue).

The fraudulently elected 444 members of the National Assembly (*Sejm*) met for the first time on 4 February 1947. The Communist government allowed the Polish Peasant Party a total of twenty-eight seats. At the first meeting, Mikolajczyk denounced the elections as fraudulent. At the second meeting, 5 February, the *Sejm* elected Boleslaw Bierut President of Poland by a vote of 408 to 25. Taking advantage of their presence in the *Sejm*, the members of the Polish Peasant Party condemned the new government, while Mikolajczyk uttered prophetic words: "By your methods you have thwarted the reconstruction of Poland and have done much to crush the creative spirit of the people." Meanwhile, the government gave up on communizing the adults (solidly opposed to Communism) and began a program of organizing and communizing the youth. This effort put the Communists in conflict with the Catholic Church which began to experience increased repression.[1]

On 18 October 1947, Mikolajczyk learned from a reliable source that three members of the parliament would be stripped of their immunity at the opening of the third session, 20–28 October. The police would seize and execute the three. They were Mikolajczyk, Stefan Korbonski, and Wincenty Bryja, treasurer of the Polish Peasant Party. Mikolajczyk worried about the attitude of the Party toward him, once the members learned of his escape. Notwithstanding, he decided to leave, believing that his death by the Communists would neither assist the Polish people nor further the interests of the Party. At the same time, he felt that in a democratic country, he could tell the full, shocking story of the debasement of their ally, Poland. By 20 October, a group of eight Poles laid plans to escape. They were Stefan Korbonski and wife, Wincenty Bryja, Maria Hulewicz and Pawel Zaleski (both Mikolajczyk's secretaries), Mikolajczyk and wife, plus Kazimierz Baginski and wife. Baginski had just been released from jail for the purpose of adding him to the three doomed Peasant Party leaders in order to create a more sensational trial. Mikolajczyk included Maria Hulewicz and Zaleski in his escape plans. He believed that they would be arrested immediately as accomplices as soon as the Communists learned of his escape, and their loyalty would be their death. The eight divided into separate parties to increase the possibility of escape. On the evening of the planned escape, Mikolajczyk thought about the good things the Polish Peasant Party had accomplished for the nation for the past two and one-half years. "Above all," Mikolajczyk later documented, "we had proved conclusively to the free world that Communist Russia is criminally guilty of depriving the Polish nation of its freedom and independence."[2]

20 October 1947 was the date set for the escape. Mikolajczyk departed Party headquarters for his home in the late afternoon. As soon as he left in his car, driven by his chauffeur Tryc, two cars with ten security agents immediately followed him. They had been shadowing him for two weeks. After picking up several small items at home, including a revolver, he got back into his car, and driver Tryc outwitted the police and sped out of sight. Mikolajczyk had arranged to meet Zaleski at 8 P.M. at the train depot where Zaleski handed Mikolajczyk two tickets to Leszno in western Poland. His third-class compartment was packed with peasants, small officials, and victims of Polish resettlement movements and their children and goods. He found a seat in a corner, held a newspaper in front of his face, and later slept. Just before reaching the town of Krotoszyn, he stepped off the train at a small station. The area was familiar to him; his father was born here. His chances of being recognized were greater but he knew

the terrain. He walked into the forest and to a small cottage of a forest guard, who was a Polish patriot. Mikolajczyk revealed his identity to the forest guard who offered to help. Together they planned the manner of crossing the border into Communist East Germany. While Mikolajczyk hid in a barn, the forest guard left on his bicycle to contact one of the smuggling bands that trafficked in goods along the border. Two days later the forest guard returned. He had good news. A smuggling group that operated out of a village near Gubin agreed to take Mikolajczyk across the border. On 24 October, a delivery truck, used by a cooperative in the area, drove up to the cottage. The driver delivered a box of "groceries"—a change of clothes for Mikolajczyk. He quickly put on his travel clothes and bade farewell to his friend. Posing as the driver's assistant, Mikolajczyk rode off toward the border. They came to a village and the home of the most prominent Communist in the village. Mikolajczyk became alarmed. The driver, however, reassured him that this Communist lets it be known that he is a Communist. The driver explained the pretense allows him to entertain many border guards, Polish and Russian soldiers. He gets them very drunk. The Communist was expecting the Pole. He led Mikolajczyk into his home to a dark upstairs bedroom where Mikolajczyk changed back into his regular clothes. The Communist told Mikolajczyk to keep his door locked, since he would entertain a group of border guards in his home. The Communist said he would return later and identify himself by knocking on the door in the "V" manner—three dots and a dash. (The savvy Communist undoubtedly held the party on the night of Mikolajczyk's break into East Germany. Most of the guards would get drunk and be absent from their border posts.) The guests gathered downstairs, and the house was soon filled with drunken Polish and Russian song and laughter. As the party grew more boisterous, Mikolajczyk heard the V knock and opened the door. The Communist said, "Come quickly." He led Mikolajczyk, as he clutched his revolver, down the backstairs. A Polish soldier stood silently in the backyard. The three walked briskly across fields for six or eight miles to a road where a jeep with a Russian

Army sergeant and a German civilian waited. The sight of the sergeant made Mikolajczyk apprehensive, but he tried to remain calm. He had to trust them. Mikolajczyk sat in the back of the jeep with his hand on the revolver. They drove silently in the night, and as they traveled he began to fear that he could be a victim of a fantastically simple plot to return him to captivity.[3]

After what seemed like an agonizing duration of time, they drove into a sleepy village. Here he noticed a German sign or two. It was five in the morning when the jeep arrived at a peasant's rambling house. An old couple expected the unknown individual. With them was a very beautiful and stylishly dressed girl. The old couple introduced her as their daughter, although Mikolajczyk suspected she was a member of the smuggling ring. The old couple led Mikolajczyk to a tiny bedroom in the rear and said goodnight. The Pole's spirits were lifted. He had safely negotiated the first leg of the road to freedom. He was in East Germany, in the Russian zone of occupation. He slept soundly for a few hours.[4]

At nine in the morning, the young lady came into the room with coffee and bread. They spoke in German with which Mikolajczyk was fluent. He offered her a cigarette. She sat down and talked with him. She advised him not to be afraid if Russian soldiers come to the house. "Just be nonchalant and give them cigarettes," she said. That evening Mikolajczyk had dinner with them. While talking casually, the three suddenly froze in fright. Mikolajczyk whipped around to look at the door, expecting to see an armed Russian soldier. But there was no one there. Then he realized what had happened. He had accidentally lapsed from German to English.

"You're not a German, as we have been told," the young woman said.

Looking straight at her, he answered. "No, I'm not."

"You're British."

Hoping to confirm her suspicion, he answered, "Yes, I'm British."

"For a moment we thought that you were a *provocateur*," she said with relief.

The knowledgeable young woman reviewed the next step in

Mikolajczyk's escape. She explained that Berlin was too well policed by the Russians to risk traveling through there. Also, the
main highway from Berlin to the British zone of occupation in
Germany was well policed. Therefore, plans had to be altered,
and the change would cost an additional five hundred dollars.
She demanded immediate payment. Mikolajczyk gave her the
money. So far, he had expended a total of fourteen hundred dollars for his secret getaway. Continuing the journey and dressed
in ragged peasant's clothes, he traveled by horse and cart to another village on 25 October. Here the driver and he were stopped
by three Russian soldiers who were repairing a telephone line.
The Russians allowed them to continue, although Mikolajczyk
had suffered another scare. Two days later, a boy drove him from
the village by horse and small cart to a railroad station. The young-
ster had timed their arrival just as the train was pulling into the
station. They abandoned the horse and cart, walked across a
platform crowded with German civilians and Russian soldiers,
and entered a third-class compartment. After traveling sixty
miles, the train made a short stop. The boy and Mikolajczyk got
off and walked five miles to another German home. The Pole
spent three nerve-wracking days in the house confined to a small
room. On the third night, a jeep with a civilian and two Russian
soldiers drove up to the house. Mikolajczyk joined them. The
group drove to a forest near the border between the Russian and
British zones of occupation. The civilian and Mikolajczyk got
out of the jeep and walked through the woods until nine o'clock
that evening. They had come to a clearing where five heavily-
armed civilians were waiting for them. "We must be very careful,"
the leader whispered. "If we fall into the hands of the Russian
guards, it means the lives of all of us." The group walked the
remainder of the night, crossing and re-crossing barbed wire
entanglements. At dawn, they came to the edge of a German
town. They stopped, and the leader told Mikolajczyk: "You're in
the British zone. We leave you here. When it is light enough, go
to that house there"—and he pointed to it. "A British officer
lives there." Mikolajczyk hid in the streets until 7:30 A.M. and

then walked to the house. A suspicious German housekeeper answered the door. She peered at Mikolajczyk through a slim opening. Mikolajczyk asked to see the British officer. "Wait," she said and closed and locked the door. At last, a young soldier came to the door and admitted the visitor. "I am Mikolajczyk," he said. A grin came over the soldier's face, and he shook the Pole's hand. "We heard over the wireless that you had escaped," he laughed. "We thought the Russians had killed you and simply put out a story that you're missing." He asked Mikolajczyk to wait while he informed the colonel. The soldier returned with a very grumpy British colonel who demanded to see Mikolajczyk's papers and could not understand why he had been unable to carry any. Mikolajczyk requested the colonel to telephone Churchill or Ernst Bevin, the Foreign Secretary. The colonel rejected the request as implausible. He remained unfriendly until the Pole mentioned the name of a British officer who had accomplished much secret and heroic work with the Polish Underground. The British colonel relaxed and conveyed a message to London. Two days later the British drove Mikolajczyk to an airport where a special plane of the Royal Air Force flew him to England. At last he was reunited with his wife and son. The war had imposed many hardships on his family. His wife had suffered through years of German concentration camps. The Germans not only deprived her of liberty but also ruined her health. His eighteen-year-old son was imprisoned in a German concentration camp and tortured. Fortunately, the Polish Underground was able to free him. Mikolajczyk was overjoyed to be with his wife and son. "Yet for myself," he vowed, "the war had not ended. It cannot end until that precious thing for which Poland bled—peace and security and democracy—is once again established on our soil."[5]

Of the eight Poles who made the break for freedom, six made it. Bryja and Maria Hulewicz, however, were caught in Czechoslovakia and turned over to the Polish Communist government which undoubtedly executed them. Bryja had lost his only son in the Warsaw Uprising against the Germans in 1944. Maria's parents had been murdered by the Germans. Maria had served as Mikolajczyk's secretary after a career as an assistant at the University of Krakow. During the German occupation she had carried out dangerous courier work as a member of the Underground. She also was the author of a book entitled *Through Women's Eyes.*[6]

Stanislaw Mikolajczyk escaped to freedom in late 1947. He immediately began to document his experiences as a member of the Polish Government-in-Exile (London), in which he also served as Prime Minister, as well as the leader of the Polish Peasant Party in Poland. His fact-filled book *The Rape of Poland* was published the next year, 1948, by the McGraw-Hill Book Company of New York. Greenwood Press reprinted the book in 1972. His book was also published in the United Kingdom. He states his purpose: "To present to free people the misfortunes of my nation, which had their beginning during the war in the political errors of appeasement of Russia and in the occupation of my country by the brutal forces of a Communist minority acting at the command of, and with the aid of, Soviet Russia under the high-sounding name of 'people's democracy.'"[7]

In the final chapter, "Conclusion," Mikolajczyk re-emphasizes the dangers of Communism and how it should be combated. "The Communist system, whose aim is to dominate the world, calls itself 'a people's democracy,'" Mikolajczyk states, "but it is in fact Red fascism." Stripped of all its democratic-sounding names, Communism turns civilians into slaves of the state. He compares the two evil systems—German Nazism and Russian Communism. The Nazis worked alone. They issued orders and carried out the orders themselves. The Communists, on the other hand, maintain a Communist Party in every country where these Communist groups are organized openly or secretly. Moscow makes decisions and issues orders. The violence and murders are carried out by the citizens of the home country. (The Communist methods appear to have been adopted by Islamic fascism in the twentieth-first century. Terrorists are supported by Islamic elements who are citizens of a country, speak the language, and carry out sabotage against their own citizens.) Both the German

Nazis and the Russians carried out the extermination of whole populations. Although the Germans were very efficient and were able to cremate up to ten thousand people daily at Oswiecim (Auschwitz), they still were too limited in space and time to destroy as many human beings as could the Communists. The Russians were neither handicapped by time nor space. The Russians worked their victims to death as a method of liquidation. The slavery of the labor camps replaced the ovens of Oswiecim.[8]

Poland's tortured existence from 1945 to 1947 demonstrated how a nation can be devoured despite strenuous efforts to win the independence pledged to it by its Western Allies. All legal opposition in Poland was crushed, proving that a police state can subjugate the majority. The Communist system is more dangerous than the Nazis which sprouted with German nationalism. Communism works under the slogan of internationalism. Therefore, there is a large number of Communists in every country ready to betray their land, to shed the blood of their people, to help install a dictatorship in their country, and place at the head of the government individuals who blindly carry out Russia's orders. Because the German Nazis were satisfied that they were the master race, they did not study the nations they swallowed. The Communists, on the other hand, have at their service in every country a host of spies and agents (*provocateurs*) speaking the language of that country, familiar with the mentality of that nation. In their propaganda, they use the slogans and catchwords native to the country. Thousands of citizens of various nationalities train in Russia and in other countries. The Russians then give secret orders to established cells in the various countries. These Communist agents pass the orders to public figures, coating all slogans with the flower of patriotism, independence, and sovereignty.[9]

Mikolajczyk stressed the great need for a coordinated global plan to combat Communism, and he points to the demonstrated treachery of the Russians. They cold-bloodedly broke the agreements signed with the United States and Great Britain at Tehran, Yalta, and Potsdam. Russia perverted the Atlantic Charter to which it had subscribed, and it violated every agreement that it had signed with Poland and other states which had since become helpless puppets.

Mikolajczyk praised the Marshall Plan that rebuilt the devastated countries of Europe. The Marshall Plan was meant to help Poland, too. But Russia would not allow it. At all costs Russia blocked the Western influence that would accompany the aid. Mikolajczyk said that Russia would not permit any aid from Western countries because such aid "threatens to elevate in some countries the greatest of all menaces to Communism—stability and a better standard of living." Poland, the first to fight and a loyal ally of the West, received no economic aid from the Marshall Plan while Germany, America's enemy during the war, received a tremendous economic boost that gave the Germans a strong economy. Nevertheless, Mikolajczyk says the devastated lands need an uplift of morale. He speaks of Poland as an example. "It's 24,000,000 people, who underwent fantastic hardship while remaining in the Allied camp during the war and who were promised freedom, are now wholly enslaved by what amounts to not even five percent of the population." The Poles sought to establish a democratic government through free elections, but the vote was stolen. The Poles looked anxiously to the Big Three to carry out the solemn promises made to what President Roosevelt once called "the inspiration of the nations—Poland." However, those pacts were callously broken by Russia with only "paper protests" from the United States and Great Britain.

Mikolajczyk stated his belief in 1948 that if Russia possessed the atomic bomb it would employ it against the United States and the West. (Russia acquired the know-how to manufacture nuclear weapons in 1949.) Russia's new capability increased the tension of the Cold War and led to a fearful strategy of mutual nuclear self-destruction. President Roosevelt had thought naively he could persuade Russia to become a co-leader with the United States for a peaceful world. Instead, Roosevelt's disastrous foreign policy ushered in the Cold War.[10]

As soon as the war ended, Russia cast off its alliance with the

United States and Great Britain that had successfully crushed Germany and now began to flex its muscles. In 1948, Russia blocked the communications lines of the United States and Great Britain to Berlin across the Russian zone of occupation. With apparent arrogant abandon, Russia decided to impose its will on the United States. This time, however, the Russians were not dealing with President Roosevelt who always appeased Stalin. Harry Truman was President. Russia's provocative action could lead to war. Truman, however, outwitted the Russians. He ordered the famous Berlin Airlift to fly in supplies of food, medicine, clothing, and even coal for the American troops and for the more numerous German residents of West Berlin. The airlift filled the skies with cargo planes and saved West Berlin from starvation and capitulation. The Russians did not interfere with the airlift. Interference with the airlift meant war. The Russians, however, confidently expected the airlift to fail. When it succeeded, the Russians called off the land blockade.[11]

Mikolajczyk proposed a working plan of free nations to band together in a united offensive against Communism. Perhaps the Berlin Airlift, among other factors, convinced the United States and other democratic countries of the urgent need to form an opposition to the Soviet Empire and its evil designs of world domination. In 1949, the United States took the lead in establishing the North Atlantic Treaty Organization (NATO), consisting of a diplomatic component of sixteen nations and a powerful military component in Europe called the Supreme Allied Command, Europe (SACEUR). NATO kept the peace and stood as a bulwark against Russian expansion into Western Europe and the Middle East (Turkey) for the next forty years.[12]

Just as Stanislaw Mikolajczyk wrote in *The Rape of Poland*, Arthur Bliss Lane likewise recorded the brutal methods of the Communists in his historically-important book *I Saw Poland Betrayed*, published in 1948, one year after his return to the United States. He wanted the American people to know the truth about Russia because the Roosevelt Administration and the media had fed the public pro-Russian propaganda during the war years. Lane wrote that the primary responsibility for the tragic condition of Poland should be placed on Adolf Hitler. Nevertheless, almost equal responsibility must be placed on the Russian government. What allowed Hitler to plunge the world into war was the secret Von Ribbentrop-Molotov Agreement of 23 July 1939 that committed both powers to attack Poland and defeat it in a swift campaign before Great Britain and France could react.

Lane condemns Russia for having deported hundreds of thousands of Poles to Siberia during the Russian occupation of Eastern Poland from 1939 until the German attack on Russia on 22 June 1941. The brutal deportation of Poles was calculated to remove nationalists and non-Communist elements and to destroy the flower of the Polish Army. The liquidation of ten thousand Polish officers (Lane's figure) was consistent with the Russian policy of systematically destroying all elements of Polish nationalism.

Despite Russia's agreement to the Yalta and the Potsdam declarations affecting Poland, Russia already had decided to subjugate Poland at the very beginning of the war in 1939. Stalin set up the "Union of Polish Patriots," consisting of Moscow-trained Communists which became the core of the Polish government. (President Truman unwittingly helped to establish the Communist-dominated Provisional Government of National Unity. Upon taking office as President in April 1945, Truman tried to unravel Roosevelt's personal and secretive foreign policy. Truman looked for knowledgeable diplomats from the Roosevelt Administration. He called on Harry Hopkins who was, indeed, very knowledgeable on matters affecting Poland and Russia. At the same time, however, Hopkins was the chief American appeaser of Roosevelt's appeasement crowd. When the Commission of three foreign ministers, charged with the selection of the members of the Polish provisional government, became deadlocked in Moscow, President Truman dispatched Hopkins to resolve the deadlock. Hopkins did, because he agreed to Stalin's demands of including a majority of Communists in the provisional government. Hopkins and Ambassador Harriman falsely called the selection a fulfill-ment of the Yalta Declaration and deceived President Truman.)

At every opportunity the Russians systematically eliminated Polish leadership opposed to Communism. Lane points to Russia's tacit agreement in August 1944 to allow Germany, a sworn en-emy, to quell the Warsaw Uprising that resulted in the loss of 250,000 Polish lives, mostly civilians. Lane emphasized that the failure of the uprising, with the Russian Army sitting idly on the east bank of the Vistula River, was the most savage blow against Polish nationalism. Lane explains what a Communist member of the Polish Provisional Government revealed to a prominent American visitor to Warsaw in 1946:

> Had General Bor-Komorowski and his underground army suc-ceeded in liberating Warsaw, they would have been the heroes of Poland and would have formed the nucleus of the government within Poland. It would have been most difficult under such cir-cumstances for the Soviet Government to maintain in power the Lublin Committee of National Liberation.[13]

The surrender of the Home Army to the Germans eliminated a powerful element of Polish nationalism. And with the subse-quent advance of Russian Armies through Poland, Russia took a firmer hold of Poland. As Russia became more arrogant, it forced the United States and Great Britain to concede to its demands at Yalta (with the pitiful acquiescence of President Roosevelt). Without the knowledge or concurrence of the Polish people, the Big Three cavalierly gave away one-half of Poland to Russia (just as Neville Chamberlin and Edouard Daladier gave away Czechoslovakia to Germany in 1938). Although at Yalta the Big Three agreed that democratic leaders from within Poland and from abroad should constitute the Provisional Government, the Communist embryo of that government-to-be was already func-tioning in Poland, backed by the Russian Army and the Russian NKVD. Under such circumstances, the truly democratic forces never had a chance to express themselves freely or to form a government clearly representative of the Polish people.[14]

Lane calls attention to another Russian diabolical trick with the arrest of the sixteen Polish leaders from within Poland that included General Leopold Okulicki who succeeded General Komorowski to the command of the Home Army. Their arrest and trial was carried out in defiance of Western public opinion. Russia was determined to liquidate all Polish leaders who might provide opposition to the Communist-dominated government. With the efficient methods similar to those of the German Gestapo, the NKVD and its Polish equivalent organized a police state so that all effective opposition would be suppressed. Arrests, torture, and assassinations were as effective under the Russian-controlled police state as under the German Nazi variety. Finally, the end of democracy in Poland occurred when the fraudulent national elections gave no voice in the new government to the popular Polish Peasant Party. Lane stressed that the world must condemn the Russian government for its ruthless action against the Polish people. Regardless, Russia rejected all condemnation and continued to pursue its evil goals.[15]

The principal responsibility for Poland's fate, Lane states, must be placed on the German and Russian governments. Nevertheless, the United States and Great Britain, Lane stresses, cannot escape a share of the tragic betrayal. Anxious to maintain close relations with Stalin during a critical period of the war, Roosevelt and Churchill agreed to Stalin's demand for Eastern Poland at Tehran in December 1943. This give-away was Roosevelt's personal decision. It was never expressed in a treaty which would have required the consent of the U.S. Senate. Roosevelt deliberately kept the shameless action from the public. It was kept a secret until after the presidential elections of 1944. Lane wrote in *I Saw Poland Betrayed* that an official of the State Department who was at Tehran told Lane some months later that he had tried to prevail on the President to take a firmer stand with Stalin on Poland. According to Lane's informant, Roosevelt replied: "You may know a lot about international affairs, but you do not understand American politics."[16]

At Yalta in February 1945, Lane writes, the United States

lost an opportunity to stand firm. Yalta confirmed the decision reached earlier at Tehran. Subsequently, the efforts of the United States, Great Britain, and the Polish Peasant Party to insure free and unfettered elections became a useless exercise. Lane asserts that Yalta "was the death blow to Poland's hopes for a democratic form of government." The United States' policy of appeasement toward Russia (the same as the gutless, appeasement policy of Neville Chamberlin at Munich) emboldened Stalin to march forward with his plan for the total domination of Poland and the other countries of Eastern Europe. Although Roosevelt stands guilty of the major share of American appeasement, the State Department, Lane claims, must also share the onus. The State Department cooperated in Roosevelt's personal and secret diplomacy. Anyone who dared to oppose Roosevelt felt his wrath. (Unresponsive diplomats could expect to suffer the fate of the Assistant Governor of American Somoa, George H. Earle.)[17]

The fate of Poland, the traditional friend of the United States, Lane says, will always be of primary interest to Americans. (Lane wrote this generous statement in 1948. This author today is less confident of Lane's sentiments.) As he had determined on his return to the United States, Lane began an intensive program of informing the American public of the appeasement of American and British Allies and of the machinations of Stalin and his Communists. Lane penned a lengthy essay "How Russia Rules Poland," published in *Life* magazine, 14 July 1947. He wanted to inform the Americans quickly of his experiences as Ambassador to Poland. The essay is a great exposé, covering many of the incidents which he later included in his book. The Polish Communist government reacted viciously to Lane's essay in *Life*. In September 1947, nine democratic leaders in Poland were seized and sentenced to death. Some of them were condemned on the charge of furnishing Lane with information used in the essay. The charge was false. Lane had lived through the repression of the Communists in Poland and knew his facts well. In his essay in *Life*, Lane included the arrest of Irena Dmochowska, an American citizen born in Chicago and an em-

FRANKLIN DELANO ROOSEVELT MEMORIAL
Statue of President Roosevelt in a wheel chair at the Memorial site that includes First Lady Eleanor Roosevelt. Designed by Lawrence Halprin, the construction of the Memorial site began in September 1991, and the dedication of the completed Memorial took place on 2 May 1997. The Roosevelt Memorial Site is located on West Basin Drive, Washington, D.C.

ployee of the American Embassy. Her task was simply to translate Polish publications into English. The Communists did not care that Dmochowska was an American citizen. They wanted to stop contact between the people of Warsaw, where she lived, and the American Embassy. Lane reminds us again that the Polish Communist government violated accepted international law. In October 1947, another American citizen employed by the Embassy, Wanda Sroka, was arrested, subjected to rough handling, and questioned by the security police, in violation of the long-established rules of international law. Intimidation and repression continued in Communist-controlled Poland.

Lane emphasizes the rights of citizens in a democratic country. He writes: "The public has a right to know when the executive branch of the government makes far-reaching commitments which affect millions of persons which might seriously endanger the security of the United States." He adds that the peace of the world requires a policy of firmness by the United States backed by military strength.

(CONTINUED FROM PREVIOUS PAGE)

When the project of a memorial to President Roosevelt was first proposed, two schools of thought emerged on the design of the statue. One group wanted a design that projected a confident and strong President, the image that the President himself had encouraged during his lifetime. The other group wished to show the President as he really was—an invalid in a wheel chair. The realists won the day, but not entirely.

The designer's statue shows an individual in a sitting position, presumably on a wheel chair, but the posture is not readily apparent because a large cape covers the body and wheel chair. A clue to an invalid condition is the walking cane on which Roosevelt rests his hands. The Roosevelt Memorial is a striking design and a tribute to Lawrence Halprin. (Photo of Roosevelt statue, courtesy of the National Park Service, Washington, D.C.)

Lane gathered a committee of some twelve prominent Americans to assist him in educating the American public about the great injustice done to subjugated Poland. Lane conducted many interviews and spoke before clubs and organizations. He did a yeoman's job. Arthur Bliss Lane proved himself to be a great American. Poland needs friends of Lane's stature. Soon, Russia's hostile actions toward the United States, like the blockade of Berlin, exposed the danger of the "Evil Empire" (so named by President Ronald Reagan).

AMERICAN LIBERAL DEFENDS ROOSEVELT'S DEALS WITH STALIN

Forty-five years after the end of World War II, Communism in Eastern Europe crumbled, and shortly after that the Soviet Empire fell apart. Nothing that President Roosevelt had done led to the downfall of Communism. In fact, Roosevelt's disastrous foreign policy ushered in the Cold War. Following the end of the war, the peaceful but relentless offensive against the Evil Empire brought down Russian tyranny. One of the first blows against Communism was President Harry Truman's firm response to Russian tactics of blackmail when Russia blocked American land lines to West Berlin in 1948. Although the Russian move was provocative and could lead to war, Truman outwitted the Russians with the successful Berlin Airlift. In 1962, President John F. Kennedy forced the Russian leader Nikita Krushchev to remove the Russian nuclear-armed missiles from Cuba. In 1981, President Reagan placed great pressure on Russia when he outdistanced and outspent Russia in a relentless arms race. He frightened Russia and the satellite countries with the deployment of the new Pershing II nuclear missile to Europe in 1985. Meanwhile, the swift advance of technology in the United States and the Western world left Russia far behind. Admittedly, Russia was able to gather its few scientists and its limited resources for a successful space program. However, the vast citizenry still wallowed in the Dark Ages and was unskilled and unprepared to operate weaponry of advanced design. Pope John Paul II brought to the papacy a strong moral force against Communism. Earlier, in 1970, dock workers at the port of Szczecin rebelled against the Polish Communist government which put down the unrest with bloodshed. Nevertheless, the Polish working class grew bolder, and in 1980 the stevedores of Gdansk went on strike and closed down the port. Under the leadership of electrician Lech Walesa, they forced the government of Edward Gierek to recognize Solidarity, the first independent and non-communist union of workers. (The author with two daughters were visiting relatives in Gdansk in August 1980 and were witnesses to an historic event when Solidarity defied the Communist government.)

An independent workers' union in a Communist country challenged Communist logic. After all, Marx and Lenin touted Communism as the defender and benefactor of the working masses. Solidarity, however, gave the lie to Communism in open view of the whole world. Russia was on the verge of invading Poland to stamp out Solidarity and independent thinking in 1981, when Polish Communist leader General Wojciech Jaruzelski persuaded his Kremlin bosses to allow him to carry our the suppression of Solidarity. He wanted to avoid bloodshed. On 13 December 1981, Jaruzelski imposed martial law and imprisoned Lech Walesa and other Solidarity officials. Nevertheless, the rumbling of discontent became louder. Seeing the handwriting on the wall, Jaruzelski invited Solidarity leaders to a Round Table Conference in Warsaw in the spring of 1989. Jaruzelski offered to share power. Half of the representatives to the parliament (*Sejm*) would be Solidarity members and half, Communist (with one additional seat to the Communists as a symbolic majority). Tadeusz Mazowiecki became Premier and Jaruzelski continued as President (but not for long. The next year Lech Walesa was elected President of Poland). Six months after the Round Table Conference in Poland where Communism first crumbled, the Germans tore down the Berlin Wall. The American media played it up. Earlier, President Reagan had aroused the attention of the world when, at the Berlin Wall, he cried out, "Mr. Gorbachev, tear down this wall!" The American media seized on the Berlin Wall as the end of Communism. Notwithstanding, Communism ended six months earlier at the Round Table Conference in Warsaw. The symbol of tearing down the wall as the end of Communism in Eastern Europe is a fabrication of the American media.

On 26 June 1990, *The Wall Street Journal* published a lengthy article by Arthur Schlesinger, Jr., in which he tries to vindicate President Franklin Roosevelt's decisions at Yalta. Schlesinger was a Professor of Humanities at the City University of New York and winner of Pulitzer Prizes in history and biography. In addition to President Roosevelt, Schlesinger, too, felt the sting of barbs hurled at Roosevelt. Schlesinger identifies the criticism that was leveled at Roosevelt for forty-five years until the fall of Communism in 1989. He admits that critics have blamed Roosevelt for the growth of Soviet power, the spread of Communism, and the rise of the Cold War. Critics have also charged Roosevelt with the error of subordinating political to military objectives and neglecting the shape of the world to come in the interest of beating Hitler (the influence of General George C. Marshall on Roosevelt). Schlesinger also mentions the criticism of Roosevelt's naivete when he handed Eastern Europe to Stalin at Yalta, and this appeasement encouraged Stalin to undertake the quest for world domination.

Schlesinger admits that Roosevelt may have been many things to many people, but he denies the President was naive. If one concedes that Roosevelt, indeed, was not naive, he was sick, physically and mentally, and unfit to make momentous decisions at Yalta. Historian William Henry Chamberlin identifies Roosevelt's disabilities: "Among the symptoms of the President's bad health was liability to severe debilitating colds, extreme haggardness of appearance, occasional blackouts of memory, and loss of capacity for mental concentration."[18]

Schlesinger calls attention to the pledges of freedom and the independence of nations in the Declaration on Liberated Europe. On Poland, he states in his letter, "The Declaration on Poland pledged 'a strong, free, independent, and democratic Poland, with free and unfettered elections…on the basis of universal suffrage and secret ballot.'" This is exactly what Roosevelt agreed to at Yalta. However, the United States and Great Britain were unable to achieve the pledged objectives, and Poland, therefore, suffered hardship, repression, and lack of industrial progress for forty-five years. And it was Roosevelt who cast Poland into Communist captivity. Schlesinger's interpretation of the results of Yalta is a vast stretch of the imagination, incongruous. He states in his letter: "Far from handing over Eastern Europe to the Russians, the Yalta accord called for precisely the democratic Eastern Europe that is finally coming into existence today."[19]

During World War II millions of individuals were killed for brutal political objectives. Poland lost one-fifth of its population: 3,000,000 Christian Poles and 3,000,000 Polish Jews.

APPENDICES

A. THE NATIONAL KATYN MEMORIAL,
BALTIMORE, MARYLAND

B. HENRY IGNATIUS SZYMANSKI,
BIOGRAPHICAL SKETCH

C. EDWARD JOSEPH YORK,
BIOGRAPHICAL SKETCH

D. ACKNOWLEDGEMENTS

THE NATIONAL KATYN MEMORIAL BALTIMORE, MARYLAND

AN IMPRESSIVE MEMORIAL in honor of 15,000 slain Polish prisoners of war of World War II rises majestically at Inner Harbor East in Baltimore, Maryland. Polonia and the people of Baltimore erected the Monument as a lasting symbol of the precious value of human life against the ruthlessness of a tyrant or a band of fanatics. The completed memorial speaks for the silence of the officer-prisoners who were methodically shot in the back of the head by the Russian secret police on the orders of Josef Stalin in the Katyn Forest near Smolensk, Russia. The Polish officers were all professionals. There were some 700 physicians, university professors, engineers, attorneys, accountants, priests, journalists, athletes, and the Chief Rabbi of Warsaw. The intellectual elite of Poland was liquidated by the brutal hand of Stalin's secret police. The motive sprang from Russia's vicious plan to eliminate the leadership of the Polish nation so that it could not oppose the subsequent subjugation of Poland.[1]

The project of the Katyn Monument began very modestly in 1970, and it expanded enthusiastically as individuals discovered it. A Marylander, Major Clement Knefel, U.S. Army, had been stationed in Poland where he learned of the Katyn Forest massacre in the spring of 1940. Moved and outraged by the discovery, Knefel and friends in Baltimore organized a lodge of the Polish

National Alliance and named it "Martyrs of Katyn Forest." Knefel began a fund-raising effort to purchase a memorial plaque to be placed in Patterson Park in Baltimore. He raised the money by selling soft drinks and sandwiches at festivals. He also collected small donations from supporters. By 1989, however, Knefel had to stop his personal fund raising. He had become ill and could no longer continue. Knefel's modest beginning did not die. Others sprang into action, notably Milan Kamski and Alfred B. Wisniewski who organized the National Katyn Memorial Committee. It was incorporated as a non-profit organization with seven officers and four directors in 1994. Enthusiasm for the project grew. The entire Polish community of Baltimore banded together for the memorial project. It soon became apparent that the project should be more than a plaque, as interest in the project and donations increased. Honorary Chair of the Katyn Memorial Committee, U.S. Senator Barbara Mikulski, obtained a generous donation from the Associated Jewish Charities of Baltimore. Richard Lansburgh, Chairman of the Board, presented Senator Mikulski a check for $36,500, and Alfred Wisniewski graciously accepted the donation for the Committee.

The Katyn Committee searched for a site in Baltimore for the monument. In a meeting with Baltimore Mayor Kurt L. Schmoke, the Committee members were delighted with the Mayor's offer of a traffic circle adjacent to the Inner Harbor as the proper site. On behalf of the Committee, Edward B. Rybczynski negotiated an agreement with the city which pledged the site and promised to make improvements and provide landscaping. It was an admirable location in a renovated area that was planned as a showplace of Baltimore.

In 1995, Pope John Paul II visited Baltimore where William Cardinal Keeler, Archbishop of Baltimore, greeted the pontiff. Subsequently, the Cardinal told the Committee: "It was a particular privilege of mine to present to Pope John Paul II on your behalf a model of the memorial. It is appropriate that this memorial stands in Baltimore as a reminder of past cruelty and a caution against future tyranny."

ALFRED B. WISNIEWSKI
Chairman, National Katyn Memorial Committee

In 1996, the National Katyn Memorial Committee held a dedication of the selected site at President and Aliceanna Streets. A
delegation from the Embassy of Poland in Washington, D.C. attended the ceremony, as well as many elected officials and
dignitaries. On this occasion, the Reverend Monsignor Zdzislaw
J. Peszkowski arrived from Poland, bringing an urn of earth from
the mass graves in the Katyn Forest. Monsignor Peszkowski was
one of a very few Poles who survived the massacre. In his remarks at the dedication, the Monsignor said: "I am a priest, who
survived the horrible tragedy of the Katyn Forest massacre in which

AERIAL VIEW OF THE NATIONAL KATYN MEMORIAL

*Located at President and Aliceanna Streets, East Inner Harbor, Balti-
more, Maryland.(Photo by Richard P. Poremski, Baltimore, Maryland)*

ANDRZEJ PITYNSKI
Sculptor

15,400 of my fellow Polish patriots were brutally murdered." The audience was moved to tears and could be seen weeping openly as they were overpowered by the emotion of the moment.

The Committee sought to engage a prominent, professional artist for the design of the monument that would adequately portray the monumental crime of Katyn. After considering several outstanding artists, the Committee chose Andrzej Pitynski, a Polish American of worldwide reputation. Among his works are portrait busts of scientist Maria Sklodowska Curie and Pope John Paul II. Pitynski also designed the monument in Warsaw dedicated to General Jozef Haller's Polish Blue Army of World War I fame. The Polish government awarded Pitynski a gold medal for artistic achievement. He also received many other awards. Pitynski was so deeply moved by the Katyn Forest tragedy that he donated his services to the Committee at substantial personal expense in time and money.

Continuing the project vigorously, the Committee contacted several foundries in the United States and Poland for the construction of a 44-foot bronze monument as conceptualized by the sculptor. The Committee chose the GZUT foundry in Gliwice, Poland (Gliwickie Zaklady Urzadzen Technicznych SA), based on cost and a reputation for monuments of quality in France, England, Germany, Austria, and Japan. The GZUT foundry built a one-quarter scale model of the monument and shipped it to Baltimore. The Committee approved the model. In the spring of 1999, Committee Chairman Wisniewski and Vice Chairman Edward B. Rybczynski traveled to Poland to examine the finished, full-scale maquette. Tadeusz Wojarski, President and Chief Executive Officer of GZUT, received the two visitors and escorted them to a huge work area in a warehouse to see the maquette. At the time, scaffolding encircled the maquette, and Pitynski assisted by three sculptors was at work. Immediately beyond the scaffolding was the one-quarter scale model. Wisniewski and Rybczynski concurred that the full-scale model maquette matched the smaller model. The two Baltimoreans conversed at length with Wojarski, Pitynski, other sculptors, and engineers. Impressed and convinced of the quality and design of the maquette, Wisniewski and Rybczynski signed documents on behalf of the Committee, signifying approval. Wojarski and Pitynski signed on, as well. In another GZUT building the two looked over a newly created, larger-than-life statue of Pope John Paul II to be dedicated in Lichen, Poland. They learned that the full size Katyn maquette would be cut into more than 100 sections, a mold made for each section, and bronze poured into each mold. The 100 sections then would be welded together to form the monument. When the monument was completed, the Committee had an opportunity to inspect the finished product, which was then shipped to Baltimore.

.   .   .

KATYN COMMITTEE MEMBERS VISIT FOUNDRY IN POLAND
Two members of the National Katyn Memorial Committee visit the
GZUT foundry in Gliwice, Poland, to examine the nearly-completed
Katyn statue, April 1999. (Photo by GZUT)

FUND RAISING

The visionary and massive scope of the Katyn Monument project posed an enormous challenge for a group of patriotic civilians. The noble purpose of the project, however, gained the enthusiasm and support of city and Maryland state officials. The National Katyn Memorial Committee decided to seek passage of a $200,000 Bond Bill during the 1997 session of the Maryland General Assembly. State Senator Perry Sfikas introduced the bill in the Senate and Delegate Carolyn Krysiak, seconded by Delegates Cornell Dypski, Peter Hammen, Speaker of the House Casper Taylor, and others introduced the bill in the House of Delegates. The Committee invited Monsignor Peszkowski to return to Maryland for the purpose of opening the sessions of the House and Senate with prayers. Legislators were impressed and deeply moved by the priest's sincerity.

Kathleen Kennedy Townsend, Lieutenant Governor of Maryland, met Monsignor Peszkowski and members of the Committee. She led the effort to obtain the support of the Maryland government. After conferring with Governor Parris N. Glendening, Townsend told the Committee: "I am happy to inform you that we are recommending (State Matching Grant Fund) of $200,000 for the National Katyn Memorial." Committee members sprang into action, lobbying the legislature for passage of the bill. Dr. William Krol directed an extensive mail campaign to reach the legislators. Thomas Rybczynski, W. Milam-Kamski, Barbara Miegon, Stella Spies, Eugene Pawlikowski aided by additional volunteers, went from door to door of the legislators' offices. The result was successful. The Maryland Legislature approved the $200,000 for the Katyn project by a combined vote of 148-3.

In association with the fund-raising campaign, worldwide media focused attention on the Katyn Memorial. Television in Poland covered the story in prime time. Radio stations in the United States broadcast stories about the tragedy. Major metropolitan newspapers such as *The Baltimore Sun* published articles and editorials in support of the monument. Fund raising continued into 1997. Three county executive officers pledged $5,000 each for the project. They were John Gary of Anne Arundel County, Eileen Rehrmann of Harford County, and C. A. "Dutch" Ruppersberger of Baltimore County.

Gary saw a broad meaning of the Katyn massacre. He observed that "When the National Katyn Memorial Committee dedicates this monument to all prisoners of war, I believe veterans from Korea and Vietnam will join with me in honoring all of our fallen comrades."

The Katyn Committee had raised about $200,000 in smaller cash contributions and had expended some of that money to pay for operating and fund-raising costs. Another $100,000 loan by the City of Baltimore allowed the Committee to complete the matching fund grant by the State of Maryland. The treasurer's report for the quarterly period, April–June 1999, gave the following summary:

Total Cost of the Katyn Memorial—	$565,000
Total Funds Available or Used—	486,000
Difference Required for Completion—	79,000

All money collected was tax deductible and not used for personal expenses or personal gain of any member. For the trip to Gliwice, Poland, as an example, all costs were borne by each member of the Committee from personal funds.

The foundry in Gliwice, Poland, fabricated the 44-foot Katyn Monument in July 2000 and prepared to ship it to Baltimore. The National Katyn Memorial Committee, therefore, set the date of 10 September 2000 for the unveiling and dedication. The monument was loaded aboard the Dutch merchant ship *Edisongracht* at Gdansk, Poland. The ship first sailed to Finland to load cargo. Heavy storms in the Baltic Sea and a temporary work stoppage in Finland delayed the ship which did not reach Gdansk until 23 August 2000. Unfortunately, the dedication planned for 10 September had to be delayed. As *The Baltimore Sun* commented: "The tallest sculpture in Baltimore was to be dedicated Sept. 10, but it was unable to make its own coming out party." After a last minute effort to persuade NATO to fly the crated monument to Baltimore failed, the Committee was forced to postpone the dedication to Sunday, 19 November 2000. The frustrated Committee cancelled diplomatic receptions, banquet reservations, concert hall rentals, and many other preparations.[2]

Earlier, the base of the monument was readied for the installation. Located on a round plaza, the site fronts the newly-built Marriott Baltimore Waterfront Hotel. The base is bright black granite, as are the tablets with names of supporters of the project. The center tablet is inscribed with a brief history of the massacre and concludes with a quotation of Poland's national poet, Adam Mickiewicz: "Should I forget them, may God in heaven forget me." Chuck Wright, construction supervisor at the site, remarked about the memorable words of Mickiewicz. Nodding his head in the direction of the tablet, Wright said: "They won't be forgotten when the memorial's here. That's for sure."

THE MONUMENT ARRIVES
IN BALTIMORE

The merchant ship *Edisongracht* arrived from Europe to the port of Baltimore on 12 September 2000. A group of Committee members came to the dock to welcome the ship (the expected arrival date had been 23 August). "I'm relieved, to say the least. Happy, of course," said Alfred Wisniewski, Chairman of the Committee. On board the ship, the statue was stored on its side in a protective cage of red steel. It was swaddled in a white plastic, revealing only its shape. Unloading the 12-ton, 44-foot bronze sculpture from the ship onto a flatbed truck called for a careful movement of machinery and manpower. As a crane hoisted the cage over the side of the ship, workers pulled at it with a long rope, positioning the cage for the descent to dry land. The cage was lowered

AT THE PORT OF BALTIMORE

Dock workers offload the crated Katyn statue in September 2000. (Photo by Richard P. Poremski, Baltimore, Maryland)

slowly to about six feet above the ground. A flatbed truck was backed into place beneath the hovering cage. Hard-hatted dock workers edged the crane down until it rested on the truck. At this moment the dock workers were surprised by applause coming from Wisniewski and Committee members. Chris Eyler, in charge of the dockyard operation, commented: "I can understand the emotion that goes into a project like this." And added: "There is a lot of cultural pride involved...and to get the statue to this point is a partial culmination of a long effort by them." To assist the unloading crew, Tadeusz Wojarski and several members from the GZUT foundry in Poland were at the dock. Next, the truck was driven to the site at night at low-traffic hours of 1 A.M. and 5 A.M. The city temporarily removed the traffic lights to accommodate the height of the statue.[3]

PLACEMENT OF THE MONUMENT

The Katyn monument is lowered onto its base at the pre-selected site at Inner Harbor East, Baltimore, Maryland, September 2000. (Photo by Richard P. Poremski, Baltimore, Maryland)

At the site near Inner Harbor East, two huge pieces of equipment from Linden Crane Services lifted the monument and held it steady as four men from the GZUT foundry worked with local crews to secure it to the base. The bright, dark-gray granite base on which the statue stands rises about eight feet above the ground. It is encircled by fifteen levels of brick steps down which streams of water trickle—"like the murmur of lost souls," whispered Wisniewski. With the beautiful monument in place, the National Katyn Memorial Committee planned to celebrate the achievement of a historic landmark project.[4]

CELEBRATION

A two-day celebration took place—a Dedication Dinner at the Pier 5 Hotel on Saturday, 18 November 2000, and the unveiling ceremony the next day at the National Katyn Memorial. Polish and American officials as well as proud Polish Americans and guests attended the banquet. Committee Vice-Chairman Edward B. Rybczynski welcomed the guests and called on Minister Bogulaw Majewski of the Embassy of Poland in Washington, D.C. to be the master of ceremonies. He introduced the members of the National Katyn Memorial Committee and presented each with a medal—the Knight's Cross of the Order of Merit of the Republic of Poland. The master of ceremonies next introduced Committee Chairman Alfred B. Wisniewski who spoke eloquently.

Cameron Munter, Director for Central Europe of the National Security Council at the White House, congratulated the Committee and the City of Baltimore for erecting a historic reminder for healing the wounds of World War II. U.S. Senator Paul Sarbanes was likewise very complimentary. He had supported the project from the beginning. The key speaker was His Excellency Przemyslaw Grudzinski, Poland's Ambassador to Washington. The dinner ended with the closing remarks of Edward B. Rybczynski. (See program, "The National Katyn Memorial Dedication Dinner" and "Dedication Ceremonies.")

CLOSE-UP VIEW OF NATIONAL KATYN MEMORIAL
(Photo by Richard P. Poremski, Baltimore, Maryland)

On Sunday, 19 November 2000, some 5000 people gathered around the National Katyn Memorial for the dedication. The 389th U.S. Army Band (AMC's Own) played military and patriotic airs as the audience eagerly awaited the opening of the ceremony and never minding the November chill. "The cold chills I have aren't from the cold," Peggy Snyder said. A choreographer for a children's Polish folk dance ensemble, Snyder explained the ceremony: "This is kind of like closure, and a dedication to the people who come to the call of their country."

Chairman Alfred B. Wisniewski rose to address the audience. However, he was so overcome by the historic moment that he could not utter a word. His brother Stanislaus read the Chairman's statement which included a message to the dead: "May your dreams now be peaceful ones, because you will always be honored. You will always be remembered." U.S. Senator Barbara Mikulski told the gathering that the prominent location of the Monument is very appropriate. The first glimpse of Baltimore of many Polish immigrants was of Fort McHenry and the cross of St. Stanislaus Church. "It is fitting," the Senator added, "that the Katyn Memorial might be another landmark that newcomers from Poland might see."

LEFT: *The design of the monument gracefully incorporates the image of fire, a universal symbol of death and destruction on the one hand and life and vitality on the other, with sufficient recognizable references to officers who died at Katyn. Emerging out of the core of the flame, one can see the silhouette of the Eagle, a symbol used by many nations, especially Poland.*

Ever since the days of classical sculpture, the artist has strived to create a sense of momentum and make the viewer aware of not only the material but the space that surrounds it and that it encompasses. The monument, standing over five stories high, will be viewed by persons below, with the sky as its backdrop. The backdrop will change each day, so the sculpture, with its open space, will offer a constantly renewing aspect to the viewer.

THE NATIONAL KATYN MEMORIAL
DEDICATION DINNER
NOVEMBER 18, 2000

The National Katyn Memorial Committee gratefully acknowledges the assistance and cooperation of The Embassy of the Republic of Poland. The Committee is honored that Minister-Counselor Boguslaw M. Majewski from the Embassy has graciously consented to be the master of ceremonies for this evening's dinner.

Welcome and Introduction by Mr. Edward B. Rybczynski, Vice Chairman, The National Katyn Memorial Committee

Dinner is served

Minister Boguslaw Majewski introductory remarks and introduction of Minister Maciej Musial representing the Prime Minister of Poland

Introduction of The National Katyn Memorial Committee

Presentation of medals by Minister Maciej Musial from the Republic of Poland to The National Katyn Memorial Committee

Introduction of Mr. Alfred B. Wisniewski, Chairman, The National Katyn Memorial Committee

Remarks by Mr. Alfred B. Wisniewski

Introduction of Mr. Cameron Munter, Director for Central Europe at The National Security Council, The White House

Remarks by Mr. Cameron Munter

Introduction of Senator Paul Sarbanes

Remarks by Senator Paul Sarbanes

Introduction of Ambassador Prezmyslaw Grudzinski

Remarks by Ambassador Prezmyslaw Grudzinski

Closing Remarks by Mr. Edward B. Rybczynski, Vice Chairman

THE NATIONAL KATYN MEMORIAL
DEDICATION CEREMONIES
SUNDAY, NOVEMBER 19, 2000

The National Katyn Memorial Committee gratefully acknowledges today's musical performance by the 389th Army Band (AMC's Own). The "AMC's Own" designation means that the band represents all of the 65,000 military and civilian personnel within the Army Materiel Command.

Welcome and introductions by Maryland State Senator Perry Sfikas
National Anthems-Pledges to the Flag: American and Polish
Invocations by Father Bogdan Palka, St. Rita Church, Dundalk, MD, and
  Rabbi Rex D. Perlmeter, Senior Rabbi, Baltimore Hebrew Congregation
Introduction of Mayor Martin O'Malley, Mayor of Baltimore City
Remarks by Mayor Martin O'Malley
Introduction of Mr. Alfred B. Wisniewski, Chairman, The National Katyn
  Memorial Committee
Remarks by Mr. Alfred B. Wisniewski
Introduction of Mr. Kurt L. Schmoke, former Mayor of Baltimore City
Remarks by Former Mayor Kurt L. Schmoke
Introduction of Senator Barbara Mikulski, U.S. Senator from Maryland
Remarks by Senator Barbara Mikulski
Introduction of Mr. Andrzej Pitynski, award-wining sculptor of the National
  Katyn Memorial
Remarks by Mr. Andrzej Pitynski
Musical Presenations
  Letter from Lt. Governor Kathleen Kennedy Townsend read by Mr. Thomas
    J. Rybczynski
  Presentation by Maryland Delegate Carolyn Krysiak and Speaker of the
    Maryland House of Delegates Casper Taylor
  Presentation of Baltimore County Councilman John Olszewski
  Presentation of message from Secretary of State Madeline Albright by Mr.
    Francisco Javier Gonzalez, Country Officer for Poland, U.S. Department of State
  Presentation by Mr. David Carroll, representing U.S. Congressman Benjamin
    Cardin
  Introduction of Msgr. Zdzislaw J. Peszkowski, a survivor of the Katyn Massacre
  Remarks by Msgr. Zdzislaw J. Peszkowski
Musical Presentations
  Introduction of Minister Maciej Musial representing the Polish Prime
    Minister
  Remarks by Minister Maciej Musial
  Presentation of a letter from the President of Poland by Ambassador
    Przemyslaw Grudzinski
Closing remarks and acknowledgment of wreaths by Senator Perry Sfikas
Mr. Alfred B. Wisniewski and Msgr. Zdzislaw Peszkowski carry an urn of soil
    from the Katyn Forest to be permanently placed in the National Katyn
    Memorial during a special musical presentation of Chopin's Funeral March.
Final Musical Presentation

THE NATIONAL KATYN MEMORIAL COMMITTEE

The Baltimore Sun reported the dedication as a day of Polish pride. Some like Peggy Snyder wore the colorful floral print skirts, the beaded vests, and the flowers that define Poland's national costume. A contingent of military re-enactors, dressed in uniforms of the 2nd Polish Parachute Brigade of World War II, marched past the stage to the music of the Army Band. The re-enactors were members of the Polish Legion of American Veterans, Staff Sergeant Joseph Jagiello Post 191. The correspondent of *The Baltimore Sun* added a bit of Polish history in his article. "Standing atop a fountain whose waters run over black granite bricks," he wrote, "the statue depicts soldiers against flames that are gilded in gold leaf." He also said the World War II soldiers are depicted alongside other great warrior heroes from Poland's history such as Boleslaw the Brave who ruled Poland in 1000 A.D. The flames also include a cut-out in the shape of an eagle, the symbol of Poland. Hanka Raczynski of Bethesda, Maryland, was emotionally struck by the dedication: "This is all so beautiful," she exclaimed. Her father, a captain in the Polish Army, was among those killed at Katyn Forest. She was seven at the time.

There is a Katyn Memorial in Jersey City, New Jersey, and others in Poland. Monsignor Peszkowski, however, described the Memorial in Baltimore as "the biggest and in some ways the most beautiful Katyn monument in the world."

———————————

LEFT: *The National Katyn Memorial Committee:*

Top row *(left to right): Frank Wesolowski, Thomas Rybczynski, Henry Wentz, Benedict A. Pokrywka, Charles Slomski, William F. Krol, Stanley Sdanowich, Richard P. Poremski, James Mislak, George Bozek, Frank Lanocha, Jerzy Miegon.*

Bottom row *(left to right): Eugene J. Pawlikowski, Sr., Zofia Graczyk, Theophilia Zamecki, Stella E. Spies, Alfred B. Wisniewski, Edward B. Rybczynski, Alfreda Jamrosz, Patricia Skurzynski. Committee members not pictured: Raymond Dombrowski, Robert Suchy.*

MONSIGNOR ZDZISLAW J. PESZKOWSKI
Survivor

At the end of the two-hour long ceremony, Monsignor Peszkowski and Chairman Wisniewski climbed into a cherry picker to place on the statue a small container of soil from the Katyn Forest in Russia. The Monsignor blessed the Memorial as the bugler played "Taps."[5]

This chapter ends with the memorable words of the Reverend Monsignor Zdzislaw J. Peszkowski, excerpted from his speech delivered in March 1999:

> The twentieth century now drawing to a close has been a pe-
> riod of tremendous advances in medicine, space exploration, and
> numerous fields of technology. But it has been a century marked
> by unspeakable crimes, by eruptions of mindless hatred and vio-

lence, directed not only against man but also against humanity as such. Two forces of evil crushed my nation—from the East by the degenerate Stalinist dictatorship and its NKVD henchmen, and from the West by Hitler's SS and Gestapo butchers. My nation was condemned to death, it was not supposed to live. Two symbols of that tragedy are **Katyn** and **Auschwitz**, with all their apocalyptic terror and perversion of truth. We should also not forget the disgraceful attitude of the other world powers—cowardly observers, who insensitively witnessed the crimes, remained silent, and bargained off the freedom of others.

No, we do not seek revenge! All we want is for the victims to be properly remembered, in accordance with truth and justice. In order to dispel every lingering shadow of evil—**I forgive, we forgive,** those who knew not what they did. **We forgive those who have trespassed against us.** That is what our nation's Christian heritage teaches us to do. We wish to contribute that unique value to the annals of mankind.

Having completed its historic mission, the Committee modified its name to "The National Katyn Memorial Foundation." Its new mission is the conduct of annual Katyn Remembrance Ceremonies at the Memorial. The Foundation also involves itself actively with the oversight, maintenance, and improvement of the Memorial and site.

HENRY IGNATIUS SZYMANSKI
COLONEL, U.S. ARMY

BIOGRAPHICAL SKETCH

HENRY IGNATIUS SZYMANSKI served the United States and his ancestral country Poland in an outstanding manner as an officer of the United States Army during World War II. Born in Chicago on 4 July 1898, he was the son of Polish immigrants, Ignacy Szymanski and Aniela (Starzyk) Szymanski. He spoke Polish from childhood, and his bilingual capability served him well as an officer in the Middle East Theater of Operations. Szymanski attended grammar and high schools in Chicago. Throughout life he was known by his nickname "Red," perhaps because he had red hair. (Few Poles are red heads. The author's father, however, had a tinge of red hair during his younger years.)

At age nineteen, Szymanski was appointed to the United States Military Academy by Congressman Gallagher of the Eighth Illinois Congressional District. He entered West Point in June 1917— just three months earlier the United States had declared war on Germany and Austria-Hungary. Consequently, Szymanski and the

Class of 1919 were put through a War Emergency Course, graduating in eighteen months as second lieutenants, 1 November 1918.
In ten days, however, the war in Europe ended with an Armistice
on 11 November. The War Department, therefore, recalled the
Class of 1919 to West Point as officer-cadets for six months of
additional schooling and training. Szymanski and the Class of
1919 completed the additional course on 11 June 1919.

At West Point Szymanski excelled in athletics. He enthusiastically participated in baseball, boxing, and wrestling. A lieutenant
in 1920, he became a member of the U.S. Olympics Wrestling
Team which competed in Belgium.

The schooling at West Point for two years was not a sufficient
time to earn a college degree. Szymanski, therefore, while on
ROTC duty at Northwestern University in Evanston, Illinois,
enrolled in courses that led to a Bachelor of Science degree in
1929. At Northwestern, Szymanski became attracted to coed Jean
Powell Burns, and they were married on 22 September 1922.
Part of his ROTC duties at Northwestern included coaching the
school's wrestling and baseball teams, 1921–1923. He also instructed recruits of Citizens Military Training Camps in boxing,
wrestling, and baseball, 1921–1924. He was assigned as director
of all physical training at Camp Custer, Michigan, when training
was held at the camp during the period of 1922–1924. As coach,
he led the National Champion Boxing and Wrestling Teams in
competitions in the Philippine Islands in 1927. Szymanski found
that service in a small, stagnant army in the 1920 decade offered
a bleak future. He resigned from the army as a first lieutenant in
1928 and entered the civilian world as an entrepreneur.[1]

Being an accomplished athlete and possessing years of experience in physical training, Szymanski conceived the idea of
establishing a physical fitness center. Still in the army in 1924,
he founded the North Shore School of Physical Development in
Evanston, Illinois. After his retirement in 1928, he devoted full-
time to the School. He personally planned and directed every
student's program. His life changed drastically when the Japanese
attacked Pearl Harbor on 7 December 1941. Volunteering to serve

his country, he entered the Army of the United States (AUS) in the grade of first lieutenant and rose rapidly in rank.

Lieutenant Szymanski was assigned to the 33rd U.S. Army Infantry Division at Camp Forrest, Tennessee. As the Morale Officer of the Division, he instructed the soldiers in physical fitness. He introduced a revolutionary kind of daily dozen. Basically it consisted of thirteen self-administered, sudden jerks and stretching motions. His system differed from the usual calisthenics which builds muscles and melts away fat. Instead, Szymanski's system gave soldiers additional stamina and ruggedness. His exercises proved so effective that the army made his booklet, "Take Your Tip from the Army," available for general sale (with the permission of Secretary of War Henry L. Stimson).

In his role of Liaison Officer to the Polish Second Army Corps of General Wladyslaw Anders, Szymanski made a lasting contribution to history. His two reports propelled him into the controversy of the Katyn Forest Massacre. His first report dealt with the Russian obstruction that prevented him from reaching the Polish troops in Russia. The Moscow government denied him entry into the country. The Russians feared that Szymanski could learn of the cruel conditions in Russian prisons. Szymanski was able to join the Polish Second Corps when it departed Russia and deployed to Iran. Here the Polish soldiers were succored to health and equipped with uniforms and arms by the British. Speaking fluent Polish, the American officer mingled with the officers and men and learned the details of the brutal murder of 5000 Polish officers at Katyn. He submitted his second report on the Katyn massacre to the War Department Military Intelligence Division G-2 which suppressed both reports.

Colonel Szymanski accompanied the Poles to North Africa and Italy. As a major component of the British Eighth Army, the Second Corps fought valiantly against the battle-hardened soldiers of Marshal Albert Kesselring who defended Monte Cassino from behind the rubble of the Monte Cassino Abbey. Fighting in the mountainous terrain, the Poles captured Monte Cassino on 18 May 1944. Of all the units of the Eighth Army engaged in the campaign to capture Rome, General Anders' Corps suffered the heaviest casualties, losing forty-two and one-half percent of its Corps strength.[2]

Field Marshal Sir Harold Alexander, Commander of Allied Forces in Italy, congratulated General Anders and his Corps: "In this great campaign against the German Army, the Poles played a part which gained them the admiration of their comrades and the respect of their enemies. They fought many a victorious battle alongside their Allies, but their greatest was at Monte Cassino."[3]

In Italy, on 30 July 1944, Colonel Szymanski was awarded the Order of Polonia Restituta, Degree of Commander, by General Kazimierz Sosnkowski, Commanding General of the Polish Armed Forces of the Polish Government-in-Exile (London). The presentation occurred in the presence of General Wladyslaw Anders and other high ranking Polish and British officers. During the ceremony, General Sosnkowski said in part:

> Colonel Szymanski of the U.S. Army was appointed Liaison officer to the Polish Army in the East as far back as 1941. As known, he was not permitted to enter Russia at that time, but he did join us early in 1942 in Persia.
>
> From that moment, however, he has been and is a sincere and loyal friend of the Polish Army in the East. He has on many occasions been of great service and assistance; he has given us valuable advice. Respected and much liked, Col. Szymanski has in accordance with historic tradition continued the friendship between Poland and the United States.

Correspondent Edd Johnson, who witnessed the award presentation, added in his report to the *Chicago Sun*: "Reports from Moscow some time ago said Szymanski is popular with the Polish people because he speaks their language fluently, yet gives it an 'interesting American accent.'"[4]

Colonel Szymanski remained with the Polish Second Army Corps until December 1944, when he was assigned to Headquarters, Allied Expeditionary Forces (SHAEF). He served on General Eisenhower's staff as Specialist in Polish Affairs. For the next year, he successfully recruited replacements for General Anders' decimated Corps from among Poles conscripted by the Germans and from interned Poles in Switzerland. He was one of the first Americans to visit the German concentration camps of Dachau and Buchenwald. At those camps he aided and adjusted the lives of thousands of Polish prisoners of war and displaced persons. With the approval of SHAEF, he organized guard battalions from the former Polish prisoners for protecting supply lines on the Western front, thereby releasing American and British soldiers for the fighting. Szymanski returned to the United States in December 1945. He retired from the U.S. Army in the rank of colonel for disability (weak heart) in 1953.[5]

Szymanski, wife Jean, and daughter Jean Pirrie made their home in Colorado Springs, Colorado. From 1955 to 1957, he served as Public Relations Director of the Exchange National Bank. In 1957, he founded the Academy Life Insurance Company and served as its president until he died on 6 November 1959. Wife Jean bade him farewell with this great tribute: "Red Szymanski's tenacious adherence to what he considered morally, spiritually, and ethically right and just remained unshaken to his last breath."

Jean Szymanski continued to live in Colorado Springs where she took part in local affairs, especially with regard to city planning and zoning. She was one of the founders and for ten years president of the largest Home Owners Association in the city, and she was active in the League of Women Voters. The Szymanski's one daughter, Jean Pirrie Milani, resided with her husband in Iran and was a teacher of biology at the University of Tehran. They had three children: Camran, Darius, and Mina.[6]

Appendix C

Edward Joseph York
Colonel, U.S. Army Air Corps/
U.S. Air Force

Biographical Sketch

This author first learned of Colonel York from Ambassador Arthur Bliss Lane who mentions him prominently in his book *I Saw Poland Betrayed* (1948). York served as Air Attaché at the American Embassy in Warsaw in 1946. When the American government provided Ambassador Lane with a C-47 cargo plane, York flew the Ambassador on diplomatic missions in Europe. On one occasion he accompanied the Ambassador to Paderewski Park in the Praga district of Warsaw,

located on the east bank of the Vistula River. Lane wanted to investigate a report that an American aircraft had crashed in Paderewski Park in September 1944 during the Warsaw Rising under General Bor-Komorowski. The United States and Great Britain were able to airlift a limited amount of supplies to the beleaguered soldiers of the Polish Home Army. Russia, however, cooperating with its arch enemy Germany, obstructed the re-supply flights. Consequently, the help was too little to be effective and the loss of aircraft was heavy. At Paderewski Park, the Ambassador and York found pieces of the downed American plane. Fluent in Polish, York learned from the residents about another downed American cargo plane in Praga. A lad led the Ambassador to the site. York found several parts that identified the plane as manufactured in the United States. The residents told York that, when the plane crashed to the ground, Russian soldiers rushed to the site and stripped the crew members of all identifying documents, including their "dog tags." Lane became outraged over the behavior of the Russians. In his book, Lane proudly points to York's role in the famous Jimmy Doolittle bombing raid over Tokyo on 18 April 1942. York piloted one of the sixteen B-25 bombers.

The future officer and pilot was born in Batavia, New York, on 16 August 1912, the son of James and Tekla Cichowski. Upon graduating from high school in Batavia, York enlisted in the United States Army in 1930 and served with the 7th Infantry Regiment at Chilkoot Barracks, Alaska. Striving to become an officer, York applied for and was accepted as a student at the West Point Preparatory School in San Francisco for eighteen months. Before continuing the Army route for an appointment to West Point, York received a senatorial appointment to the U.S. Military Academy in 1934. After four years of schooling and military training, he was graduated in the top third of his class on 14 June 1938. Prior to graduation, he changed his surname regrettably from Cichowski to York. Nevertheless, his friends and associates called him "Ski" throughout his military service.

Choosing the Army Air Corps as his branch of service, York took flight training at Randolph Field, Texas, where he received the wings of a military pilot in 1939. While at Randolph Field, Lieutenant York met and married Mary Elizabeth Harper of San Antonio. Together they reported to his first duty station, March Field, California. At the outbreak of World War II, York commanded the 95th Bombardment Squadron at McChord Field, Washington. In early 1942, York volunteered for a top secret project led by Lieutenant Colonel James Doolittle who selected

York as the operations officer. In this capacity, York trained a group of pilots for the Doolittle raid at Eglin Field, Florida. Prepared for the mission, Colonel Doolittle loaded sixteen B-25 Bombers and their crews aboard the aircraft carrier U.S.S. *Hornet*. Just before loading the aircraft aboard the carrier, York discovered that his B-25 had its special carburetors removed by mistake and replaced by standard carburetors. Notwithstanding, York decided to fly the mission without the special carburetors despite the reduced range he could expect. On 18 April 1942, sixteen B-25 bombers were launched from *Hornet* some 760 miles from Japan rather than the planned 400 miles. The bombing raid was successful. The pilots bombed their assigned targets over Tokyo. York now determined that his plane did not have sufficient fuel to reach the planned destination in China. York, therefore, flew the shorter distance to Vladivostok, Siberia, where he landed safely, but the Russians interned him and the crew. York and his team were held for thirteen months before they escaped Vladivostok in April 1943.

Shortly after his return to the United States, York volunteered for combat duty in Italy where he was assigned as Deputy Commanding Officer of the 483rd Bombardment Group. He flew twenty-four combat missions over southern Europe before he was recalled home due to the policy of keeping former internees from participating in combat missions. His stay was short. In early 1945, York was assigned as Air Attaché at the American Embassy in Warsaw until January 1947. While in Warsaw, York became a certified Polish language translator.

At Lackland Air Force Base, San Antonio, Texas, he served as Commandant of the Air Force Officers Candidate School. In 1950, he joined the Military Advisory Assistance Group (MAAG) in Copenhagen, Denmark. He returned to the United States to attend the Air War College (1953) and then to Headquarters, U.S. Air Force, to run the Air Attaché Branch. For the next five years he served with the Military Air Transport Service (MATS) at Andrews and Travis Air Force Bases, followed with a one-year duty with the Air Materiel Command.

When the Air Force gained the mission of deploying and oper-
ating long range surface-to-surface missiles, York was appointed
commander of a Site Activation Task Force at Larson Air Force
Base, Washington, where he devoted two and one-half years of
dedicated effort. His final assignment took him to San Antonio
as Chief of Staff of the U.S. Air Force Security System. After
three years in this assignment for which the Air Force awarded
him the Legion of Merit, York retired from active duty on 13
August 1966.

Colonel York was awarded the Distinguished Flying Cross for
the Doolittle Bombing Raid on Tokyo, Legion of Merit with oak
leaf cluster, Air Force Commendation Medal, and the Order of
Lun Hui (Chinese), plus numerous theater and campaign medals.

York retired in San Antonio, Texas, after thirty-one years of
service. He received the position of city manager of Olmos Park,
a suburb of San Antonio, that he ran for more than nine years.
He died at his home on 31 August 1984 and is buried at Fort Sam
Houston National Cemetery. He was survived by wife, Mary Elizabeth Harper York, son, Edward J. York, Jr. who was graduated
from the U.S. Air Force Academy in 1970, daughter Tina York
Daniel, and four grandchildren.

Those who knew Ski York have always treasured his dedication to DUTY, HONOR, COUNTRY, and his unfailing humor.
General James Doolittle eulogized York: "Ski and I served together, I am proud to say, during the raid over Tokyo. He was the
only West Pointer in the group and as operations officer added
his knowledge and expertise to the mission. We were all grateful
for his attention to detail and thorough follow through. Not only
was Edward a fine officer but an excellent individual. We miss
him, but remember his terrific spirit."

APPENDIX D

ACKNOWLEDGEMENTS

Library of Congress
Manuscripts Division and Photoduplication Service
Washington, D.C.

Carla Tomaszewski
Piney Point, Maryland

El Paso Public Library
Interlibrary Loan Division
El Paso, Texas

Library
University of Texas at El Paso
El Paso, Texas

Terry Adams
Chief Photographer
National Park Service.
Washington, D.C.

Colonel Casimir I. Lenard (AUS-Ret)
Executive Director, Washington Office
Polish American Congress
Washington, D.C.

Jadwiga Szmidt
Polish Library, London
United Kingdom

Notes

Chapter 1. Germany and Russia Plunge the World into War

1. Norman Davies, *God's Playground: A History of Poland* (2 Vols) (New York: Columbia University Press, 1984), II: 435.
2. Stefan Zaloga and Victor Madej, *The Polish Campaign 1939* (New York: Hippocrene Books, Inc., 1985), p. 156.
3. Robert Wernick and Editors, *Blitzkrieg* (Alexandria, Virginia: Time-Life Books, 1977), p. 21.
4. Zaloga and Madej, *The Polish Campaign*, p. 110.
5. Davies, *God's Playground*, II: 438-39.
6. Zaloga and Madej, *The Polish Campaign*, p. 156.
7. B. H. Lidell-Hart, *History of the Second World War* (New York: G. P. Putnam's Sons, 1978), p. 3.
8. Davies, *God's Playground*, p. 439.

Chapter 2. Russia Tries to Destroy the Soul of Poland

1. The introduction to the *The Dark Side of the Moon*, following T. S. Eliot's preface, speaks of the vastness and remoteness of the Siberian and Asian landscapes and quotes Arthur Koesler who writes in his book *The Yogi and the Commissar*: "This reality, the every day life of people in Kazan, and Saatov, Ashkabad and Tomsk, even in the very suburbs of Moscow, not to speak of the Forced Labor Camps on the White River, is as remote from the Western observer as the dark side of the moon from the stargazer's telescope."
2. Zoe Zajdler, *The Dark Side of the Moon* (New York: Charles Scribner's Sons, 1948), Preface.
3. *Ibid*, p. 3.
4. *Ibid*, p. 79.
5. *The Erie Times*, 28 April 1950.

6. Zajdler, *The Dark Side of the Moon*, p. 98.

7. *Ibid*, p. 127.

8. *Ibid*, p. 135.

9. *Ibid*, p. 138.

10. *Ibid*, p. 143.

11. *Ibid*, p. 176.

12. *Ibid*, p. 273 (Epilogue).

Chapter 3. Russia Murders 15,000 Polish Prisoners of War

1. J. K. Zawodny, *Death in the Forest: The Story of the Katyn Forest Massacre* (South Bend, Indiana: The University of Notre Dame Press, 1962), p. 5.

2. *Ibid*, pp. 6-10; and *The Dark Side of the Moon*, pp. 210-11.

3. Zawodny, *Death in the Forest*, pp. 15-19.

4. Norman Davies, *Rising '44: The Battle for Warsaw* (New York: Viking-Peguin, 2003), pp. 115-16.

5. Zawodny, *Death in the Forest*, pp. 20-24.

6. *Ibid*, pp. 17-20.

7. *Ibid*, pp. 29-33; and Jan Ciechanowski, *Defeat in Victory* (Garden City, New York: Doubleday & Company, 1947), p. 159.

8. *New York Times*, 19 November 1943.

9. Zawodny, *Death in the Forest*, pp. 42-43; and Roosevelt to Stalin, 5 May 1943, *Stalin's Correspondence*, II: 63-64.

10. Zawodny, *Death in the Forest*, p. 43.

11. *Ibid*, pp. 49-51.

12. *Ibid*, pp. 52-55.

Chapter 4. The Polish Underground State 1939-1945

1. Norman Davies, *God's Playground: A History of Poland* (2 Vols) (New York: Columbia University Press, 1984), II: 446.

2. Stefan Korbonski, *The Polish Underground State 1939-1945* (New York: Columbia University Press, 1978), pp. 16-17.

3. Michael Alfred Peszke, *The Polish Underground Army, the Western Allies, and the Failure of Strategic Unity in World War II* (Jefferson, North Carolina, and London: McFarland & Company, Inc., Publishers, 2005), p. 53; and *Zgoda* (Chicago), 1 August 2006.

Chapter 5. Poland's Home Army

1. Martin Middlebrook, *The Peenemunde Raid* (Indianapolis-New York: The Bobbs-Merrill Company, Inc., 1982).

2. Stefan Korbonski, *The Polish Underground State 1939-1945* (Columbia University Press, 1978), pp. 60-61; and Jozef Garlinski, *Hitler's Last Weapon* (New York: Times Books, 1978), pp. 149-65.

3. Wladyslaw Kozaczuk and Jerry Straszak, *Enigma: How the Poles Broke the Nazi Code* (New York: Hippocrene Books, Inc., 2004), pp. vii-viii.

4. Kozaczuk and Straszak, *Enigma*, p. 1.

5. Korbonski, *The Polish Underground State*, p. 68.

Chapter 6. Tehran and Yalta Conferences

1. Winston S. Churchill, *The Hinge of Fate* (Boston: Houghton Mifflin Company, 1950), p. 20.

2. Mark Clark, *Calculated Risk* (New York: Harper & Brothers, 1950), pp. 368-71.

3. Michael Alfred Peszke, *The Polish Underground Army, the Western Allies, and the Failure of Strategic Unity in World War II* (Jefferson, North Carolina and London: McFarland & Company, 2005), pp. 107-08.

4. Mikolajczyk, *The Rape of Poland* (New York: McGraw-Hill Book Company, 1948), pp. 95-107.

5. *Ibid*, pp. 96-100.

6. *Ibid*, p. 101.

7. Frances Perkins, *The Roosevelt I Knew* (New York: The Viking Press, 1946), p. 395.

8. Wittmer, *The Yalta Betrayal*, p. 78.

9. Edward R. Stettinius, Jr., *Roosevelt and the Russians: The Yalta Conference* (Garden City, New York: Doubleday & Company, 1949), pp. 346-47.

10. Ellis M. Zacharias with Ladislas Farrago, *Behind Closed Doors: The Secret History of the Cold War* (New York: G. P. Putnam's Sons, 1950), p. 58.

11. William Henry Chamberlin, *America's Second Crusade* (Chicago: Henry Regnery Company, 1950), p. 216.

12. Wittmer, *Yalta*, p. 82.

13. Robert E. Sherwood, *Roosevelt and Hopkins: An Intimate History* (New York: Harper & Brothers Publishers, 1948), pp. 874-75; and Churchill, *Triumph and Tragedy*, p. 401.

14. Diane Shaver Clemens, *Yalta* (London and New York: Oxford University Press, 1970), p. 175; and Churchill, *Closing the Ring*, p. 453.

15. Mikolajczyk, *The Rape of Poland*, pp. 66-67.

16. *Ibid*, p. 67.

Chapter 7. Harry Truman Becomes President

1. Chamberlin, *America's Second Crusade*, p. 225.

2. *Memoirs by Harry S. Truman: Year of Decision* (Garden City, New York:

Doubleday & Company, Inc., 1955), pp. 24-25.

3. *Ibid*, p. 26.

4. *Ibid*, p. 39.

5. *Ibid*, pp. 38-39.

6. *Ibid*, pp. 41, 50, 71-72.

7. *Ibid*, pp. 76-78.

8. *Ibid*, pp. 77-79.

9. *Ibid*, pp. 80-81.

10. *Ibid*, pp. 85, 107-08.

11. *Ibid*, p. 263.

12. *Ibid*, p. 263.

13. Stanislaw Mikolajczyk, *The Rape of Poland*, p. 114; and Truman, *Year of Decision*, p. 263.

14. Truman, *Year of Decision*, p. 322.

15. *Ibid*, p. 320; *New York Times*, 16 May 1945, p. 28; and Winston S. Churchill, *Triumph and Tragedy* (Boston: Houghton Mifflin Company, 1953), pp. 488, 497-98.

16. Mikolajczyk, *The Rape of Poland*, pp. 111-13, 129.

17. Churchill, *Triumph and Tragedy*, pp. 583-84; and Truman, *Year of Decision*, p. 339.

18. Truman, *Year of Decision*, pp. 341-42.

19. *Ibid*, p. 353; and Truman, *Years of Trial and Hope*, p. 111.

20. *Ibid*, p. 361.

21. *Ibid*, p. 366.

22. Leahy, *I Was There*, p. 396.

23. Truman, *Year of Decision*, pp. 370-73, 387, 395, 400.

24. *Ibid*, p. 405.

25. *Ibid*, p. 412; and Byrnes, *Speaking Frankly*, p. 87.

Chapter 8. A Valiant Try for Poland

1. Mikolajczyk, *The Rape of Poland*, pp. 118-19.

2. Arthur Bliss Lane, *I Saw Poland Betrayed* (Indianapolis: Bobbs-Merrill Company, 1948), p. 29.

3. *Ibid*, p. 55.

4. *The New York Times*, 12 October 1944, p. 1; Lynne Olson and Stanley Cloud, *A Question of Honor* (New York: Alfred A. Knopf, 2002), p. 36; and Lane, *I Saw Poland Betrayed*, pp. 60-61.

5. Lane, *I Saw Poland Betrayed*, pp. 79-82.

6. Norman Davies, *God's Playground: A History of Poland*, (2 vols) (New York: Columbia University Press, 1984). Vol. 1, Chapter 5.

7. Lane, *I Saw Poland Betrayed*, p. 84.

8. *Ibid*, pp. 126, 131.

9. *Ibid*, pp. 133-34.

10. *Ibid*, pp. 18-19.
11. *Ibid*, p. 20-21.
12. *Ibid*, p. 27.
13. *Ibid*, p. 136.
14. *Ibid*, p. 137.
15. *Ibid*, pp. 138-39.
16. *Ibid*, p. 140.
17. *Ibid*, p. 141.
18. *Ibid*, p. 148.
19. *Ibid*, pp. 150-51.
20. *Ibid*, pp. 151-52.
21. *Ibid*, pp. 155-56.
22. *Ibid*, pp. 158-59.
23. *Ibid*, p. 161.
24. *Ibid*, p. 162.
25. *Ibid*, p. 163.
26. *Ibid*, pp. 163-65.
27. *Ibid*, pp. 167-68.
28. *Ibid*, p. 169.
29. *Ibid*, p. 170.
30. *Ibid*, pp. 171-72.
31. *Ibid*, p. 52. Colonel York was a West Pointer, Class of 1938. He entered the U.S. Military Academy in 1934 as Edward Joseph Cichowski. Prior to graduation and regrettably, he changed his surname to York.
32. Lane, *I Saw Poland Betrayed*, p. 174.
33. *Ibid*, pp. 175-77.
34. *Ibid*, p. 178.
35. *Ibid*, p. 178.
36. *Ibid*, p. 52.

Chapter 9. The Fraudulent National Elections

1. Lane, *I Saw Poland Betrayed*, pp. 179-81.
2. *Ibid*, pp. 182-84.
3. *Ibid*, p. 184.
4. *Ibid*, p. 185.
5. *Ibid*, pp. 185-86.
6. *Ibid*, p. 187.
7. *Ibid*, pp. 188-89.
8. *Ibid*, p. 191.
9. *Ibid*, p. 192.
10. *Ibid*, p. 197.
11. *Ibid*, pp. 198-200.
12. *Ibid*, p. 201.

13. *Ibid*, pp. 203-04.
14. *Ibid*, pp. 204-05.
15. *Ibid*, pp. 206-07.
16. *Ibid*, p. 209.
17. *Ibid*, pp. 213-14.
18. *Ibid*, pp. 241-42.
19. *Ibid*, pp. 243-44, 254.
20. *Ibid*, pp. 261-62.
21. *Ibid*, pp. 268, 271-75.
22. Mikolajczyk, *The Rape of Poland*, p. 188.
23. Lane, *I Saw Poland Betrayed*, pp. 277-80.
24. *Ibid*, pp. 280-82.
25. *Ibid*, pp. 283-84.
26. *Ibid*, p. 285.
27. *Ibid*, pp. 284-85.
28. *Ibid*, p. 288.
29. *Ibid*, pp. 289-94, 300-02.

Chapter 10. U.S. Congress Finds Russia Guilty

1. Obituary (Spring 1960) of Henry Ignatius Szymanski, published by the Association of Graduates, United States Military Academy, West Point, New York, p. 93.
2. *The Van Vliet Report (Reconstructed)*, Lieutenant Colonel John H. Van Vliet, Jr., Fort Lewis, Washington, 11 May 1950. (Entry on the internet of ElectronicMuseum.com).
3. Eugene Davidson, *The Trail of the Germans: Nuremberg* (New York: The Macmillan Company, 1966), pp. 71-72; and "George Howard Earle II," *Dictionary of American Biography*, Supplement 9: 1971-1975 (New York: Charles Scribner's Sons, 1994.)
4. Zawodny, *Death in the Forest*, p. 184.
5. Janusz K. Zawodny, "The Katyn Forest Massacre: Morals in American Foreign Policy," *The Minnesota Review*, 1963; and Davidson, *Trial of the Germans*, p. 24.
6. Zawodny, *Death in the Forest*, pp. 66-70.
7. "Final Report of the Select Committee to Conduct an Investigation and Study of the Facts, Evidence, and Circumstances on the Katyn Forest Massacre, U.S. House of Representatives (Washington: Government Printing Office, 1952), pp. 1-2, 19-21.
8. *Ibid*, pp. 3-4.
9. *Ibid*, pp. 4-5.
10. *Ibid*, pp. 4-5.
11. *Ibid*, pp. 4-5.
12. *Ibid*, pp. 7-8.

13. *Ibid*, p. 9.
14. *Ibid*, p. 9.
15. *Ibid*, p. 10.
16. Zawodny, *Death in the Forest*, p. 74.
17. "Final Report of the Select Committee," pp. 11-12.
18. Zawodny, "Katyn Forest Massacre," *The Minnesota Review*, p. 9.

Chapter 11. Documenting Poland's Tragic Betrayal

1. Mikolajczyk, *The Rape of Poland*, pp. 204-05, 222.
2. *Ibid*, 240-41.
3. *Ibid*, pp. 247-48.
4. *Ibid*, p. 248.
5. *Ibid*, pp. 249-50.
6. *Ibid*, p. 243-45.
7. *Ibid*, p. 251-54.
8. *Ibid*, p. 255.
9. *Ibid*, p. 253.
10. Truman, *Memoirs: Years of Trial and Hope* (Vol 2), pp. 123-31.
11. *Ibid*, pp. 240-51.
12. Lane, *I Saw Poland Betrayed*, p. 303.
13. *Ibid*, p. 304.
14. *Ibid*, pp. 304-05.
15. *Ibid*, p. 305.
16. *Ibid*, p. 306.
17. *Ibid*, p. 310-11.
18. Chamberlin, *America's Second Crusade*, p. 206.
19. *The Wall Street Journal*, 26 June 1990 (containing Arthur Schlesinger, Jr.'s opinion article).

Appendix A. The National Katyn Memorial

1. The data of Appendix A are based on documents and publications provided by Richard P. Poremski of the National Katyn Memorial Committee of Baltimore, Maryland.
2. *The Baltimore Sun*, "Polish officers monument delayed," 29 August 2000, p. 1B.
3. *The Baltimore Sun*, "A Monumental arrival," 13 September 2000, and *The Port of Baltimore*, "A Monumental Task," December 2000, p. 24 (published by the Department of Transportation).
4. *The Port of Baltimore*, p. 24.
5. *The Baltimore Sun*, 30 November 2000, p. 9A.

Appendix B. Biographical Sketch of Henry Ignatius Szymanski

1. Szymanski's West Point File, The Association of Graduates, U.S. Military Academy, West Point, New York.
2. John Ellis, Cassino: *The Hollow Victory* (New York: McGraw-Hill Book Company, 1984), p. 469.
3. Anders, Lt-General W., C. B., *An Army in Exile: The Story of the Second Polish Corps* (Nashville: The Battery Press, 1981), p. v.
4. Johnson, Edd, *The Chicago Sun*, 30 July 1944.
5. Szymanski's Obituary, Association of Graduates, U.S. Military Academy.
6. Entry for Colonel Henry I. Szymanski, *Fifty-Year Book*, Class of Nineteen-Nineteen, United States Military Academy (Washington, D.C.: Published by the Class, August 1963), p. 121.

Appendix C. Biographical Sketch of Edward Joseph York

Obituary of York published by the Association of Graduates, U.S. Military Academy (OB, March 1991).

BIBLIOGRAPHY

I. PRIMARY SOURCES

1. Books and Articles.

Anders, Lt-General W. *An Army in Exile: The Story of the Second Polish Corps.* Nashville: The Battery Press, 1982.

Byrnes, James R. *Speaking Frankly.* New York: Harper & Brothers, 1947.

Ciechanowski, Jan. *Defeat in Victory.* New York: Doubleday & Company, Inc., 1947.

Churchill, Winston S. *The Gathering Storm.*

———————. *Their Finest Hour.*

———————. *The Hinge of Faith.*

———————. *The Grand Alliance.*

———————. *Closing the Ring.*

———————. *Triumph and Tragedy.*

Boston: Houghton Mifflin Company, 1948-1953.

Korbonski, Stefan. *The Polish Underground State: A Guide to the Underground, 1939-1945.* New York: Columbia University Press, 1978.

Lane, Arthur Bliss. *I Saw Poland Betrayed: An American Ambassador Reports to the American People.* Indianapolis: The Bobbs-Merrill Company, Publishers, 1948.

———————. "How Russia Rules Poland," *Life*, 14 July 1947.

Leahy, Fleet Admiral William D. *I Was There: The Personal Story of the Chief of Staff to Presidents Roosevelt and Truman Based on His Notes and Diaries Made at the Time.* New York: McGraw-Hill Book Company, 1949.

Mikolajczyk, Stanislaw. *The Rape of Poland.* New York: McGraw-Hill Book Company, 1948.

Perkins, Frances. *The Roosevelt I Knew.* New York: Harper & Brothers, Publishers, 1946.

Post, Krystyna Sokolowska. *Krystyba: A Chronicle of Life and War.* Colorado Springs, Colorado: Mary Jo Meade, 2005.

Stettinius, Edward R. *Roosevelt and the Russians: The Yalta Conference.* Garden City, New York: Doubleday & Company, 1947.

Truman, Harry S. *Memoirs*, 2 Vols, *Year of Decision* (1955) and *Years of Trial and Hope* (1956). Garden City, New York: Doubleday & Company, Inc.

[Zajdler, Zoe]. *The Dark Side of the Moon.* Preface by T. S. Eliot. New York: Charles Scribner's Sons, 1948.

Newspapers

The Baltimore Sun
The Erie Times
The New York Times
The Chicago Sun

II. SECONDARY SOURCES

Chamberlin, William Henry. *America's Second Crusade.* Chicago: Henry Regnery Company, 1950.

Clemens, Diane Shaver. *Yalta.* London and New York: Oxford University Press, 1970.

Davies, Norman. *God's Playground: A History of Poland*, 2 Vols. New York: Columbia University Press, 1984.

_____. *Rising '44: The Battle for Warsaw.* New York: Viking Penguin, 2003.

Garlinski, Jozef. *Hitler's Last Weapons: The Underground War against the V-1 and V-2*. New York: Times Books, 1978.

Katyn w Dokumentach Kongresu USA (Katyn in the Documents of the USA Congress). Pelplin-Warsawa-Londyn: 2003. Monsignor Z. Peszkowski and Dr. S. Z. Zdrojewski, editors.

Keegan, John. *Six Armies in Normandy*. New York: The Viking Press, 1982.

Kozaczuk, Wladyslaw, and Straszak, Jerzy. *Enigma: How the Poles Broke the Nazi Code*. New York: Hippocrene Books, Inc., 2004.

Middlebrook, Martin. *The Peenemnde Raid*. Indianapolis-New York: The Bobbs-Merrill Company, Inc., 1982.

Peszke, Michael Alfred. *The Polish Underground Army, the Western Allies, and the Failure of Strategic Unity in World War II*. Jefferson, North Carolina: McFarland & Company, Inc., Publishers, 2005.

Sherwood, Robert E. *Roosevelt and Hopkins: An Intimate History*. New York: Harper & Brothers, Publishers, 1948.

Wittmer, Felix. *The Yalta Betrayal: Data on the Decline and Fall of Franklin Delano Roosevelt*. Caldwell, Idaho: The Caxton Printers, Ltd., 1953.

Wood, Thomas E., and Jankowski, Stanislaw. *Karski: How One Man Tried to Stop the Holocaust*. New York: John Wiley & Sons, 1994.

Zacharias, Ellis M., with Ladislas Farago. *Behind Closed Doors: The Secret History of the Cold War*. New York: G. P. Putnam's Sons, 1950.

Zawodny, J. K. *Death in the Forest: The Story of the Katyn Forest Massacre*. Notre Dame, Indiana: University of Notre Dame Press, 1962.

Zayas, Alfred M. de. *Nemesis of Potsdam: The Anglo-Americans and the Expulsion of the Germans*. London: Routledge & Keegan Paul, 1977.

INDEX

Berlin Airlift, 211
Berlin Wall, 219
Berman, Jakub, 130, 133
Biddle, Ambassador A. J. Drexel, Jr., 189
Bierut, Boleslaw, 29, 30, 94, 101, 126, 143, 147
Bismarck State College, North Dakota, xi
Bissell, General Clayton:
    Assistant Army Chief of Staff for Intelligence, G-2, 178; receives report of Lieutenant Colonel John J. Van Vliet, Jr. on the Katyn Forest Massacre, 178; testifies he forwarded the Van Vliet report to State Department (Julius Holmes) followed by a second letter to the State Department (Frederick B. Lyon) who both testify under oath they never received the report, 191; the Army apparently never punishes him for his crime of perjury, but he retires from the military service in disgrace.
Bletchley Park, England, 71
Blitzkrieg (book), 6
Bohlem Charles E., 120
Bolton, Congressman Woman Frances P., 147
Brda River, Poland, 6
Brindisi, Italy, 67, 70, 144
British Labour Party, 106
British Minister of Information, 41
Brown Shirts (Germany), 158
Brown, Spencer Curtis, 29, 32
Bryja, Wincenty, 202
Brzura River, Poland, 6
Buchenwald, 251
Bug River, Poland, 68
Bulganin, Nikolai A., 85-86
Bulgaria, 179
Burns, Jean Powell, 248
Butz, Herr Doktor, 177
Buzul'uk, Russia, 26, 37
Bydgoszcz, Poland, 50
Byelorussia, 50

Byrnes, Secretary of State James R., 106, 140-41, 148, 153, 163

C

Cairo, Egypt, 76
Carter, John F., 179
Cavendish-Bentinck, Ambassador Victor, 158, 168
Chamberlin, Prime Minister Neville, 1, 10
Chamberlin, William Henry, 86, 91, 220
Charles Scribner's Sons, New York, 11,
Chiang Kai-Shek, 76
Chicago, Illinois, 174
Ciechanowski, Ambassador Jan, 41, 120
Cichowski, James Joseph, 254
Cichowski, Tekla, 254
Chief Rabbi of Warsaw, Poland, 225
China, 23, 24,
Chmielewski, Captain Jerzy, 67, 69-70
Christian Labor Party, 79, 148
Chrusciel, General Antoni, 131
Churchill, Winston:
    Six-volume history of World War II, 14; at Tehran Conference, 30, 77; appeals to Stalin to allow British planes to fly supplies to beleaguered Polish Home Army during Warsaw Rising, 144; meets with Roosevelt and Stalin for Yalta Conference, 75; abandons recognition of Polish Government-in-Exile (London) and establishes diplomatic relations with the Polish Provisional Government of National Unity formed by Russia, Great Britain, and United States, 102; reports the results of Yalta to House of Commons and receives favorable reaction, although a small group of Conservatives reject the agreement, 87; states that Czechoslovakia should have resisted by military action the German conquest

of that country in 1939, 89.
City University of New York, 220
Clark, General Mark, 77
Clemens, Diane Shaver, 87-90
Collins, General J. Lawton, 178
Colorado Springs, Colorado, 251
Columbia, 119
Comintern, 28
Committee of National Liberation, 30
Commonwealth of Poland, 4, 79
Communism, 52
Communist East Germany, 204
Congressional Record, 186
Copernicus, Nicholas, 48
Crossbow Committee (British), 70
Curie, Maria Sklodowska, 229
Curzon Line, 30, 76, 79, 81, 88
Czechs, 1
Czechoslovakia, 1, 8, 89
Czestochowa, Poland, 149

D

Dabrowski, Dr. _____, 134
Dachau, Germany, 251
Daily Worker (British), 41
Daladier, Edouard, 48
Daniel, Tina York, 256
Danzig (See Gdansk)
Dark Ages, 12, 18, 218
Davis, Elmer, 193-94
Davidson, Eugene, 183
Davies, Joseph E., 42, 100
Davies, Norman, 7, 74
Deane, General John R., 75, 98
Death in the Forest, viii, 35
Detroit, Michigan, 181
Dillon, Thomas P., 156, 168
Dmochowska, Irena, 138, 156-57, 215
Doolittle, General James, 256
Dondero, Congressman George A., 185
Dnieper River, Russia, 178
Drake, Colonel Thomas D., 179
Drohobycz, Poland, 20, 76

Duben, Germany, 178
Dunkirk, France, 9
Dunn, James, 95
Durbrow, Elbridge, 120
Dypski, Cornell, 232

E

Earle, George H. II, 179, 190
East Prussia, viii
Eden, Foreign Secretary Anthony, 36, 66, 79, 90, 94
Edisongracht (ship), 233-34
Ehrenburg, Ilya, 16
Eighth Illinois Congressional District, 247
Eisenhower, General Dwight D., 125, 141-45
Eliot. T. S., viii, 12
Embassy of Poland, Washington, D.C., 227
Emilia Plater Street, Warsaw, 138
Enigma (Secret Code), 71
Erie, Pennsylvania, 15
Estonia, 48, 55
Exchange National Bank, Colorado Springs, Colorado, 251
Eyler, Chris, 235

F

Federal Communications Commission (FCC), 188, 184
Finland, 233
Fischer, Dr. Ludwig, 73
Flood, Congressman Daniel J., 185
Fogg, Michael, 133
Forrestal, Secretary of the Air Force James, 97
Fort McHenry, Baltimore, 239
Fort Sam Houston National Cemetery, Texas, 256
France, 1, 2, 4, 6, 9, 182

"Tempest" (command), 89

Terman, Chaplain (Colonel) Curtis L., 112

The Baltimore Sun, 233-34, 243

The Campaign in Poland 1939, 8

The Dark Side of the Moon, viii, 11

The Polish Underground State, viii

The Rape of Poland, ix, 101

The True Glory (film), 158

The Ultra Secret (book), 71

The Voice of the Soldier, 166

Thompson, Dorothy, 168

Thompson, Llewellyn E., 164

Time-Life Books, 6

Tobruk, Libya, 131

Tokarzewski, Geneal Michael, 56-57

Tokyo, Japan, 25

Tonesk, Lieutenant William, 125, 132, 149

Townsend, Lt. Governor Kathleen, 232

Treaty of Riga (1921), 123

Treaty of Versailles (WW I), 1, 9, 123

Treece, Major Lawrence, 130

Through Woman's Eyes (book), 208

Tryc (driver), 203

Tsar Nicholas II, 12

Tukhachevsky, Marshal Mikhail, 28

Turkish Army, 25

Truman, President Harry S.:

The Memoirs of Harry S. Truman (2 vols), ix; becomes U.S. President, 12 April 1945, 91; placed at great disadvantage by Roosevelt's secret foreign policy, 91; sets out to become knowledgeable rapidly, 92; opposes Russia's recognition of Communist Lublin group to be the provisional government of Poland, 92; coordinates foreign policy with Churchill, 93; meets privately with Harry Hopkins, 93; coordinates proposed American and British messages to Stalin on approved Polish leaders for the Provisional Government, 94; confers with his diplomatic and military advisors, 96-98; meets with Russian Foreign Minister Molotov in Washington and tells the Russian to carry out agreements reached at Yalta, 98; sends Hopkins and Harriman to Moscow to resolve impasse over the composition of the Polish Provisional Government, 100; Truman's choice of Hopkins is disastrous for Poland, 102; accepts Stalin's recommendation to meet at Potsdam, Germany, 100; Hopkins agrees with Stalin's demands and Truman approves the list, 102; Truman and Churchill recognize the new Polish Provisional Government and abandon their wartime ally, the Polish Government-in-Exile (London), 5 July 1945, 102; Russian trial of sixteen Polish leaders of the Underground Government shocks Truman, 102; holds conference at Potsdam with Stalin and Churchill, 16 July – 2 August 1945, 105; meets Stalin for the first time, 106; agrees to place German land east of the Oder-Neisse Rivers under Polish administration, 113; at end of Potsdam Conference flies to England to meet King George VI, 116; concludes from his impressions at Potsdam that Russia is bent on world conquest, 116.

Tsar Nicholas II, 12

Tupaj, Stanislaw, 138

Turkish Army, 15

U

Ukraine, 50, 79

Ukrainians, 55, 124

Union of Polish Patriots (Communist), 29

United Nations, 94

United Press, 148

ABOUT THE AUTHOR

FRANCIS CASIMIR KAJENCKI was graduated from the U.S. Military Academy and commissioned second lieutenant in January 1943. He served in the Pacific Theater in World War II, followed by staff and command assignments over a span of thirty years. He retired as Colonel and Assistant Chief of Information, Department of the Army, in 1973.

Kajencki earned three Masters degrees: from the University of Southern California in Mechanical Engineering, 1949; University of Wisconsin-Madison in Journalism, 1967; George Mason University in History, 1976. Upon retiring from the army, he took up historical research and writing that led to nine published books on American history.

The author was born in Erie, Pennsylvania, November 15, 1918. A widower with four adult children, he resides in El Paso, Texas.

Typography, book and cover design, and map production by Vicki Trego Hill of El Paso, Texas. Text was set in 11 pt. Caslon 224 Book with 14 pts. leading; chapter headings were set in Caslon 3 Roman Small Caps.

Printing/Binding by Thomson-Shore, Inc. of Dexter, Michigan. The text was printed on 60-pound Natures Natural, an acid-free paper with an effective life of at least three hundred years.